P9-DIA-261

UNION COLLEGE LIBRARY
BARBOURVILLE KY 40906

MEDIEVAL TEXTS & CONTEMPORARY READERS

# Medieval Texts & Contemporary Readers

*Edited by*

Laurie A. Finke

*and*

Martin B. Shichtman

*Cornell University Press*

ITHACA AND LONDON

UNION [illegible] LIBRARY
BARBOURVILLE, KY. 40906

809.02
M489
C1

Copyright © 1987 by Cornell University

All rights reserved. Except for brief quotations in a review, this book, or parts thereof, must not be reproduced in any form without permission in writing from the publisher. For information, address Cornell University Press, 124 Roberts Place, Ithaca, New York 14850.

First published 1987 by Cornell University Press.

International Standard Book Number (cloth) 0–8014–2003–2
International Standard Book Number (paper) 0–8014–9463–X
Library of Congress Catalog Card Number 87–47545

Printed in the United States of America

*Librarians: Library of Congress cataloging information appears on the last page of the book.*

*The paper in this book is acid-free and meets the guidelines for permanence and durability of the Committee on Production Guidelines for Book Longevity of the Council on Library Resources.*

# Contents

## PART II
## *Intertextuality*



## PART III
## *The Reader*

# Editors' Preface

> Persse went to see the head of his department, Professor Liam McCreedy, and asked if he could take a sabbatical in the coming term.
>
> "A sabbatical? This is a rather sudden request, Persse," said McCreedy, peering at him from behind the usual battlement of books. Instead of using a desk, the Professor sat at an immense table, almost entirely covered with tottering piles of scholarly tomes—dictionaries, concordances, and Old English texts—with just a small area in front of him cleared for writing. The visitor on the other side of these fortifications was placed at a considerable disadvantage in any discussion by not always being able to see his interlocutor...
>
> "Er, what would you be wanting to be doing during this leave, exactly?"
>
> "I want to study structuralism, sir," said Persse.
>
> The announcement sent the Professor diving for cover again, into some slit trench deep in the publications of the Early English Text Society, from which his voice emerged muffled and plaintive. "Well, I don't know that we can manage the modern literature course without you, Mr. McGarrigle."

David Lodge's depiction of the medievalist Liam McCreedy, in his novel *Small World*, explains perhaps better than anything we might write why we wanted to collect together the essays of *Medieval Texts and Contemporary Readers*. Professor McCreedy, the embattled scholar hiding behind his fortress of primary texts and reference materials, is, of course, a caricature of how the academy's community of critics often views medievalists. The perception is not without some justification.

Many medievalists have found contemporary theory a strange and threatening field, and medieval studies have, for the most part, lagged behind other disciplines in recognizing the importance of much recent critical thought. At the same time, however, many proponents of contemporary critical theory have been unwilling to acknowledge that the study of the Middle Ages can advance their own work. A growing number of medievalists—among them the contributors to this volume—have begun to think about the implications of recent critical theory for their research. Unfortunately they continue to encounter difficulty in finding forums that will allow for open communication both with more traditionally minded colleagues and with those whose interest in theory is well advanced.

We began this volume envisioning a book that would look, Janus-like, both backward and forward in time, that would attempt to bridge two diverse fields: medieval studies and contemporary literary and cultural theory. We hope that our efforts, and the efforts of our contributors, will initiate a dialogue between the skeptical and the converted, a dialogue that has been too long delayed. We believe that the essays included in this book offer the traditionalist a sampling of the innovative work in literary theory being done by medieval scholars, and at the same time they demonstrate that medievalists may engage the issues raised by contemporary theory in productive ways. Because contemporary theory seems at times a bewildering maze of schools, isms, and fashions, crossing disciplinary boundaries into sociology, anthropology, history, psychology, and even science, the purpose of our volume is necessarily heuristic rather than authoritative. We do not intend this book as a comprehensive, systematic introduction to contemporary theory, nor do we advocate any single position or attitude toward contemporary theory. We envision it as an exploration of the potential for a dialogue between medieval texts and contemporary thought. We see it as a means of bringing together the Liam McCreedys of our profession and their critically fashionable detractors to consider the possibilities engendered by the interaction of their disciplines.

As editors of this volume we have benefited from the generous support of many involved in our project. Chief among these, of course, are our contributors, whose cheerful patience and cooperation were surpassed only by the quality of the work they produced. There were many others with whom we corresponded while planning the volume, others whose encouragement and thoughtful advice both aided and sustained us. In this regard we owe special thanks to Paul Bové, R. Howard Bloch, E. Talbot Donaldson, George D. Economou, Edward B. Irving, Jr., Barbara Johnson, Stephen G. Nichols, and Eugene Vance. We appreciate the efforts of Patrick Bigelow, Juliet Flower MacCannell, and R. A. Shoaf, who helped get this volume off the ground. Portions of the book received careful readings from Robert Con Davis, David Gross, and Ronald Schleifer. We can never adequately thank Robert Markley, who read almost all of the manuscript and offered sound advice and editorial wisdom at every stage of the project. Financial assistance and clerical help were provided by G. Andrew Rembert, Dean of Faculty at Lewis and Clark College, and Donald F. Drummond, Dean of Arts and Sciences at Eastern Michigan University. For their insightful and detailed responses to the manuscript, we also thank the readers for Cornell University Press, Peter Allen and Sherron Knopp. Finally, we express our gratitude to our editor at the Press, Bernhard Kendler, for helping us in so many ways as we prepared our manuscript for publication.

The section from *Small World* with which this Preface opens is reprinted with permission of Macmillan Publishing Company. Copyright © 1985 by David Lodge. A portion of Robert Hanning's essay appeared in *Studies in the Age of Chaucer* 7 (1985), and we gratefully acknowledge permission of the editors to reproduce these pages.

Simply working together—collecting the contributions, editing the manuscript, in short melding a group of twelve separate essays into a coherent book—fulfilled our best hopes about the joys of scholarly collaboration. This book also benefited, however, from another kind of collaboration. For their love, understanding, and support, we thank our closest collaborators, our spouses, Robert Markley and Maryann Shichtman.

Laurie A. Finke and
Martin B. Shichtman

*Portland, Oregon,*
*and Ypsilanti, Michigan*

Medieval Texts &
Contemporary Readers

# Introduction: Critical Theory and the Study of the Middle Ages

LAURIE A. FINKE AND
MARTIN B. SHICHTMAN

Contemporary readers never experience medieval texts directly, unambiguously, or ahistorically. Their reading is always mediated in highly complex ways by the scholarly activities that make these texts accessible: the editions, glosses, textual notes, manuscript facsimiles, transcriptions, and translations through which medieval literature is filtered and transmitted. The sheer bulk of the scholarly apparatus on Dante, Chaucer, or Langland should remind us constantly how historically distant, how alien these poets really are.[1] Yet, paradoxically, the activity of reading often effaces such differences, bringing writers of the tenth through the fifteenth centuries into the domain of a textual scholarship that domesticates them, seeks to identify definitive readings, and turns the differences, the anomalies, preserved by the tradition of manuscript transcription into something approaching (or governed by) a contemporary theory of copy-text.[2] We know that we cannot really

1. See Hans Robert Jauss, "The Alterity and Modernity of Medieval Literature," *New Literary History* 10 (1979), 181–229.

2. For a particularly enlightening study of the current state of medieval textual criticism, see Derek Pearsall, "Texts, Textual Criticism, and Fifteenth Century Manuscript Production," in *Fifteenth-Century Studies*, ed. R. Yeager (New Haven: Yale University Press, 1983), pp. 121–36. Although Pearsall does not identify his work with any contemporary critical school, his article raises important questions about medieval studies as an institution.

read Chaucer's *Canterbury Tales,* or anything resembling Chaucer's poem, without a trip to the Huntington or the Bodleian, but we still talk in our scholarly journals, professional meetings, and classrooms about "what Chaucer meant" as if the notion of meaning—of authorial intention or historical reconstruction—was itself unproblematical.

The problem of meaning has preoccupied medieval studies for decades. Throughout the New Critical debates of the 1960s and 1970s, critics talked almost exclusively about the poem's meaning and about interpreting texts, whether they asserted that a text should yield a univocal meaning or acknowledged several plausible interpretations. As early as 1960, with Dorothy Bethurum's *Critical Approaches to Medieval Literature,* the terms of the debate were set by R. E. Kaske and E. Talbot Donaldson.[3] Kaske, in his defense of patristic exegesis, championed "the role of the entire exegetical tradition as a sort of massive index to the traditional meaning and associations of most medieval Christian imagery." Exegesis, he argued, would lead to "the close analysis of the traditional associations which such imagery usually brings with it into literary works, and the interpretation of whatever artistic use has been made of them" (p. 28). Indeed, Kaske and other critics (most notably D. W. Robertson and his followers), whether consciously or unconsciously, seemed to find the critical paradigm for their enterprise in the very texts they were analyzing, appropriating hermeneutic models on the basis of what they frequently perceived as an unwavering belief on the part of medieval writers in the authoritative rhetoric of the Bible and patristic tradition.

In contrast, Donaldson argued in his critique of patristic exegesis that these readings were too narrow and limiting, because they located meaning within an institutionalized rhetoric rather than in the poem or the poet:

> It is scarcely necessary to reassert the right of a poem to say what it means and to mean what it says, and not what anyone, before or after its composition, thinks it ought to say or mean.... To give a reader a flat injunction to find one specific meaning in Middle English poetry is anything but the ideal way to prepare him to understand something old and difficult and complicated; for in his eagerness to find out what must be there he will likely miss what is there; and in so doing he may

3. Dorothy Bethurum, ed., *Critical Approaches to Medieval Literature* (New York: Columbia University Press, 1960). Subsequent citations are noted parenthetically in the text.

> miss a meaning arising from the poem that is better than anything that exegesis is able to impose upon it. (p. 2)

Despite their sharp disagreement, both Kaske and Donaldson would agree (at least they would have done in 1960) on two premises. First, the meaning of a text inheres in the poem, or the author's intention, or both (criticism, for Kaske, is the interpretation of "whatever artistic use has been made of [traditional associations]"; for Donaldson, "a poem means what it says and says what it means"). Second, the critic's task is to uncover that meaning (the exegetical tradition for Kaske is a "massive index" to interpretation; Donaldson claims the exegetical critic will "miss what is there," a meaning "better than anything exegesis is able to impose"). In short, good criticism discovers latent meaning; bad criticism imposes it.

Significantly, this debate in the 1950s and 1960s over textual meaning and patristic exegesis was accompanied by textual and editorial activity nearly rivaling that of the philologists of the nineteenth century. This work was indispensable: it made accessible beyond the rare book libraries previously obscure or unavailable medieval texts. In many instances the production of "new readings" of old texts would not have been possible without the work of such scholars as E. Talbot Donaldson, George Kane, Eugene Vinaver, and others. But many editors transferred their critical biases to the task of editing. Some were conscious of the complexities involved and the prejudices they brought with them to the text. Others invoked "objective" and "scientific" theories of manuscript recension which, as Derek Pearsall has argued, simply glossed over the critical activity that was in fact taking place.[4]

Through the 1970s, then, medievalists had hardly questioned the ways in which they elided the historical differences between their work and the works they studied. In the 1980s we have begun to examine how medieval studies, as an institution, mediates between what has survived of medieval culture and its reception in the twentieth century. Medievalists, because of their institutionalized commitment to both editing and interpretation, to recuperating as well as reading texts, have understandably been slow to respond to the challenges posed by contemporary literary and cultural theories, primarily because, as Jonathan Culler has argued, much contemporary theory challenges the

4. Pearsall, "Texts," p. 125.

assumptions on which the quest for stable meanings is based.[5] On the other hand, however, the ideas addressed by contemporary theoretical debates may provide both a vocabulary and a new set of questions that will enable medievalists to reevaluate their critical thinking. That process will be neither rapid nor easy, but it has already begun in the works of such continental critics as H. R. Jauss, Paul Zumthor, and Roger Dragonetti and in the essays included in the 1978 and 1984 special issues of *New Literary History* on medieval literature and contemporary theory.[6] Even a traditionalist such as Morton Bloomfield has recognized that it is time for medievalists to consider, however belatedly, the issues raised by contemporary theory: "Just as it was some fifteen years before the New Criticism reached Chaucer in the 1950s, so is it the case with the new literary theorizing, which is now about ripe to reach Chaucer."[7]

The twelve original essays in *Medieval Texts and Contemporary Readers* question assumptions that contemporary criticism has nothing to say about medieval literature and that medieval studies can remain insulated from the issues of contemporary criticism. Because neither medieval literature nor contemporary critical theory is of a piece, we have brought together essays on a wide variety of texts and critical philosophies which reflect the interdisciplinary nature of historical and theoretical criticism. We have included essays on medieval philosophy, history, and religion, as well as essays on British and continental literature. The essays are united not by a single outlook, critical rhetoric, or perspective but by their commitment to questioning traditional perceptions of medieval texts and the fictions and ideologies that structure these perceptions. Our purpose is not to develop a new orthodoxy based on any single postmodern model—the volume does not, finally, advocate a deconstructive, psychoanalytic, Marxist, feminist, or even pluralistic approach to medieval texts. Rather, by bringing together competing as well as complementary critical strategies, we hope to explore how the variety of contemporary theoretical approaches may broaden our understanding of both the Middle Ages and our own critical values and assumptions.

5. Jonathan Culler, *The Pursuit of Signs* (Ithaca: Cornell University Press, 1981).
6. See *New Literary History* 10 (1979) and 16 (1984).
7. Morton Bloomfield, "Contemporary Literary Theory and Chaucer," in *New Perspectives in Chaucer Criticism*, ed. Donald Rose (Norman, Okla.: Pilgrim, 1981), p. 25.

Many critics have argued that contemporary literary theory—the work of the structuralists, poststructuralists, semioticians, and psychoanalytic critics—is more or less of a fad, merely the most recent way of reinterpreting individual texts. This view is hardly uncommon; observers in all fields of literary study still see postmodern criticism as merely a reshuffling of the deck, a reorganization rather than a subversion of traditional categories and perceptions of literature. This view, we feel, requires serious consideration. Indeed, one of the purposes of this book is to stimulate debate around such issues: What do we mean by "theory" and how should we define its purposes? What kinds of criticism should we be practicing?

To focus the debate on the relationship between theory and strategies of reading, we have divided *Medieval Texts and Contemporary Readers* into three sections that reflect what we consider three important emphases of contemporary critical thought: "Textuality," "Intertextuality," and "The Reader." The essays on the poststructuralist notion of textuality examine the play of signifiers and difference in medieval literary and philosophical texts. Essays on intertextuality move beyond the traditional notion of the text as an autonomous, privileged, or originary object; they examine the relationships among medieval literary works and other philosophical, historical, and religious texts. Finally, the essays dealing with the reader explore medieval texts in light of contemporary reader-response criticism. Our contributors suggest in several ways that contemporary literary theory should not imply a simplistic rejection of traditional medieval scholarship but rather encourage an ongoing reevaluation of the critical assumptions currently structuring the discipline. Because the essays in our volume present themselves as continuations of, as well as challenges to, traditional ways of viewing medieval writers, the tripartite division of the book is intended to disclose the underlying assumptions of the three basic concerns of traditional medieval scholarship: textual study, source study, and the historical situation of the reader in the Middle Ages. At the same time the essays provide new directions for work in these areas.

Our contributors rely on a variety of rhetorical and critical strategies to define the significance of literary theory for a new generation of medievalists, but their strategies generally fall along a continuum between two basic positions. Not all writers are ready to break utterly with the past. Some, like H. Marshall Leicester in the opening essay and Alain Renoir in the concluding essay, apply new terminologies, and their accompanying contemporary critical methods, to traditional problems. Leicester, calling upon Derridean models, examines a long-standing problem for medievalists, the evolving manuscript tradition of the Middle Ages. He argues that whereas oral culture assumes the possibility of "univocal meaning," the manuscript tradition emphasizes the transcribing, copying, editing, and translating that mediate between the medieval author and the reader. Renoir, in his wide-ranging essay on oral-formulaic rhetoric, uses an anthropological approach to re-create the kind of audience that could appreciate poetry composed orally. Leicester describes cultures whose literatures were primarily oral as "logocentric"; Renoir calls them "high-context." Both terms suggest that oral culture tends to flatten out difference whereas writing introduces it, transforming literature from a communal to a private experience. Robert Hanning incorporates seemingly traditional terminology to examine questions that are strikingly contemporary. In discussing the interpretive functions of the medieval gloss, he argues that "the idea that a gloss manipulates rather than explains its text may seem a peculiarly modern one, but medieval scholars and satirists were by no means unaware of the possibilities of such textual harassment."

At the other end of the continuum are essays that apply new methodologies with the aim of radically altering the questions that are asked of medieval texts. Louis Mackey, for instance, employs deconstructive strategies to undermine the logical certainties that modern scholars often perceive in medieval philosophies. Mackey calls into question Western philosophy's search for logocentric meaning and stable representation (of the Divine) and ends up deconstructing his own text as well. Like the Derridean texts it emulates—and sometimes parodies—Mackey's essay is often obscure and demanding, inviting the reader to take up the challenge to traditional forms of critical rhetoric. This essay was originally presented at the University of Oklahoma's Conference on Deconstruction at Yale; at the same conference, in a symposium on Marxism and Deconstruction (with Barbara Johnson and J. Hillis Miller), Mackey articulated his view that the deconstructive reader, like the Marxist and Freudian reader, "practice[s] a form of what Ricoeur called 'the hermeneutics of suspicion'; that is, you just don't take the text at its word, but you say 'what in the world is going on here that isn't obvious?' " Unlike the Marxist or Freudian, however, "the deconstructive reader is not supposed to start off with preconceptions about what he is going to find."[8] This same openness requires that the reader sensitize him or herself to the possibility of Anselm's *Proslogium* undoing what it attempts to demonstrate. Mackey does not "impose" a deconstructive reading on the *Proslogium* but takes the reader through the deconstructive process. Because language is the subject of philosophy as well as the medium in which it is conducted, philosophy, as Derrida has argued, is its own limit.[9] According to Mackey, Anselm's proof takes place at the level of the signifier: it succumbs to its inability to yield the signified—"God."

The rhetorical and critical strategies of the essays in this book run the gamut from Martin Shichtman's reassessment of traditional views of Arthurian literature in the light of contemporary historiographical theory to Alexandre Leupin's examination of "originality" in the *Poetria Nova.* Both Shichtman and Leupin focus on the notion of medieval writing as re-vision, the revitalization of a past perceived only obscurely. Shichtman's essay, perhaps more than any other in the volume, demonstrates that the language and issues of recent theory can be used to advance traditional scholarly concerns, to provide new directions for research. In suggesting that Wace and Laȝamon rewrote the past for audiences eager to valorize their own cultures, Shichtman does not require a domestication of either contemporary theory or traditional scholarship but rather insists upon an interchange that can illuminate both areas.

But if these essays concern themselves with strategies by which contemporary readers come to terms with medieval texts, they also seek to overcome the frustrations some medievalists feel at the ways in which the Middle Ages are perceived or simply ignored by postmodern theorists. Occasionally one gets the impression that contemporary theory can ask questions relevant only to post-Enlightenment texts or that the problems they define did not exist for medieval writers.[10] The "modernist" bias inherent in much postmodern theorizing, we feel, is un-

8. Louis Mackey, Barbara Johnson, and J. Hillis Miller, "Marxism and Deconstruction," *Genre* 17 (1984), 80.

9. Jacques Derrida, "The Supplement of Copula: Philosophy before Linguistics," in *Textual Strategies: Perspectives in Post-Structuralist Criticism,* ed. Josué V. Harari (Ithaca: Cornell University Press, 1979), pp. 82–120.

10. For another expression of this view, see Peter Haidu, "Romance: Idealistic Genre or Historical Text," in *Craft of Fiction: Essays in Medieval Poetics,* ed. Leigh Arrathoon (Rochester, Mich.: Solaris, 1984), pp. 1–7.

necessarily limiting, and we wish to explore and challenge it in this volume. In his essay on Geoffroi de Vinsauf, "Absolute Reflexivity," Alexandre Leupin explores further the relationships between modern theory and medieval practice. He notes that our own age tends to trace its "modernity" back only to the Romantic era. His essay teases out the problem of *modernitas* in Geoffroi's *Poetria Nova,* arguing that medieval writers show neither "idolatrous respect for a tradition they would complacently repeat nor the anguish of innovation conceived as rupture." The essay traces the development of "originality" in Geoffroi's work and argues its relation to history. Elsewhere Leupin has suggested that "medieval studies could play a crucial role in ongoing discussions of literary theory.... What we are discovering is the ability of medieval writers to ask us quite relevant questions in some of our own most recently named fields."[11]

Nowhere do the issues addressed by Leupin surface more tellingly than in the poststructuralist notion of textuality. Several of our contributors attempt to demonstrate that the problems of language and referentiality seemed as difficult for medieval writers as they do for modern critics. Many of the concepts we recognize as the products of modern semiotics are already present—albeit in a different and therefore historically problematic vocabulary—in such medieval works on language as Augustine's *On Christian Doctrine.* Although we do not claim ahistorically that Augustine "anticipated" poststructuralism, we do suggest that an examination of *On Christian Doctrine* in the light of contemporary semiotic theory can be mutually illuminating: in the heightening of textual anxiety during the Middle Ages we begin to trace the evolution of those textual concerns which play such a prominent part in contemporary critical debates. The task of evaluating the Augustinian sign system has already begun in the works of Marcia Colish and Eugene Vance.[12] It is extended here in an essay by Laurie Finke. Finke refers to the passage in *On Christian Doctrine* in which Augustine describes the dilemma faced by the Christian whose language is insufficient to express the ineffability of God and yet whose mission

11. Alexandre Leupin, "The Middle Ages, the Other," *Diacritics* 13 (1983), 22.

12. See Marcia Colish, *The Mirror of Language: A Study in the Medieval Theory of Knowledge* (Lincoln: University of Nebraska Press, 1983), and Eugene Vance, "Saint Augustine: Language as Temporality," in *Mimesis: From Mirror to Method, Augustine to Descartes,* ed. John D. Lyons and Stephen G. Nichols (Hanover: University Press of New England, 1982), pp. 20–35.

it is precisely to glorify God in words.[13] Augustine's failed attempt to incarnate representation—to ensure allegory's meaning and truth through the divine Logos—suggests that the problems of signification he examines are also problems of faith. The contradictions and silences within Augustine's theory of signs undermine both language and rational, demonstrable faith. In this sense the Augustinian dilemma is not so much "passed over in silence" (as Augustine advises) but explored by Langland and other medieval writers whose texts are often characterized by the tensions between the traditional language of knowledge and the apprehensions of an inarticulate faith.

Textuality, however, is never pure, never simply a freeplay of signifiers divorced from social, historical, and literary contexts. The notion itself implies a transgression of the limits of the "text"; textuality, in other words, exists as a form of intertextuality, the complex interaction among texts, ideologies, and traditions, the play of cross-references, echoes, and cultural symbols. Peggy Knapp's essay on Alisoun and Augustine furthers Finke's argument, demonstrating that the Augustinian sign system articulated in *On Christian Doctrine* functions throughout the Middle Ages as a vehicle for the church's deployments of institutional power while at the same time it provokes destabilizing challenges to that authority. This Bakhtinian analysis of Christian logocentrism traces a complex intertextuality that stretches from Augustine through the institutionalizations of biblical glossing, the Wife of Bath, and the Lollards, down to present-day commentaries on medieval scholarship. Knapp's essay explores "the dialogically agitated and tension-filled environment" of medieval glossing, the interplay of "institutional forces of centralization that attempt to contain and stabilize" interpretation and "insurrectionary forces" that destabilize it and open it up to heterodoxy. Her analysis of recent interpretations of Chaucer's Wife of Bath demonstrates that the same dialogic tensions accompany the interpretive activity of academicians no less than of churchmen.

Another way of looking at intertextuality is through Harold Bloom's notion of the anxiety of influence, which explains a poem's coming into being as the result of a poet's willful "misprision" of a precursor text. Bloom's theories, however, simply assume that before Milton

13. Saint Augustine, *On Christian Doctrine,* trans. D. W. Robertson, Jr. (Indianapolis: Bobbs-Merrill, 1958), pp. 10–11.

influence was unproblematic. The essays by Rachel Jacoff and Sheila Delany both reexamine the anxiety of influence by looking at the receptions that medieval writers afforded their precursors. Jacoff offers a revision of Bloom, arguing that medieval writers did not pay idolatrous respect to the traditions they imitated. Exploring Dante's re-vision of Virgil's *Aeneid,* she maintains that, for Dante, "influence" privileges the relationship between his poem and its predecessors. Dante's text offers commentary on previous texts at the same time as it is securing its own authoritative place in the tradition. Delany begins with the "creative misprisions" of Bloom's work by gender-oriented critics such as Susan Gubar, Sandra Gilbert, and Annette Kolodny. She challenges feminist theorists to examine thoroughly the historical and social contexts in which women of the past wrote—even as they provide us with positive female role models. Using Christine de Pizan as an example, she argues that women writers cannot be evaluated in a vacuum. Rather, the contemporary reader of the medieval woman writer must come to terms with his or her own ambivalences about her by understanding both her successes and her failures.

By their very natures, then, textuality and intertextuality describe the complex processes of *reading,* of examining not merely the text itself but the ways in which it shapes its audience. Reading, in this respect, is not a static process but a range of critical possibilities. Medieval culture's valorization of tradition over originality, its method of producing texts, and the performative nature of even its most "readerly" literature make the reader a pivotal figure, for it is in the act of reading that medieval texts are created.[14] Peter Travis finds in medieval writers an acute awareness of the heuristic and even therapeutic value of their readers' responses as they actualize a text's meaning. Drawing on a wide range of Continental and American reader-response critics, Travis attempts to extend Jauss's *Rezeptionsästhetik* as it applies to medieval literature. Whereas Jauss sees the masterpiece as effecting a one-time shift in the "horizon of expectations" through its adversarial relationship to its original audience, Travis argues that a masterpiece

14. Roland Barthes's view of the reader as collaborator rather than consumer, his belief that the reader in a real sense produces the literary text, should come as no surprise to even the most traditional scholar of the Middle Ages. See Barthes, "From Work to Text," in Harari, *Textual Strategies,* pp. 73–81. For more concerning Barthes's position on reader response, see Vincent Leitch, *Deconstructive Criticism: An Advanced Introduction* (New York: Columbia University Press, 1983), p. 107.

can effect change by reaffirming shared values and beliefs. This reaffirmation does not, however, necessarily allow for complacency, and in the Corpus Christi play, for instance, it forces the audience to confront its own spiritual indifference. Marina Scordilis Brownlee demonstrates how reader-response criticism rejects formalism and the belief in an autonomous text; literature is culturally determined, and only within a cultural context can it be read. She explores, within the culture of the Middle Ages, the process of reading itself as a means of examining from another perspective the politics of intertextuality and misogyny. Reading therefore is a temporal as well as a linear and circular process. In the *Corbacho* the reader reads retrospectively as well as progressively, constantly revising and adjusting assumptions in a process that ultimately undercuts the authority of the poet's didactic voice.

The essays in this volume examine various aspects of English, French, Italian, Spanish, German, and Latin literature of the Middle Ages from a variety of perspectives—rhetorical, historical, anthropological, philosophical. Some essays are more radical or more explicitly theoretical than others; all are theoretically aware. Some adopt a language that is deliberately challenging, even difficult; others strive to make the complexities of contemporary theoretical rhetoric accessible to readers. Ultimately what unites these essays is their authors' shared belief that the study of the Middle Ages can and must contribute, in significant ways, to ongoing discussions of literary theory. Although we have sought to represent contemporary theoretical debates as comprehensively as possible, we have by no means exhausted our subject. No single collection of essays can hope to cover every issue relevant to the relationships between medieval studies and contemporary criticism. By bringing together essays on a wide range of historical and theoretical topics, we hope to foster both communication and debate, to expand rather than reinforce the boundaries that currently define the study of medieval literature and culture.

# PART I

# *Textuality*

# Oure Tonges *Différance*: Textuality and Deconstruction in Chaucer

H. MARSHALL LEICESTER, JR.

I take my title from Book I of *Troilus and Criseyde,* a passage where the narrator prepares to give us the first love song Troilus made to Criseyde:

> And of his song naught only the sentence,
> As writ myn auctour called Lollius,
> But pleinly, save oure tonges difference,
> I dar wel seyn, in al that Troilus
> Seyde in his song, loo! every word right thus
> As I shal seyn; and whoso list it here,
> Loo, next this vers he may it fynden here. (I, 393-99)[1]

This is one of the most striking of numerous passages in Chaucer's poetry which explicitly raise and make problematic the issue of what is nowadays called textuality. The original love song of Troilus was, as the text points out, written or sung in a different language and is only summarized as "sentence" in Chaucer's (fictional) "source," Lollius—yet the speaker claims that he will give us every word. Moreover,

A version of this essay was originally delivered to the Chaucer Section of the MLA, New York, December 1981.

1. All quotations from Chaucer are from F. N. Robinson, ed., *The Works of Geoffrey Chaucer,* 2d ed. (Boston: Houghton Mifflin, 1957).

not only is Lollius apparently a fiction, a composite of at least five actual sources in three languages (Dares, Dictys, Benoit, Guido, and Boccaccio), but the song Chaucer gives us in the next stanzas (I, 400–420)—set off by the Latin rubric *Canticus Troili*—is actually a translation of Petrarch's sonnet to Laura, number 88, "S'amor non e." Like the opening of Book II of *Troilus and Criseyde,* in which words for speaking and reading, writing and listening, are sharply and discordantly juxtaposed,[2] this passage presents us with traces of an enormously complex system of textual mediations and transpositions between us and Troilus's original performance yet appears to disregard those mediations to treat the song as a *meaning* whose essence can be conveyed without them. The passage thus appears to subscribe to a set of so-called logocentric illusions: that meaning is univocal and unchanging, that writing is a supplementary or secondary medium that preserves and delivers meaning transparently, and that it does so in the mode of presence—as if the speaker and the audience were present to one another (Chaucer's frequent references to his audience as, for example, "ye loveres that ben here" [II, 1751], seem to support this assumption). We, by insisting on the difference between speaking and writing, can bring out the awkward questions, contradictions, and paradoxes that the passage raises, embodies, and begs: Where did the speaker get the song if it isn't in his source? How can he know what he claims to know? Where is the *here* of "next this vers," and how can we *hear* what *isn't spoken* "here"? As one can only write literally or speak phonically, isn't "speaking literally," which is what the passage claims to do, an oxymoron or undecidable, one of those structures that simultaneously and irreconcilably mean one thing and its opposite? Jacques Derrida, under such names as *hymen, pharmakon, supplément,* and *différance,* has so put his signature on this phenomenon that I am tempted to call it *la chose Derridienne,* or simply Jacques' Thing ("construeth that as yow lyst, I do no cure," as Chaucer remarks in the prologue to the *Legend of Good Women*).[3]

2. For example: "Of no sentement I this endite, / But out of Latyn in my tonge it write." (II, 13–14); "Ek though I speeke of love unfelyngly" (19); "if it happe in any wyse, / That here be any lovere in this place / That herkneth, as the storie wol devise" (29–31); "Ek som men grave in tree, some in ston wal, / As it betit; but syn I have bigonne, / Myn auctour shal I folwen, if I konne." (47–49): "As I shall synge, on Mayes day the thrydde" (56).

3. F, 152. The context, as will emerge, is relevant to the argument of this essay. For logocentrism and the problem of presence, see particularly Jacques Derrida, *Of*

What I have just outlined is the beginning of a deconstructive reading of the passage from *Troilus and Criseyde.* In a consideration of the entire poem the reading could be extended to include such things as a demonstration not only of the impossibility of the presence of speaker and audience one to another[4] but also of the impossibility of self-presence or identity, of the radical discontinuity of time and therefore of the impossibility of history, and finally to a general critique of all signifying systems, including social and religious institutions and language itself—the whole catalogue of logocentric, or meaning-centered, assumptions. What interests me, however, is that Chaucer seems to have anticipated such a reading and to have done it himself in his own writing. The very conspicuousness with which the passage begs the questions I have raised suggests that Chaucer wants to raise them, that he, like Derrida, is *miming* a certain sort of discourse in such a way as to bring out the assumptions that make it possible and to question them. In *Troilus and Criseyde,* for example, the first three books of the poem represent an experimental playing out or miming of logocentric ideals. These books embody a deliberate attempt to conflate past and present, here and there, speaker, audience, and characters, and "vapour eterne" with love "in tymes" (III, 11), in a transparency of meaning that can be felt to exist in some unmediated way *beyond* the text, the words. In Book III itself the failure of this attempt is enacted in various ways, many of them having to do with the expressed feeling that the lovers' consummation which is the principal event of the book cannot sustain the symbolic weight that has been put upon it. Significantly, the feeling is represented as arising from a failure of language to do justice to the intensity of an imagined experience "That is so heigh that al ne kan I telle" (III, 1323). This failure drives the narrator to a slightly nervous apology for his inadequacies (III, 1324–36) and a request that his readers, "yow that felying han in loves art" (III, 1333), in effect rewrite the text themselves in the light of their

---

*Grammatology,* trans. Gayatri Chakravorty Spivak (Baltimore: Johns Hopkins University Press, 1976). *Supplément* is discussed on pp. 141–64. For *hymen,* see "The Double Session," in Derrida's *Dissemination,* trans. Barbara Johnson (Chicago: University of Chicago Press, 1981), pp. 173–286, and for *pharmakon,* "Plato's Pharmacy" in ibid., pp. 61–172. For *différance,* see "Différance" in the same author's *Speech and Phenomena and Other Essays on Husserl's Theory of Signs,* trans. David B. Allison (Evanston: Northwestern University Press, 1973), pp. 129–60.

4. See Derrida, "Signature Event Context," trans. Samuel Weber and Jeffrey Mehlman, *Glyph* 1 (1977), 172–97, especially 196.

superior experience, "encresse or maken dymynucioun / Of my langage" (III, 1335–36). It seems to me no accident that the sense of separation from the experience of the lovers is represented as a fall into textuality, a movement from a magical, imaginative seeing and saying to a baffled reading and writing dominated by uncertainty as to whether one's attempts to convey the "sentence" of "myn auctor" have been "in eched for the beste" (III, 1329).

In the last two books of the poem Chaucer himself deconstructs the ontological and logocentric pretensions of the first three, in part by calling attention more explicitly to the textuality of his own text. In Book V, where he uses the locution "thow redere" for the first time in the poem (V, 270), he also presents the "story" as a collection of documents—letters between the erstwhile lovers reproduced verbatim (V, 1317–1421, 1590–1631), a summary of the *Thebaid* "as men in bokes fynde" (V, 1463–1519),[5] a group of portraits drawn from Joseph of Exeter's translation of Dares (V, 799–840) containing, among other matter, what "they writen that hire syen" (816) about Criseyde, and so forth. The conspicuous gaps between these various documents put us all in the same position—the reader's position—as the narrator. They destroy the illusion of connected narrative and, as Robert W. Hanning has finely put it, "make a definitive interpretation of the poem intentionally impossible."[6] They do so, moreover, in such a way as to call into question not only the meaning of the end of the story but, retrospectively, the whole previous conduct of its telling. What began by pretending to be the presentation of an experience to listeners ends by identifying the activity it embodies as the construction for readers of a text whose meaning has yet to be determined. At the end of the poem Chaucer calls attention to the textual phenomenon of *absence,* the way a text is a kind of orphan, bereft of its maker, and equally uncertain of its destination, of who will receive it and how: "Go, litel bok, go litel myn tragedye. . . . That thow be understonde, God I biseche!" (V, 1786, 1798).[7]

5. Robinson's notes to this passage (pp. 835-36) point out that "a Latin argument," further summarizing the twelve books of Statius's poem "is inserted in the MSS, after l. 1498." Though it is almost never printed as part of the poem, this insertion further contributes to the "look" of a manuscript as a collection of heterogeneous texts and probably belongs on the page.

6. "The Audience as Co-Creator of the First Chivalric Romances," *Yearbook of English Studies* 11 (1981), 20. The whole discussion of *Troilus and Criseyde* is of interest.

7. Derrida takes the notion of the text as orphan from Plato, *Phaedrus* 275e, and

In *Troilus and Criseyde,* therefore, the issues central to deconstruction are made a central focus of the poem, and Chaucer uses the literary imitation of oral discourse in such a way as to bring out a textual critique of logocentrism. This pattern is constant in Chaucer and central to his art. All the early dream-visions exploit the distinction between the dream originally dreamed and the subsequent process of writing it down. I have called attention elsewhere to this process as it operates in the *Parlement of Foules,* a poem that is in large part about the difficulties generated by the multiplication of texts in the poet's world.[8] The dream itself was, the poem makes clear, a dream about texts, whose characters were drawn from the poet's reading—Macrobius, for instance, or a Nature who looks and speaks "right as Aleyn, in the Pleynt of Kynde, / Devyseth" [*PF,* 316–17]—and the text provides reasons for believing that the dream functioned originally as a kind of logocentric fantasy, an imaginary making-present of the *auctores* it contained. In the poem, however, this visual and immediate experience is retextualized, reread, and reinterpreted in such a way as to stress its still unresolved character. What is finally produced is not a definitive summation of the "sentence" of the poet's reading but yet another text to be added to the pile of conflicting versions of the nature of love.

The Prologue to the *Legend of Good Women* (especially the F version), written after *Troilus and Criseyde* and centrally concerned with the longer poem's reception, makes the problem of the independent life of texts one of its principal themes. In the poem the line I have already quoted with reference to Derrida follows a description of the birds in the poet's dream as they celebrate the return of spring:[9]

> And therwithalle hire bekes gonnen meete,
> Yeldyng honour and humble obeysaunces
> To love, and diden hire other observaunces
> That longeth onto love and to nature;
> Construeth that as yow lyst, I do no cure. (F, 148-52)

---

develops it in "Plato's Pharmacy," pp. 75–84. See also "Signature Event Context," p. 181.

8. See H. Marshall Leicester, Jr., "The Harmony of Chaucer's *Parlement:* A Dissonant Voice," *Chaucer Review* 9 (1974), 17. For the distinction between the time of dreaming and that of writing, see for example lines 113–19, where the poet presents himself, momentarily, as suddenly understanding for the first time that the dream was inspired by Cytherea, something he did not realize even "whan I began my sweven for to write" (118) some sixteen stanzas earlier.

9. The passage is heavily intertextualized, not only with its general source in Guillaume de Lorris but also, at line 145, to Chaucer's own *Parlement.*

The poet's comment is directed to the reader, who cannot see the absent scene. Here as in my use of it earlier, the line calls attention to something that might be read as an indelicacy, a breach of decorum, not in the scene but in the text (and thereby makes it more likely that it will be read that way). The poem is full of such awkward moments, many of which stress the poet's position as the nervous center of unwelcome attention. The funniest and most chilling of these is perhaps the moment when the entourage of the God of Love surrounds, "a-compas environ," the poet and the daisy beside which he is kneeling (F, 300ff.) and maintains a pregnant silence "the mountance of a furlong wey of space" (F, 307)—the time it takes to walk the length of two football fields—while the poet waits to be noticed. When he is noticed, he is taken to task for his previous writings, especially *Troilus and Criseyde* and the *Romance of the Rose,* which, according to the God of Love, have demonstrated the poet's hostility to love "in pleyn text, withouten nede of glose" (F, 328).

Clearly the poet's texts have gotten beyond his control. Temporal displacements, for instance "Construeth that as yow list" or the disclaimer of partisanship in the debate of Flower and Leaf (F, 188–96), suggest that the anxiety generated by the misunderstandings of readers such as the God of Love in the past has continued into the present of writing. It is as if the poet were attempting to forestall further misreadings by supplying clarifying glosses in the very act of writing his text. The fiction of the poem, the dream, shows how the audience of *Troilus and Criseyde,* far from being a unified group with a common understanding and a shared world, has fragmented into a set of *readers* who have variously (mis)understood or (mis)taken the text, and the textualizing of the dream is conducted in such a way as to suggest that once such a breach in the transparency of meaning has occurred, it can never be repaired. The society depicted in the Prologue to the *Legend* has to deal with the independent life and agency of texts in the world by patching up a new and precariously ad hoc agreement regarding how to take them, how to allocate blame for the trouble they cause, and what to do about it. It seems fitting that, here as in the *Parlement,* the "solution" arrived at involves, ironically, the potentially endless production of further texts, the legends, "while that thow lyvest, yer by yere" (F, 481).

The modern theory of the text has, by and large, addressed historical issues only in terms of a single problem, the development of modernism out of bourgeois culture.[10] It seems to me, however, that medieval society provides a natural field for examination in these terms because, as everyone recognizes, its institutional structure is a complex blend of oral and written elements and exhibits a slow drift over time from the predominance of the former to that of the latter.[11] This drift from oral to written is roughly parallel to, and connected with, a drift from a traditional, face-to-face, logocentric culture of presence to a textual, disseminated modern culture of absence based in writing, where strangers read one another. Traditional societies that rely on oral transmission of cultural information are, as Claude Lévi-Strauss suggests,[12] virtually by definition "structuralist" cultures, because their institutions are embedded in a mechanism that almost automatically mystifies the actors and conceals from them the extent to which they are responsible for the creation and maintenance of culture. In line with this mystification, such cultures typically privilege the "logocentric" qualities of discourse. Oral delivery implies a relatively small group, whose members all know one another and whose most common mode of interaction is face-to-face, that is, present to one another. The assumption of presence supports the assumption of a shared world, the cultural consensus of "what everybody knows," because in face-to-face situation any misapprehension can supposedly be corrected by the performer "in person." At the same time, however, the apparent freedom and originality of spontaneous self-disclosure in the immediacy of oral performance is in fact extremely constrained. Even if a performer chooses and is permitted to make fun of traditional stories or to change them radically, such deformations disappear with the last echo of the performance itself. What is remembered is what the society has *structured as memorable:* the traditional, the formulaic, the orthodox. What lasts is not what an individual does, but what everybody knows. Logo-

10. I have in mind the writings of Roland Barthes, particularly *S/Z,* trans. Richard Miller (New York: Hill & Wang, 1974) but also such things as the historical assumptions of "To Write: An Intransitive Verb?" in *The Structuralist Controversy*, ed. Richard Macksey and Eugenio Donato (Baltimore: Johns Hopkins University Press, 1970), pp. 134–45. See the discussion by Hayden White, "The Question of Narrative in Contemporary Historical Theory," *History and Theory* 23 (1984), 10–15.

11. Brian Stock, *The Implications of Literacy* (Princeton: Princeton University Press, 1983), chap. 1 "Oral and Written," pp. 12–87, has an excellent discussion covering several areas of culture and an extensive bibliography. See also Paul Zumthor, *Essai de poétique médiévale* (Paris: Seuil, 1973).

12. For example, in *The Raw and the Cooked,* trans. John and Doreen Weightman (New York: Harper, 1975), "Overture," pp. 1–32.

centrism, the metaphysics of the Word, is predicated on taking all language communication on the model of face-to-face discourse, in which the assumption of a shared world, that is, of the very possibility of univocal meaning, is protected by the co-presence of the actors, who can "say what they mean" to one another.[13]

Writing is the serpent in this paradise because it is capable of preserving the deviant, subversive, or simply different interpretations that tend to be lost in oral transmission. No single text is likely to raise much trouble, but as divergent texts multiply and are more widely disseminated, it becomes easier for what would have been merely idiosyncratic performances in oral culture to turn into *quaestiones disputatae*. That is in fact what happened in the Middle Ages, as a glance at the diversity of written authorities who have to be reconciled by any *summa* will verify.[14] As in the *Parlement of Foules* and the *Legend of Good Women*, writing creates more writing, and over the long haul textual culture is almost inevitably poststructuralist, whether it wants to be or not—it deconstructs itself.

But again, I am arguing that Chaucer does not merely contribute to this long-range process like any other writer. He is an *active* deconstructionist whose historical moment comes far enough along in the process to present him with a world in which the phenomena of textuality are readily available for his use. His work depicts a society in which much of culture is mediated through writing—we are a long way from the bard who transmits the wisdom of the tribe in oral formulas[15]—and a society that exhibits the relative fragmentation, self-

13. The clearest brief explanation of many of these matters is Barbara Johnson's "Translator's Introduction" to Derrida, *Dissemination*, pp. vii–xvi. See also Eric A. Havelock, *The Literate Revolution and Its Consequences* (Princeton: Princeton University Press, 1982), and Walter J. Ong, *Orality and Literacy: The Technologizing of the Word* (New York: Methuen, 1982).

14. See my discussion in "The Harmony of Chaucer's *Parlement*," pp. 18–19. In addition to the sources there listed, Erwin Panofsky, *Gothic Architecture and Scholasticism* (New York: Meridian, 1957), is extremely helpful.

15. The critical perspective enabled by textuality may, however, be adopted whenever there are texts and in fact occurs much earlier than Chaucer in medieval culture. For an analysis of the *Beowulf* manuscript's textual critique of the oral *scop*, see Harry Berger, Jr., and H. Marshall Leicester, Jr., "Social Structure as Doom: The Limits of Heroism in *Beowulf*," in *Old English Studies in Honor of John C. Pope*, ed. Robert B. Burlin and Edward B. Irving, Jr. (Toronto: University of Toronto Press, 1974), pp. 37–79.

consciousness, and alienation of a "modern" age. But this culture still tries to mystify itself, to treat its institutions *as if* they were still supported by the logocentric guarantees of common understanding and a shared world. Chaucer's typical practice is to begin by assuming and miming the conventions that try to sustain the logocentric coherence of "what everybody knows." In the General Prologue to the *Canterbury Tales,* for example, in the opening lines and in the portraits at least through the Wife of Bath's, the speaker's confident and relatively neutral tone is sustained by his ability to allude to estates conventions and traditional notions of hierarchy which tend to obscure his responsibility for the tacit judgments he makes.[16] But here as in *Troilus and Criseyde* this miming of traditional attitudes is conducted in such a way as to bring out contradictions and the dilemmas they lead to. As the prologue proceeds, the traditional categories seem less and less adequate to capture the complexities of the individual pilgrims; the poet's judgments become more explicit and more explicitly his own; and by the end of the prologue the question of what it means to judge or categorize one's fellows has become an issue in the poem. We are presented once again with an image of the poet as nervously isolated, surrounded by the silent attention of *readers* whose misunderstanding of his text and potentially hostile reaction to it he must endeavor to forestall (*CT* I, 715–46)—a situation already familiar from the end of *Troilus and Criseyde* and the Prologue to the *Legend.* It is this awareness of the way one inevitably embodies oneself in a text which contributes to Chaucer's intense interest in self-presentation, the central preoccupation of the *Canterbury Tales* as a whole.[17] When self-disclosure no longer takes place in the sustaining presence of others to whom one may explain oneself face-to-face, when it is indirect and deferred, one must be much more careful to control the image of self that is carried by the orphaned text across the gap between those original strangers, reader and writer. The "scene of writing" seems to have made Chaucer sharply aware of "oure tonges *différance,*" of the way language itself (because it is a medium, not meaning itself) both defers our access to final meaning and

16. See Jill Mann, *Chaucer and Medieval Estates Satire* (Cambridge: Cambridge University Press, 1973).

17. For further discussion of self-presentation in the *Tales,* see my "The Art of Impersonation: A General Prologue to the *Canterbury Tales,*" *PMLA* 95 (1980), 213–24.

inscribes its own ability to keep generating new meanings endlessly into the gap it creates; and this can be matter for uneasiness.

But this situation also has its opportunities and rewards. The *Canterbury Tales* as a whole refers to, or mimes, a face-to-face oral situation in which the participants tell one another traditional stories. Here as elsewhere, however, the illusions of presence are subjected to a textual deconstruction. This deconstruction produces a new world in which the modes of interpretation proper to reading, writing, and textuality are the fundamental conditions of individual and social existence. Many of the tales are shown to "fail" as oral performances on the fictional pilgrimage: one has to think only of the Pardoner or the Wife of Bath, whose performances are, by the pilgrims on the spot who hear and respond to them, respectively condemned and then hushed up, and briefly and slightingly dismissed. These failed performances are revalued by being preserved in Chaucer's text, where the absent tellers emerge more coherently and more complexly than they were able to do "in person."[18] This is nowhere more evident than in Chaucer's own tales in Fragment VII. On the one hand, *Sir Thopas* is "saved" from the misprision of the Host, preserved for readers who may have a better understanding of the tale's "entente" as parody. More interesting still, on the other hand, is *Melibee,* which is conspicuously presented as a tale that could not have been told as we have it.[19] I am something of a believer in the "Chaucer's revenge" theory of *Melibee,* though I must admit that the revenge seems somewhat misdirected, for Harry Bailly did not have to read the tale (or even listen to it in the form it comes to us)—and I, poor dedicated Chaucerian, do. But revenge becomes an issue precisely because of the way the text raises the question of how context and use transform and undermine the traditional, logocentric message presented in the preceding link about the irrelevance of words "moore and . . . lesse" to underlying "sentence" *(CT* VII, 940–66).

*Melibee* is a subversive text, not least in the way it plays with and

18. I have developed this point in more detail in "Answer to Robert Burlin," *PMLA* 95 (1980), 881–82, and in " 'Synne Horrible': The Pardoner's Exegesis of His Tale, and Chaucer's," in *Acts of Interpretation: The Text in Its Contexts, 700–1600,* ed. Mary J. Carruthers and Elizabeth D. Kirk (Norman, Okla.: Pilgrim, 1982), pp. 45–50.

19. The best account of *Melibee,* with particular reference to the function of the text in the Canterbury framework, is Daniel R. Kempton, "Chaucer's Tale of Melibee: 'A Litel Thyng in Prose,' " forthcoming in *The Journal of Narrative Technique.* I have used it with profit in this discussion.

undermines nearly to the point of obliteration the whole idea of voicing, the notion that words are proper to whoever speaks them.[20] Here, however, I concentrate on the way that the tale's presentation alters its literal meaning. The insistent textuality of the *Melibee*—its inordinate and undramatic length, its relentless listing of proverbs and citations, the gaps in it that have forced editors to supply passages from the French version of the source to get the text to make sense—such features call attention to the possibility that Chaucer may have interpolated into his written account a text radically different from what he "performed" on the pilgrimage. This possibility in turn suggests that the text we have represents something like what Geoffrey would have liked to do to the Host, because it supplies the "doctrine" the latter asks for with a vengeance and infects the tale with an aura of social conflict and resentment which stretches from the fictional moment of Geoffrey's humiliation over *Sir Thopas* on the pilgrimage (VII, 919–5) through the time of writing to the all-too-actual now of reading. This is a story that urges temperance and patience in a way that is both monstrously intemperate and an affront to the reader's patience; as such it inflicts on the reader the results of a continuing power game between the Host and the poet. In context the tale portrays Chaucer's ineffectuality in the face-to-face encounter on the pilgrimage and simultaneously calls attention to the power of the writer as the man whose *scripta manent,* who has the last word in, and as, the text. I suspect that the tale may finally function as a comment on the deadening and coercive power of "traditional wisdom," which can deform life exactly as Prudence's proverbs do the plot. In any case, Chaucer's contextualization makes of *Melibee* something quite different from the harmless collection of *sententiae* it appears to be as a literal statement in isolation from any context; his handling of the text decenters its "original" logocentric meaning as stable, timeless wisdom and transforms it into a text of aggression.

20. Among the elements in *Melibee* which establish its recontextualization in the *Canterbury Tales*—that make it *Chaucer's* tale of Melibee—is an extensive and explicit set of intertextualities with other tales, most notably those of the Wife of Bath ("And sire, by youre leve, that am nat I," VII, 1087; cf. III, 111) and of the Merchant (VII, 1098–1101; cf. IV, 1361–74). This is perhaps an argument for the Ellesmere order of the tales, insofar as it makes a bit more sense for "Chaucer" to quote the Wife and the Merchant than for either of them to quote Prudence. But the real point, as I say in the text, is that the sense of individual voicing, irony, and intensive personal meaning that these passages take on in the tales of the other pilgrims is flattened—"ghosted," as Kempton puts it—and finally denied by the relentless march of Prudence's "ensamples."

UNION COLLEGE LIBRARY
BARBOURVILLE, KY 40906

The contextualization of *Melibee* is an example of the more general message embodied in all the poems I have discussed here: texts do not *mean,* they are *used.* "Meaning," as in German *meinen,* is not a thing, it is an action. The form of the message is consistently deconstructionist in the way it is consistently linked to issues of speaking and hearing, reading and writing. Chaucer's portrayal of the various ways people in his culture actually use their texts, the traditional, logocentrically packaged material they inherit, constitutes his *différance.* He uses and inflects textuality as a technique for deferring traditional or expected meanings (the official ideologies of the culture), in order to suggest and explore *different* ones, what people actually do.

# "I Shal Finde It in a Maner Glose": Versions of Textual Harassment in Medieval Literature

ROBERT W. HANNING

To the twentieth-century student, no term in the medieval lexicon of interpretation seems at first sight so comfortably unambiguous as *glossa* and its Latin and vernacular derivatives. But a closer look at the word reveals that during the Middle Ages its lexical meaning and cultural significance varied widely from century to century, language to language, and context to context. As an explanatory technique, glossing belonged primarily to the schools and the pulpit, but as a concept it achieved much broader cultural currency, functioning as a metaphor for all kinds of language manipulation, even what might be called textual harassment, that is, the forcible imposition of special meanings on single words or entire verbal structures.

Glossing, as technique and as metaphor, passed into vernacular literature in the course of the twelfth century. Eugene Vinaver has explicated its contribution to "the discovery of meaning"—that is, the virtuosic elucidation of character, motive, and situation—in courtly narratives of love and adventure.[1] More can profitably be said about the technical and metaphorical uses of the gloss in medieval literature,

I am grateful to Prof. Sandra Pierson Prior for reading an earlier version of this essay and making cogent suggestions for improving it.

1. Eugene Vinaver, *The Rise of Romance* (Oxford: Clarendon Press, 1971), pp. 15–32.

especially as an instrument of poetic self-consciousness. In this essay I examine instances of glossing, by poets and by their characters, in twelfth-century French texts and in the poetry of Chaucer. In addition to showing medieval literary imaginations responding inventively to an indigenous and widespread interpretive phenomenon, my examples also illustrate an interesting transference of meaning whereby glossing, instead of signifying a scholarly operation performed on texts, becomes a strategic and usually coercive operation performed on people. Before proceeding to literary analysis, however, I believe a bit of cultural background is in order.

## I

In classical Latin, *glossa* (from the Greek word for tongue and, by extension, language) originally denoted a foreign or obsolete word that needed explanation. The plural *glossae* and the derived singular, *glossarium,* came to mean a collection of such words and their definitions.[2] In the Christian Middle Ages, however, *glossa* took on new and important dimensions of meaning with respect to inherited texts that, because of their canonical status within the culture, could not be allowed to become foreign or obsolete.

From its earliest years, to be sure, Christianity had to deal with the problem of interpreting and understanding its canonic texts. The first Christian communities assimilated the Hebrew Scriptures—the record of the "old" covenant between God and Israel—by treating them as a collection of types or shadows of the full truth revealed in the life, death, and resurrection of Jesus.[3] Later ages applied complicated, multileveled exegesis to the Old and New Testaments (especially to the Revelation of Saint John) to preserve and explain their relevance to the persecuted church, then to the triumphant and established imperial church, even later to the heroic age of early medieval monasticism, and in all ages to the moral life and development of the individual Christian.

By the late eleventh century, at the burgeoning monastic and cathedral schools in northern France, the systematic study of major classical (i.e., pagan) texts, as well as of the Bible, had led to the increasing use

2. C. T. Lewis and C. Short, *A Latin Dictionary* (Oxford: Clarendon Press, 1879), s.v. *glossa, glossae, glossarium.*

3. See Jean Danielou, *Sacramentum futuri: Les figures du Christ dans l'ancien testament* (Paris: Beauchesnes, 1950).

of the marginal or interlinear gloss as a technique for teaching and studying.[4] The master supplied discontinuous, specific explanations for difficult, or indeed for all, passages of the text under discussion, explanations that could be passed along with the text—whether a book of the Bible, Virgil's *Aeneid,* or Plato's *Timaeus*—as it was copied and recopied. The production and compilation of glosses was no mere act of philological or archeological piety toward inherited classics, designed to elucidate their original meanings; on the contrary, it was frequently an exertion of mastery over such works, a focusing of intellect or belief to reclaim and domesticate alien institutions or perceptions.

For example, William of Conches's twelfth-century *Glosae super Platonem* undertakes to reconcile the cosmology of Plato's *Timaeus* with Christian beliefs about the creation of the world. William knew the *Timaeus* only in Calcidius's fourth-century free translation with integrated commentary.[5] And his understanding of the creation as recounted in Genesis was thoroughly conditioned by the Platonizing Christian gloss on it which constitutes the opening of the Johannine gospel. In other words, William's *Glosae* comes at the end of a centuries-long process of glossing, that is, of teasing and distorting texts with radically different world views into harmony one with another.

The idea that a gloss manipulates rather than explains its text may seem a peculiarly modern one, but medieval scholars and satirists were by no means unaware of the possibilities of such textual harassment. According to Beryl Smalley, for instance, the thirteenth-century Parisian masters Peter Comestor and Stephen Langton, in their lectures on biblical interpretation, reminded students that allegorical or tropological glossing offered greater freedom for the exegete than literal explanation. They recognized that, in Smalley's words, "the spiritual exposition may give quite an opposite sense to the literal," provided that the allegory conforms to Christian faith.[6] Such interpretive freedom and ingenuity did not always go unchallenged: Langton disapprovingly mentions an impious observer who, "hearing that the red colour of

4. See Beryl Smalley, *The Study of the Bible in the Middle Ages,* 2d ed. (Oxford, 1952; rpt. Notre Dame: Notre Dame University Press, 1978), pp. 46–66.

5. Guillaume de Conches, *Glosae super Platonem,* ed. Edouard Jeauneau (Paris: Vrin, 1965); Calcidius, *Commentarius in Timaeum Platonis,* ed. J. H. Waszink (London: Warburg Institute, and Leiden: E. J. Brill, 1962).

6. Smalley, *Study of the Bible,* p. 258.

the cow [Num. 19.2], which the Law commanded as a sacrifice, prefigured the blood of the Passion," responded, " 'it would be all the same if the cow had been black; the allegory is worthless; whatever the colour of the cow, some sort of allegory could be found for it.' " Such an attitude may well have gained ground despite the self-justifications of the *magistri;* by the mid-thirteenth century, Smalley tells us, the word *glossa* "was acquiring a pejorative meaning. It implied 'glossing over' instead of stating frankly what the author intended."[7]

It was at this time that the newly founded mendicant orders began their work of preaching and evangelizing among the common people, and not surprisingly the Franciscans, at least, seem in their early years to have distrusted the technique of glossing. John Fleming speaks of the respect for the Word of God in its pure form shown by Francis and of the saint's analogous insistence (perpetuated in later Franciscan legends about his life) that the text of his Rule should not be glossed. In one such legend the voice of Christ exhorts Francis, "I wish the Rule to be obeyed to the letter, to the letter, without a gloss, without a gloss." Accordingly, says Fleming, "primitive Franciscan texts . . . insist on the rhetorical simplicity of evangelical preaching," a simplicity allied to deep sincerity and emotional intensity.[8]

However, the friars soon invaded the universities, became biblical scholars, and produced new kinds of consecutive glosses (*postillae*); in reciprocation the interpretive techniques of the universities appeared more and more frequently in mendicant preaching, where they mingled with the virtuosic retelling of exemplary stories and the intense rhetoric of affective piety to create a rich, compelling homiletic brew. To maximize the impact of the gospel, mendicant preachers also developed different rhetorical styles to appeal to audiences of varied estates in life—a strategy, known as the *sermo ad status,* that involved further manipulation of biblical texts and their message.[9]

7. Ibid., pp. 261, 271.

8. John V. Fleming, *An Introduction to the Franciscan Literature of the Middle Ages* (Chicago: Franciscan Herald Press, 1977), pp. 23–26, 56, 116. The example is from the Prologue of the *Speculum perfectionis,* written ca. 1318.

9. See Fleming, *Introduction,* pp. 156–59, on the *Communiloquium* of John of Wales, a handbook for preachers. Cf. R. A. Pratt, "Chaucer and the Hand That Fed Him," *Speculum* 41 (1966), 619–42, for Chaucer's use of the *Communiloquium.* On the *sermo ad status* see also E. Vance, "Mervelous Signals: Poetics, Sign Theory, and Politics in Chaucer's *Troilus,*" *New Literary History* 10 (1979), 296–97; Vance refers to Umbertus Romanus, *De eruditione praedicatorum,* of which the second part "un-

The pulpit effectiveness and versatility of the friars brought them into conflict with the parish clergy and later with puritanical Lollards, who castigated the mendicants for their abuses as preachers and especially for self-aggrandizing exegesis or glossing. The anonymous author of *Jack Upland* (ca. 1420) asks, "Frere, whi preche ȝe fals fabils of freris and feined myraclys, and leuen the gospel that Christ bade preche?" (233–34). The later *Upland's Rejoinder* accuses a mendicant writer who replied to *Jack Upland*'s charges of "lesynges with losengery, cursynges and false glose" (4) and of beguiling "symple hertes, / With thi gildyn glose" (72; cf. 251).[10] Similarly, in the Prologue of the C-Text of Langland's *Piers Plowman,* Will sees amidst the Feld ful of Folk "of freris all the foure ordres, / Prechyng the peple for profyt of the wombe, / And glosede the gospel as hem good likede" (56-58).[11]

Even when friars were not involved, the concept of glossing evoked ambivalent responses in late medieval England, as demonstrated by the thorough mix of positive and negative meanings attested to in Middle English: the noun "glose" signified not only "comment, explanation, description" but also "specious or sophistical interpretation, the pursuit of favor by adulation, flattering or deceitful speech." The verb "glosen" signified "to interpret, explain," but also "to interpret falsely, obscure the truth, gloss over, falsely embellish, disguise, cajole, flatter, coax." A "gloser" could be a commentator but also a sycophant or flatterer; "glosynge" was interpretation but also smooth or deceitful talk, cajolery, or flattery.[12]

We see here a cultural disillusionment with (or suspicion of) scholars and scholarship; we also see how the lexical focus of that disillusionment and suspicion—terms originally describing the learned manipulation of texts—undergoes a shift in meaning and a change of venue. By Chaucer's day, the late fourteenth century, glossing had come to

---

dertakes as its task to describe the *sermones ad status* which the preacher must master if he intends to preach to any given group in society. Umbertus's classification of social groups by *status* provides no less than one hundred different categories of audience to be found among the species of man" (p. 297).

10. Parenthetical references are to line numbers; all references and quotations are from *Jack Upland, Friar Daw's Reply, and Upland's Rejoinder,* ed. P. L. Heyworth (Oxford: Clarendon Press, 1968).

11. William Langland, *Piers Plowman: An Edition of the C-Text,* ed. Derek Pearsall (Berkeley: University of California Press, 1979), pp. 30–31.

12. See *Middle English Dictionary,* ed. Hans Kurath and Sherman M. Kuhn (Ann Arbor: University of Michigan Press, 1930–), under these entries.

mean shady, tricky, self-aggrandizing discourse in general, and it could turn up in all spheres of society, not just in the academy. Such a generalization provided ample opportunities for quibbling on the various meanings of glossing, an opportunity not lost on satiric writers, especially when attacking the friars. Thus in *Upland's Rejoinder* the friar is told, "thou approvest ȝour capped maisters with a glasen glose [i.e., a sophistical interpretation, presumably of a biblical text; cf. *MED, glasen,* lb] / Which galpen after grace, bi symonye ȝour sister, / And after sitten on hie dece and glosen lordes and ladies" (357–59). In this accusation one kind of glossing leads naturally to the other: the tongue that twists language to justify clerical abuses easily becomes the tongue that flatters the rich to open their money bags.

II

The authors of the new vernacular fictions written for the twelfth-century courts of northern France and England include the notion of glossing among the many creative and interpretive issues they explore self-consciously in their works. For example, Marie de France begins her collection of *Lais* with a prologue in which she offers a rationale for the study and glossing of ancient texts:

Custume fu as anciens,
Ceo testimoine Preciens
Es livres ke jadis feseient
Assez oscurement diseient
Pur ceus ki a venir esteient
E ki aprendre les deveient,
K'i peussent gloser la lettre
E de lur sen le surplus mettre.

The custom among the ancients—
as Priscian testifies—
was to speak quite obscurely
in the books they wrote,
so that those who were to come after
and study them
might gloss the letter
and supply its significance from their own wisdom. (9-16)[13]

13. Marie de France, *Lais,* ed. A. Ewart (Oxford: Blackwell, 1947); all references to Marie's *Lais* follow this edition. All translations are from R. W. Hanning and J. M. Ferrante, trans., *The Lais of Marie de France* (New York, 1978; rpt. Durham, N.C.:

For Marie, the textual heritage of her civilization—its *auctores*—incorporates a salutary challenge to those who come after: the opportunity to *gloser la lettre,* adding a *surplus*—that is, discovering or imposing new significances—from their *sens,* which I take to mean their fund of intelligence, critical acumen, and imagination. The activity of glossing thus becomes part of that communication of one's wisdom and insight which Marie commends in the opening lines of the Prologue:

> Ki Deus ad dune escience
> E de parler bon eloquence
> Ne s'en deit taisir ne celer,
> Ainz se deit volunters mustrer.
>
> Whoever has received knowledge
> and eloquence in speech from God
> should not be silent or secretive
> but demonstrate it willingly. (1–4)[14]

In *Guigemar,* the first (and next to longest) lai of her collection, Marie demonstrates the ingenuity with which she can integrate glossing into her art as a vehicle of meaning, mastery, and wit. Under the guise of explaining a painting, for instance, she uses glossing techniques to express her lai's antagonism to a classical, Ovidian view of love. The painting adorns the walls of the room in which the future beloved of the young knight Guigemar has been imprisoned by her jealous old husband. In the image, Marie tells us, Venus is depicted instructing neophytes in "cument hom deit amur tenir / E lealment e bien servir" (237–38) [how to behave in love, and to serve love loyally]. The goddess also burns Ovidian texts that subvert her teaching and excommunicates those who read them. Here Marie's *surplus* transforms a classical deity into a medieval bishop and a rival love poet into a heretic whose books

Labyrinth, 1982). See further, concerning this passage in the Prologue, K. Brightenback, "Remarks on the 'Prologue' to Marie de France's *Lais,*" *Romance Philology* 30 (1976), 168–77; B. E. Fitz, "The Prologue to the *Lais* of Marie de France and the *Parable of the Talents* and Money Metaphor," *Modern Language Notes* 90 (1975), 558–64; D.W. Robertson, "Marie de France, *Lais,* Prologue, 13–15," *Modern Language Notes* 64 (1949), 336–38.

14. For other examples of the topos of *communiquer sagesse,* see the opening lines of Chretien de Troyes's *Erec et Enide,* the anonymous *Roman de Thebes,* and Benoit de Saint-Maure's *Roman de Troyes.*

deserve destruction. By using her Christian *sens* in this way with respect to Venus and Ovid, Marie shows her awareness of how a modernizing "gloss" (albeit presented as an ecphrasis) can be used to manipulate and subvert the "text" it sets out to explain.

Earlier in *Guigemar,* Marie assigns the task of glossing to an unusual surrogate: the marvelous androgynous deer that Guigemar, the self-absorbed, love-scorning, adolescent knight, shoots while out hunting. The arrow rebounds and wounds its launcher, whereupon the deer unexpectedly speaks, imposing its (and Marie's) *surplus* of meaning on the bizarre incident:

> ...tu, vassal, ki m'as nafree,
> Tel seit la tue destinee:
> Jamais n'aies tu medicine!
> ...N'avras tu james garisun
> De la plaie ke as en la quisse,
> De si ke cele te guarisse
> Ki suffera pur tue amur
> Issi grant peine e tel dolur
> Ke unkes femme taunt ne suffri:
> E tu referas taunt pur li,
> Dunt tut cil s'esmerveillerunt
> Ki aiment e ame avrunt
> U ki pois amerunt apres.
>
> ...You, vassal, who wounded me,
> this be your destiny:
> may you never get medicine for your wound!
> ...You will never be healed
> of that wound in your thigh
> until a woman heals you,
> one who will suffer, out of love for you,
> pain and grief
> such as no woman ever suffered before.
> And out of love for her, you'll suffer as much;
> the affair will become a marvel
> to lovers past and present,
> and to all those yet to come. (107–21)

The beast's explanation serves Marie's purposes in a variety of ways. It suggests, first of all, that Guigemar's pierced thigh is a euphemism, an external emblem for the onset of sexual desire—a suggestion confirmed almost four hundred lines later when Marie describes love as "plaie dedanz cors" (483), an internal wound. The gloss also reveals the metaphor on which the plot will hang: Guigemar's physical pain can be alleviated only by a woman who will give him, and receive from him, equivalent emotional suffering through love. The wounded thigh is not only a symbol but a type or foreshadowing of the wounded heart.[15] Finally, through her glossing intermediary, Marie inserts in her poem a portrait of its ideal audience: past, present, and future lovers who (like Gottfried von Strassburg's *edlen herzen* [noble hearts]) will respond with proper intensity to Guigemar's fate.

A final instance from *Guigemar* confirms Marie's seriocomic knowledge of the import of her age's penchant for glossing. At the climax of the lai's first section, the protagonists confess their passion for each other and agree to become lovers. They exchange words, hugs, and kisses (527–32). So much for what we might call love by the book; but Marie slyly adds, "bien lur convienge del *surplus,* / De ceo que li autre unt en us!" (533–34) [I hope they will enjoy whatever else / others do on such occasions]. The *surplus* of a love story, the part not normally described in a decorous courtly text, is in fact the real, sexual climax of a love relationship. Guigemar and his beloved must, using their sensual *sens,* add their *surplus* to their own words of wooing, and we must add ours to Marie's words of telling, fleshing out the story (as it were) from our own *sens* about what succeeds love's preliminary embraces. (Marie may again be contrasting her art to Ovid's *Ars amatoria,* which invades the bedchamber with quasi-clinical specificity.) [16] That

15. On the symbolic import of Guigemar's self-wounding, see Hanning and Ferrante, *The Lais of Marie de France,* pp. 56–57 (commentary to *Guigemar*), and R. W. Hanning, "Courtly Contexts for Urban *Cultus*: Responses to Ovid in Chretien's *Cliges* and Marie's *Guigemar,*" *Symposium* 34 (1981), 47–49. One should also note that the word for wound, *plaie,* and *plait,* the word for the knots that symbolize the lovers' fidelity to each other in the latter part of *Guigemar,* form a quibble around which Marie constructs the entire lai about Guigemar's most important *plait* (undertaking, affair; see line 526).

16. See Ovid, *Ars amatoria,* trans. J. H. Mozley, Loeb Classical Library (London: William Heinemann, and Cambridge, Mass.: Harvard University Press, 1929), 3.769–808. Two of Chretien's romances contain references relevant to the point made here. In *Le chevalier de la charette,* ed. Mario Roques, CFMA 86 (Paris: Champion, 1965), when Lancelot and Guinevere enjoy sexual union, the narrator declares, "Tant li est ses jeus dolz et buens, / et del beisier, et del santir, / que il lor avint sanz mantir / une joie et une mervoille / tel c'onques ancor sa paroille / ne fu oie ne seue; / mes toz jorz iert par moi teue, / qu'an conte ne doit estre dite. / Des joies fu la plus eslite / et la plus delitable cele / que li contes nos test et cele" (4674–84) [Their game of kissing and touching is so sweet and good that in all truth they experienced a joy and marvel whose equal was never known or heard of; but I'll certainly keep quiet about that, because it

is, sexual instincts or experience—the lovers' within the tale, the audience's outside it—provide the wherewithal for an effective gloss (elucidation, expansion, application) of the language of love, whether uttered by knights and ladies or by courtly poets. Marie's evocation of *surplus* at this climactic moment of *Guigemar* not only invites her audience to recognize their own "glossatorial" involvement in the overall meaning and effect of her lai; it also elevates her text to the level of those *livres* of the *anciens* which stimulate their readers to *gloser la lettre.*

An episode in the Ariostesque romance *Ipomedon,* by Marie's Anglo-Norman contemporary Hue de Rotelande, offers a paradigm of glossing quite different in its understanding and evaluation of the process.[17] La Fiere Pucele, the duchess of Calabria, has vowed to marry only the knight who performs the greatest deeds of prowess. When she discovers that an unknown young squire visiting her court—a handsome lad and a fine huntsman but completely uninterested in martial combat—has been smitten by her beauty, she decides to discourage him before he shames himself publicly. But how to accomplish her aim discreetly? "La Fiere en pense en meinte guise / Coment poreit, par qel qeintise, / Ensi parler qe cil l'oist / E qe il la glose entendist" (825–28) [La Fiere thought about it in many ways; how could she—by what strategem—speak in such a way that he would hear it and comprehend the hidden meaning]. What kind of text can she create to prompt in its intended

shouldn't be spoken about in a story. The story hides from us by its silence precisely that joy which was of all joys the most unique and delightful]. And a bit earlier, when Lancelot is preparing for his tryst with the queen by pretending to be tired and retiring early, the narrator comments, "Bien poez antendre et *gloser,* / vos qui avez fet autretel, / que por la gent de son ostel / se fet las et se fet couchier" (4550–53; emphasis mine) [You who have done such things can well understand and interpret that it was for the benefit of his retinue that he pretended to be tired and to go to bed]. In *Le conte du graal,* ed. Felix Lecoy, vol. 1, CFMA 100 (Paris: Champion, 1978), when the young Perceval is about to leave home to seek Arthur's court, his mother advises him concerning women he may meet in his travels "De pucele a mout qui la beise; / s'ele le beisier vos consant, / le *soreplus* vos en desfant, / se lessier le volez por moi" (544–47; emphasis mine) [He who kisses a maiden has received much; if she consents to kiss you, I forbid you the rest, if you wish to forego it for my sake].

17. All quotations and references follow Hue de Rotelande, *Ipomedon,* ed. A. J. Holden (Paris: Klincksieck, 1979). See Holden's introduction, pp. 52–57, for a critique of recent estimations of the romance, including my own: "*Engin* in Twelfth-century Romance: An Examination of the *Roman d'Eneas* and Hue de Rotelande's *Ipomedon,*" *Yale French Studies* 51 (1974), 82–101.

student the proper glossarial response—the *surplus* that comes from the *sens* of the writer rather than the interpreter?

We see that, in this model, the maker of the text—the analogue of Marie's *anciens*—and the text itself will manipulate its glossator rather than vice versa. La Fiere hits upon the scheme of delivering the rebuke intended for Ipomedon to her young kinsman Jason in Ipomedon's presence and counting on the squire to make the required transference of meaning to his own situation. Accusing Jason of falling in love with her *demeisele,* Ismeine, La Fiere scolds him for doing so before he can deserve consideration for his acts of valor, and ends by declaring, "E pur vostre bien vus chasti; / il ne fet pas mult grant folie / cil ke par autrui se chastie" (902–4) [And I am chastising you for your own good; he doesn't commit great folly who can take correction at the hands of others (or: can correct himself by applying someone else's situation to himself)].

La Fiere says this, Hue reminds us, not for Jason but "pur autri; / Cil meymes pur qi il fut dit / mult apertement l'entendit" (906–08) [for another; the one for whom it was really said understood it very clearly]. Jason subsides into silent anger, a misperceiving victim of La Fiere's textual strategy, while Ipomedon, performing the proper decoding immediately and accurately, grieves in equal silence and escapes from the court at the earliest possible moment. He thereupon begins a life of wandering prowess and constant role playing; the latter activity translates La Fiere's technique of covered speech into an experiential strategy of disguises and deceptive behavior, and in the process reveals its dangers. Time and again, those who observe the outrageous antics of Ipomedon in exile are deliberately misled by him into egregiously mistaken estimations of his worth. We can say, then, that from Hue's cynical perspective, the activity of interpretation looks much less rewarding than it does to Marie: the alternatives open to the would-be glossator confronted by obscure texts, and their equivalent in the realm of experience, seem to be the discovery of unpleasant, unsettling truths and the inability to discover the truth at all.

Another contemporaneous perspective on glossing, this one outspokenly comic, appears in the second part of Gautier d'Arras's multigeneric narrative *Eracles* (ca. 1180).[18] The Roman emperor Lais, having

18. All quotations and references follow Gautier d'Arras, *Eracle,* ed. Guy Raynaud de Lage, CFMA 102 (Paris: Champion, 1976).

chosen, with the help of Eracles' infallible judgment, the best woman in Rome as his wife, suddenly becomes the archetypal jealous husband of the medieval fabliau and attempts to forestall his wife's infidelity while he is away at war by placing her under constant guard. This treatment so offends the innocent empress, Athanais, that she decides to embark on a love affair with a handsome young nobleman, Parides. The intrigue profits from the assistance of a stereotypically greedy old crone who serves as go-between. At one point Athanais, wishing to deliver a message to Parides, tells the old woman, to whom she owes a gift, to expect it the next day. The go-between may have the gift itself for her use but must promise to pass on its *sorplus* (4356) to Parides with the instruction that he obey the *escrit* of the empress if he loves her as he claims (4353–60). Athanais writes a letter to Parides containing a plan for an assignation and slips it under the crust of a fresh-baked *paste*. She puts the pie on a silver tray and sends it to the old woman, for whom it creates an acute problem of interpretation: what is the present that is hers and what the *sorplus* that goes to the suitor? In her vexation the go-between decides "ci n'a autre present / ne mais cest paste seulement, / et li surplus est li argens" (4427–29) [There's no other present here except this pie, and what's left over is the silver tray]—a situation that seems to her most unjust, because it means that she, in her poverty, gets only a pastry, while Parides, in his wealth, gets a valuable tray. So annoyed is she that she smashes the pie, only then finding the letter inside. Realizing the truth at last, she babbles in delight, "c'est li surplus que je voi chi, / c'est li surplus que il i a" (4444–45) [It's the *surplus* that I see here, this is the *surplus* that's here"]; she then appropriates the tray and sets out at once to bring the letter to its proper recipient.

In this incident Gautier establishes a heirarchy of appetites: basic hunger, satisfied by the pie; greed, satisfied by the silver platter; and sexual desire (itself, on Athanais's part, the surrogate of a deeper desire for revenge), forwarded by the letter. The pie represents, if you will, a received text; the tray is the empress's marginal gloss, intended for the crude *sens* of a plebeian audience (the crone); the letter, meanwhile, can be seen as a kind of interlinear gloss aimed at a more sophisticated reader. From another point of view, we can say that Athanais uses her *sens*, her ingenuity sparked by resentment, to put the *sorplus* into the pie, a *sorplus* that, like that of Guigemar and his beloved, satisfies sexual desires. But for the *sorplus* to reach its intended audience, a mediating act of exegesis must take place: the discovery of the letter. Seen in this way, the pie becomes a comic version of the poetic fiction or *integumentum,* a concept dear to twelfth-century expositors and glossators of pagan poetry because it justifies their most fanciful manipulations of the canonic text.[19] The old woman's angry assault on the *paste,* which inadvertently discovers its hidden content of "higher meaning," provides a wonderfully amusing image of the frustrated exegete harassing a text and, quite by accident, discovering or recovering salutary truths. Gautier's comic linkage of the gloss-as-*sorplus* and the integument that must be pried open—intellectual operations different in theory but closely intertwined in twelfth-century literary practice—suggests his awareness, at some level, of the contingencies, inadvertencies, deceptions, and self-aggrandizement of the interpretive act.

Such an ironic view of textual study turned textual harassment may find a parallel, albeit a more trenchant one, in Chretien's *Cliges,* in the episode where three physicians from Salerno, learning of the supposed death of Fenice, intuit that her mortal illness was fraudulent and undertake to revive her, or at least to discover and reveal "tot le voir" of her condition (5810).[20] The learned doctors recall that one of Solomon's wives had tricked him, out of hatred, by pretending death (5802–4); guided by this literary exemplum, they begin their attempts to make Fenice speak, first by false promises (5863–73) and, when words fail, by beating her till she bleeds and by pouring molten lead into the palms of her hands. The healers-turned-torturers want Fenice to supply a truthful gloss that explains and exposes the integument of her false death. Their increasingly brutal *sens* will extract that *sorplus* from their supine "text," if they must destroy the text in the process. Is this odd episode the first instance in our tradition of a poet's critique of exegetes who all but annihilate the poetic value of a text—its tricky

19. See Bernard Silvestris, *Commentary on the First Six Books of Virgil's Aeneid,* trans. Earl G. Schreiber and Thomas E. Maresca (Lincoln: University of Nebraska Press, 1979), Preface, p. 5: "The integument is a type of exposition which wraps the apprehension of truth in a fictional narrative, and thus it is also called an *involucrum,* or cover." On the *integumentum* as a didactic and intellectual concept, see Winthrop Wetherbee, *Platonism and Poetry in the Twelfth Century* (Princeton: Princeton University Press, 1972), pp. 36–48, and Brian Stock, *Myth and Science in the Twelfth Century* (Princeton: Princeton University Press, 1972), pp. 49–62.

20. All quotations and references follow Chretien de Troyes, *Cliges,* ed. A. Micha, CFMA 84 (Paris: Champion, 1965).

language, its ambiguous symbols—in their effort to pry from it its more profound message of *caritas* or some other Christian truth? Given Chretien's many subversive presentations of "ideal" knights and lovers, in *Cliges* and elsewhere, we cannot rule out the possibility that he is here taking aim against not only physicians but text-torturing scholars as well.

## III

In Book IV of *Troilus and Criseyde* and in Fragment 3 of the *Canterbury Tales* (the tales and links of the Wife of Bath, Friar, and Summoner), Geoffrey Chaucer exploits the lexical and conceptual ambiguities of glossing which we have already discovered within the culture of late medieval England.[21] Furthermore, through two of his most memorable characters, Criseyde and the Wife of Bath, Chaucer capitalizes poetically upon the extension of meaning whereby "glosynge" comes to signify deceitful cajolery or flattery. The grammatical result of this development is that people can now be, literally, the object of the verb "to gloss." And this fact becomes in Chaucer's hands a potent symbol for the dehumanization inherent in the practice of deceit and manipulation. People thus "glosed" are reduced to the status of texts that the wily glossator can "explain" (i.e., control) as he pleases.

Book III of *Troilus* contains some of the poet's grandest set pieces of poetic language: Troilus's various prayers, songs, and exclamations (705f., 1254f., 1744f.); Criseyde's lament over the transitoriness of human happiness (813f.); and the narrator's rhapsodic account of the lovers' joy, accompanied by the confession of his inability to do it justice in his verses (1311f.). Surrounding these great arias are brilliantly varied recitatives, highlighted by Pandarus's tart colloquialisms (736–37, 890f.), Criseyde's quasi-epigrammatic expressions of passionate sincerity (869–70, 1210–11), and the narrator's fussy rationalizations of his characters' thoughts and actions. And, to introduce the book's feast of language, Chaucer composes a marvelous comic trio in which, at Deiphebus's house, Troilus and Criseyde first exchange words of love face to face while Pandarus, shifting from role to role and voice to voice, fills in the conversation's awkward pauses (50–203).

21. All Chaucer references and quotations follow *The Complete Poetry and Prose of Geoffrey Chaucer*, ed. John H. Fisher (New York: Holt, Rinehart & Winston, 1977).

By contrast, the language of Book IV frequently unsettles, disorients, stymies us. It is a book of strange rhetorical bedfellows—subtle mythological allusions, opaque scholastic analysis, inept and self–subverting suasoria—that provide, at several levels of Chaucer's fiction, glosses on his protagonists and their inner resources (or lack of them) as they confront the moment of greatest crisis in their love affair. For instance, references to classical myths by the narrator and the characters form a quasi-continuous universalizing gloss that heightens or complicates the significance of the lovers' impending separation. One example must stand for all: when Troilus and Criseyde sorrowfully embrace in the latter's bedchamber, the narrator invokes Myrrha (1139), the woman transformed because of her incestuous lust into the myrrh tree in the tenth book of Ovid's *Metamorphoses*.[22] Not only does Myrrha provide a hyperbolic standard by which to judge the bitterness of the tears shed by Troilus and Criseyde; she also comments ironically on Criseyde's situation, for Myrrha won infamy and divine punishment for her inability to stay away from her father, and Criseyde is about to manifest a parallel (albeit differently motivated) inability to avoid the Greek camp and her father, Calchas.

The two protagonists themselves demonstrate the uses, limits, and dangers of glossing in the course of Book IV. Using as his occasion Troilus's long, Boethian soliloquy in a temple (957f.), Chaucer manhandles a favorite text—he quotes only half of, and thus distorts, the discussion of predestination and free will in the fifth book of the *Consolation of Philosophy*[23]—while simultaneously poking fun at the clerical penchant for abstract argument about insoluble problems and demonstrating how we can all use supposedly objective or logical analysis to justify (and perpetuate) the limitations of our temperament or character. Instead of planning to prevent Criseyde's departure for the Greek camp, Troilus becomes engrossed in rehearsing an internalized scholarly disputation: "But natheles, allas, whom shal I leve? / For ther ben clerkes grete many on / That destyne thorugh argumentez preve; / And som men seyn that nedely ther is noon, / But that fre choys is yeven us everychon. / O welawey, so sley arn clerkes olde / That I not whos opynyoun I may holde" (967–73). Undismayed by the differences

22. Ovid, *Metamorphoses,* trans. F. J. Miller, Loeb Classical Library (London: William Heinemann, and Cambridge, Mass.: Harvard University Press, 1916), 10. 298–502.

23. See Chaucer's translation, *Boece,* Fisher ed., pp. 891–92.

of "opynyoun," Troilus plunges ahead, summarizing the opposing "argumentez" of those who, in his quaint periphrasis, "han hire top ful heighe and smothe yshore" (996), that is, clerical intellectuals. Amazingly (and amusingly), the Trojan prince passes quickly from the status of confused novice to that of authoritative commentator, glossing the free will position out of existence by line 1036 and then adding forty more lines of explanation to establish unassailably the predestinarian school of thought. The irony of Troilus's achievement is that his mastering the challenge of academic discourse allows him to escape the challenge of mastering experience. Earlier in the fourth book Troilus has justified to Pandarus, on prudential grounds, his refusal to take the initiative and run away with Criseyde. Now he can justify the same refusal to himself on intellectual grounds. Troilus's exercise in interpretation culminates in his surrender of responsibility for himself: he prays that God will either let him die or undertake his rescue. Glossing allows Troilus, in the words of Pandarus, to indulge once again his "lust to ben [his] owen fo" (1089).

It is around the figure of Criseyde, however, that we find gathered Book IV's most problematic forms and ambiguous connotations of glossing. When the lovers are alone together, for the first time in the book, Criseyde sensibly proposes (1254f.) that instead of lamenting their misfortune, they get on with the task of seeking its remedy. But her method of doing so pleases neither Troilus nor us. She first tries to convince Troilus that matters are not as bad as they seem: the lovers are forced to separate, but she "shal wel bryngen it aboute / To come ayen, soone after that I go" (1275–76). Accordingly, Troilus should think positively, concentrating on her proximate return rather than on their parting. They have often, out of discretion, kept apart for longer than the ten days she proposes to remain among the Greeks. Furthermore, her father will not prevent her from returning once he learns that his flight has not caused her to be despised in Troy or has otherwise abridged her happiness there. And the rumors that there will soon be peace, with Helen returned (an ironic parallel to her own situation), should encourage Troilus because peace will bring constant intercourse between Greeks and Trojans; but even without peace, she could not stay among the Greeks.

These arguments, piled upon and not necessarily consistent with one another, constitute a dubiously optimistic set of readings (or glosses) of the lovers' desperate situation in Troy. Criseyde's intention as an interpreter is obviously to persuade (ME: *glose*) Troilus not to fear her departure from him. But then (1366f.), like an ingenious glossator, she proposes yet "another wey" Troilus can understand their situation, another optimistic gloss to impose on the "text" of their love, "if so it be / That al this thyng [i.e., her explanations until now] ne may yow not suffise" (1366–67): once at the Greek camp she will easily trick her father into allowing her to return to Troy. She will tell Calchas tales of treasure that she can bring from the city if he will let her return; she will also promise to plead his case with Priam after the war has ended.

Criseyde intends to overcome her father's objections by purely verbal means: "So, what for o thyng and for other, swete," she tells Troilus, "I shal hym so enchaunten with my sawes, / That right in hevene his sowle is shal he mete" (1394-96). The problem her strategy poses for us is that it shows Criseyde "glosynge" Calchas to win his acquiescence to her return in exactly the way she is "glosynge" Troilus to win *his* acquiescence to her departure. Criseyde, in this scene, seems to see the world through rose-colored glosses; she may be fooling (or "glosynge") herself, and even her well-wishing narrator, in doing so, but she does not fool Troilus—who will soon (1440–98) refute her arguments and expose the flaws in her strategies—and she certainly does not fool us.

Criseyde anticipates that Calchas will try to test the veracity of her various stories and excuses. Her proposed method of thwarting his inquiry further subverts, instead of strengthening, the case she is making to Troilus:

> And yf [Calchas] wolde aught by hys sort it preve
> If that I lye, in certayn I shal fonde
> Distourben hym and plukke hym by the sleve,
> Makynge hys sort, and beren hym on honde
> He hath not wel the goddes understonde—
> For goddes speken in amphibologies,
> And for o soth they tellen twenty lyes.
> Eke drede fond first goddes, I suppose—
> Thus shal I seyn—and that his coward herte
> Made hym amys the goddes text to glose,
> Whan he for fered out of Delphos sterte. (1401–11)

These lines, with their image of Criseyde interrupting Calchas's priestly task of divination, rebound on their speaker by suggesting that her actual speech to Troilus is a verbal counterpart of her proposed harassment of her father; both are feeble and futile gestures of obfuscation designed to stave off a deep and tragic truth. Just as she will "distourben" Calchas to upset his auguries, Criseyde has been trying to "distourben" Troilus out of his dark understanding of their situation. Criseyde, not Calchas, "hath not well the goddes understonde," that is, has not perceived the desperation of her and Troilus's position in the face of the Trojan War. She, not the gods, is engaged in telling "twenty lies" instead of "o soth." And it is her "coward herte"—recognized even by the narrator when he subsequently characterizes her as "slydynge of corage" (V, 825)—that leads her to "glose amys" the "text" of the lovers' situation, putting a favorable interpretation on it so as to avoid having to face the harsh alternatives: loss of honor (in escaping Troy with Troilus), or loss of love (in leaving Troy without him).

Faced with the task of dramatizing Criseyde's climactic decision to leave Troy despite her love for Troilus, Chaucer shows his heroine attempting to exploit, but instead falling prey to, the ambiguities of glossing as his age understood them. Criseyde's dealings with Troilus cannot finally be distinguished from her dealings with Calchas; her well-intentioned explanations (glosses) to the former and her deceitful persuasions ("glosynge") of the latter are two sides of the same debased coinage of phrase. In Book IV of *Troilus and Criseyde,* Chaucer's heroine becomes an emblem of the use of language ostensibly as an instrument of clarification and comfort but actually to persuade, manipulate, and impose our will on other people, even as a scholar uses glossing to impose his meanings on other texts.

Chaucer's interest in the social applications of language manipulation is as strong in the *Canterbury Tales* as in *Troilus and Criseyde.* Indeed, glossing provides a unifying concept for the stories and tellers—the Wife of Bath, the Friar, and the Summoner—of Fragment 3 of the *Tales.* Mary Carruthers has already ably demonstrated how Chaucer used the contrast between letter and gloss to establish theme and character in the Friar's and Summoner's Tales.[24] I concentrate, in the remainder of this essay, on the Wife of Bath, the first taleteller of the fragment, whom Chaucer presents in part as a human "text" struggling

24. Mary Carruthers, "Letter and Gloss in the Friar's and Summoner's Tales," *Journal of Narrative Technique* 2 (1972), 308–14.

against the restrictive, negative gloss that others have sought to impose upon her and upon women in general.[25]

Although at the beginning of her Prologue the Wife of Bath establishes a dichotomy between authority and experience, and seems to ally herself with the latter, we cannot ignore the fact that she, more than any other Canterbury pilgrim, is obsessed with authoritative texts and traditions and with the uses that men have made of them in their dealings with women. The Wife, to be sure, sets out in her Prologue to tell us the story of her five marriages. What could be more experiential than that? And what could be less textual, less bookish, less abstract than the way she "folwede [hir] appetit" for life's pleasures—bright clothes, gadding about, food and drink, and of course dalliance? Nevertheless, she spends more time responding to texts and glosses (and glossators) than recounting her actual experiences, except when her encounter with a book becomes the very stuff of experience.

In the first 160 lines of her Prologue, Alisoun confronts the ranks of biblical and ecclesiastical authorities arrayed against her many marriages and counterattacks with the cleric's own weapons of text and gloss: "How manye myghte she have in mariage? / Yet herde I nevere tellen in myn age / Upon this nombre diffinicioun. / Men may devyne and glosen up and down, / But wel I woot, expres, withoute lye, / God bad us for to wexe and multiplye; / That gentil text can I wel understonde" (23–29). Even when she seems to controvert authority with experience, as in her discussion of the purpose of sexual organs, her argument soon falls back on books:

> Trusteth right wel, they [genitalia] were nat maad for noght.
> Glose whoso wole and seye bothe up and doun
> That they were maked for purgacioun
> Of uryne, and oure bothe thynges smale
> Were eek to knowe a femele from a male,
> And for noon oother cause—say ye no?
> The experience woot wel it is noght so.
> So that the clerkes be nat with me wrothe,
> I sey this, that they beth maked for bothe,

25. The remainder of this essay appears, in slightly different form, as a section of "Roasting a Friar, Mis-taking a Wife, and Other Acts of Textual Harassment in the *Canterbury Tales*," *Studies in the Age of Chaucer* 7 (1985), 3–22, and is used here with permission.

> This is to seye, for office and for ese
> Of engendrure, ther we nat God displese.
> Why sholde men elles in hir bookes sette
> That a man shal yelde to his wyf hir dette? (119–30)

After the Pardoner's interruption, the Wife ostensibly turns her attention to describing life with her five husbands; in fact, most of her account of the first three, old, ones recapitulates antifeminist commonplaces that she falsely attributes to them in her drunkenness, to put them on the defensive.[26] Although a few of these misogynous slurs appear in the Bible, they are all practical rather than theoretical or theological in nature, and Chaucer follows a strategy of comic decorum in having Alisoun report them as the verbal ammunition of domestic rather than pulpit warfare. His strategy also involves adjusting the Wife's mode of counterattack to fit her adversaries: whereas with clerics she pitted text against text (an appropriate reply to a scholastic's principled objection to multiple marriage), her husbands' supposed expressions of personal animosity she counters with the equally emotional weapon of withering scorn, for example, "After thy text, ne after thy rubriche, / I wol nat wirche as muchel as a gnat" (346–47).

Alisoun closes the Prologue, following a brief interlude provided by husband number four, by describing at length her marriage with Jankyn the cleric. Jankyn is both a domestic and a scholastic adversary: he beats her, and he reads to her nightly from his book of wicked wives.[27] In an episode embodying the ultimate coalescence of experience and authority, the Wife tears pages from the hateful book and precipitates the climactic battle of the marriage, leading to her obtaining mastery over Jankyn. This incident serves to remind us that throughout her matrimonial career Alisoun has in fact been fighting books more than people—books symbolized by Jankyn's omnibus volume and comprising a strong antifeminist, antimatrimonial current that flowed through medieval culture, fed by several tributaries: an ecclesiastical, celibate tradition based on biblical texts, pagan philosophers, and their patristic interpretations; a legacy of exempla from classical history and mythology; a tradition of scheming, lustful women in literature from Ovid

26. "Lordynges, right thus, as ye have understonde, / Baar I stifly myne olde housbondes on honde / That thus they seyden in hir dronkennesse; / And al was fals" (Wife of Bath's Prologue, 379–82).

27. See R. A. Pratt, "Jankyn's 'Book of Wikked Wyves': Medieval Antimatrimonial Propaganda in the Universities," *Annuale Medievale* 3 (1962), 5–27.

through the *Roman de la Rose* and beyond; and a pool of popular, proverbial lore about the wiles of wives and the "wo that is in mariage."[28]

It is no accident that Chaucer constitutes the "experience" of his liveliest, earthiest Canterbury pilgrim almost entirely from these traditions, and it is no accident that for most of her Prologue Alisoun directs her pugnacity against texts rather than actual men, even texts that she puts in the mouths of, and in effects substitutes for, three of her husbands. Through the Wife of Bath, Chaucer explores the paradoxes of a culture in which one half of humanity is defined not in its own words, nor by observation of its actual deeds, but by an autonomous, nonexperiential tradition of exemplary texts composed, handed on, and interpreted by a small elite drawn entirely from the other half of humanity—an elite, moreover, sworn by its clerical vocation to eschew legitimate sexual or familial relationships with those about whom it is writing. The corporeal men and women from whose harmonious or adversarial interaction a real history of the sexes might be compiled are absent from the Wife of Bath's Prologue and Tale; in their place we find only texts speaking to, controverting, and manipulating other texts. Alisoun's real opponents are not her husbands but texts—by Ovid, Jerome, Walter Map, Jean de Meun, Eustache Deschamps—that perpetuate stereotypes of women as temptresses, gold-diggers, whores, and termagants or construct fearful symmetries out of classical exempla: "Of Lyvia tolde he me, and of Lucye: / They bothe made hir housbondes for to dye / That oon for love, that oother was for hate" (747–49). Such a purely literary structure easily supports the weight of its maker's partisan moralizing: "And thus algates housbondes han sorwe" (756).

Alisoun, of course, knows precisely what (and whom) she is up against: "For trusteth wel, it is an inpossible / That any clerk wol speke good of wyves, / But if it be of hooly seintes lyves / [another literary genre, we note in passing] Ne of noon oother womman never the mo.

28. See, on various aspects of this legacy, W. Matthews, "The Wife of Bath and All Her Sect," *Viator* 5 (1974), 413–43; F. L. Utley, *The Crooked Rib: An Analytical Index to the Argument about Women in English and Scots Literature to the End of the Year 1568* (Columbus: Ohio State University Press, 1944); D. W. Robertson, *A Preface to Chaucer* (Princeton: Princeton University Press, 1962), pp. 317–330; *Sources and Analogues of Chaucer's Canterbury Tales* ed. W. F. Bryan and G. Dempster (Chicago, 1941; rpt. New York: Humanities, 1958), pp. 207–22; and Pratt, "Jankyn's Book."

/ Who peyntede the leon, tel me who? / By God, if wommen hadde writen stories, / As clerkes han, withinne hire oratories, / They wolde han writen of men moore wikkednesse / Than al the mark of Adam may redresse" (688–96). As long as "stories," issuing from isolated bastions of clerical privilege, pass on authoritative dicta about one sex or the other, the result always will be portraits of "wikkednesse" embodying the writer's hurts and frustrations. To quote the Wife again, "The clerk, whan he is oold and may noght do / Of Venus werkes worth his olde sho, / Thanne sit he doun and writ in his dotage / That wommen kan nat kepe hir mariage" (707–10).

Alisoun seems to attempt to break out of the closed world of transmitted authority by basing her own clerical expertise on experience: "Yblessed be God that I have wedded fyve, / Of which I have pyked out the beste, / Bothe of here nether purs and of here cheste. / Diverse scoles maken parfyt clerkes, / And diverse practyk in many sondry werkes / Maketh the werkman parfit sekirly; / Of fyve husbondes scoleiying am I" (43–44f.). But her very choice of (or entrapment in) a scholastic metaphor suggests, given the cultural parameters within which she is working, the hopelessness of her enterprise. Chaucer dramatizes this bind for woman and poet alike by creating, as I have already suggested, his most vivid, original character almost entirely out of recycled components from the various literary traditions of antifeminism. Even as she combats the guardians of those traditions, she recapitulates their clichés, emerging from her portrait in the General Prologue, her Prologue, and her Tale as a paradigm of female lust, bellicosity, greed, prodigality, and deviousness. Chaucer also stresses her disorganized loquacity, even to the point of having her lose her place in her discourse: "But now, sire, lat me se, what shall I seyn? / Aha, by God I have my tale agayn" (585–86). He does so not just to exploit another venerable female stereotype but because the quality serves him as a useful emblem of the labyrinthine meanderings of the various antifeminist traditions that intersect and feed on one another quite without reference to external reality. The Wife is lost in a world of words of which she is also a constituent. She exists as a literary creation of men, a system of texts and glosses which she repeatedly attacks but always ends up confirming, as in this passage:

> Wel koude I daunce to an harpe smale,
> And synge, ywis, as any nyhtyngale,

> Whan I had drunke a draughte of sweete wyn.
> Metellius, the foule cherl, the swyn,
> That with a staf byrafte his wyf hir lyf
> For she drank wyn, thogh I hadde been his wyf,
> He sholde nat han daunted me fro drynke!
> And after wyn on Venus moste I thynke.
> For al so siker as cold engendreth hayl,
> A likerous mouth moste han a likerous tayl.
> In woomen vinolent is no defence—
> This knowen lecchours by experience (457–68)

—but more by authority.

The Wife is thus an ironic representation of Chaucer's awareness of how, by imposing identity on others by means of transmitted authorities, we let them choose only between conforming to stereotypes and being attacked—and in the latter case, conforming to counterstereotypes. When we "gloss" people, we make them mean for us what we want them to and can thus use them either to satisfy our needs, if they accept our self-aggrandizing interpretation of them, or to justify our fears and hatreds, if they do not. Jankyn's treatment of Alisoun produces both results. He can, she tells us, transform her by his words into an obliging sex-object even in the face of his aggression against her: "But in oure bed he was so fresshe and gay, / And therwithal so wel coude he me glose, / Whan that he wolde han my *bele chose,* / That thogh he hadde me bet on every bon, / He koude wynne agayn my love anon" (508–12). (Note that although the basic meaning of "glose" in line 509 is "flatter, coax," Chaucer reminds us of the word's original connection with interpreting texts by requiring us, in the very next line, to gloss mentally a French euphemism for the Wife's pudenda.) On the other hand, by reading constantly to Alisoun about wicked wives who variously assault their husbands, Jankyn goads her into assaulting him, and thus into corroborating the book's thesis:[29]

> And when I saugh he wolde nevere fyne
> To reden on this cursed book al nyght,
> Al sodeynly thre leves have I plyght
> Out of his book right as he radde, and eke

29. As Evan Carton puts it ("Complicity and Responsibility in Pandarus' Bed and Chaucer's Art," *PMLA* 94 [1979], 47), "By ripping out three pages" from Jankyn's book, "Alisoun symbolically denies the book's authority (even if she confirms its estimation of a woman's temperament)."

> I with my fest so took hym on the cheke
> That in oure fyr he fil bakward adoun.
> And up he stirte as dooth a wood leoun,
> And with his fest he smoot me on the heed
> That in the floor I ley as I were deed. (788–96)

When the Wife says of this episode, "I was beten for a book" (712), we might well add that she was also beaten *by* a book.

Although Alisoun tells us that she finally subdues Jankyn, as she had subdued all her other husbands, we must remember that she has asked her pilgrim audience's indulgence "If that I speke after my fantasye" (190). She is, by her own admission, an accomplished liar, and her Prologue, like her obviously fantastic Tale of a rapist tamed and an old hag rejuvenated, may be a self-serving "gloss" on her experiences with men—may, that is, be her equivalent of the "stories" clerks have written about women "withinne hir oratories." Chaucer certainly holds open such a possibility in this most literary presentation of a character who, for all her advocacy of *maistrye,* demonstrates again and again the subjection of herself and her sex to the tyrannical harassment of text and gloss.

# Truth's Treasure: Allegory and Meaning in *Piers Plowman*

LAURIE A. FINKE

I

In the *Institutio Oratoria,* Quintilian defines allegory as a trope that "means one thing in the words, another in the sense."[1] This definition, the basis of all rhetorical descriptions of allegory in the Middle Ages and Renaissance, presupposes a stable relationship between words and things and assumes that signs reflect unproblematically what they signify. It does so by hierarchically ordering significance and meaning, by promising that allegories will yield up stable meaning if the initiated reader applies the proper "code" to translate the message. Taken a step

1. Quintilian, *Institutio Oratoria,* Loeb ed. (Cambridge: Harvard University Press, 1953), 8.6.44. Quintilian's definition has passed virtually unquestioned into modern discussions of allegory. Angus Fletcher, echoing Quintilian, writes that "allegory says one thing and means another. It destroys the normal expectations we have about language that words 'mean what they say' "; Northrop Frye argues that "we have allegory when the events of a narrative obviously and continuously refer to another simultaneous structure of events or ideas"; Mary Carruthers, echoing Augustine, writes that "all visible things, including language, are signs which point to something beyond themselves." See Fletcher, *Allegory: The Theory of a Symbolic Mode* (Ithaca: Cornell University Press, 1964), p. 2; Frye, "Allegory," in *Encyclopedia of Poetry and Poetics*, ed. Alex Preminger (Princeton: Princeton University Press, 1965), pp. 12–15; Carruthers, *The Search for St. Truth: A Study of Meaning in Piers Plowman* (Evanston: Northwestern University Press, 1973), pp. 10–11.

further, this definition suggests that allegorical texts produce stable meanings and mirror unequivocal truths. If allegory inserts another level of signifiers into the signifying process—the words yield up the sense, which, by virtue of its difference from the words, points to the "true" meaning—it never seriously questions the existence of a kernel, a truth, at the end of the process. By positing a split between words and what they signify, allegory conceals meaning from the uninitiated while making it visible for those with "eyes to see and ears to hear." Hence, for Augustine, figural language exists so that "by means of corporal and temporal things we may comprehend the eternal and spiritual."[2]

However, the recent rehabilitation of allegory in the wake of post-structuralist debates about the nature of signs has called into question both its classical definition as a kind of translation and the assumptions about meaning and truth upon which it is based.[3] Paul de Man and J. Hillis Miller, in particular, have suggested that allegory verges on being a self-canceling trope, that it simultaneously holds out the promise of truth and demonstrates the inadequacy of its linguistic formulations. The tension they perceive between the poet's desire to reveal truth and the poet's recognition that stable meaning may be subverted by an equivocating language is central to the genre of allegory. The language of allegory, de Man and Miller argue, is never simple, never simply the

2. Augustine, *On Christian Doctrine,* trans. D. W. Robertson (Indianapolis: Bobbs-Merrill, 1958), p. 10. All subsequent citations are to this edition and are noted parenthetically in the text.

3. One recent critic who has rejected the classical definitions of allegory while at the same time distancing herself from poststructuralist notions of it is Maureen Quilligan. In *The Language of Allegory: Defining the Genre* (Ithaca: Cornell University Press, 1979), she rejects the "vertical conception of allegory" (p. 28), arguing instead that allegories are "webs of words," pointing to the "possibility of an otherness, a polysemy, inherent in the very words on the page" (p. 26). Quilligan's redefinition of the terms by which we discuss allegory have inspired my own rethinking of allegory. But although her definition seems closely to resemble Derrida's notion of dissemination, of signifiers pointing to other signifiers, endlessly deferring the signified, Quilligan argues explicitly for the logocentrism of allegory. If deconstruction insists "on the disjunction between meaning and word, between sign and signified," she writes elsewhere, "narrative allegory always pursues the goal of coherence." Allegorical texts such as the *Roman de la Rose* insist upon the "congruence between word, physical fact, and divine intention." See her "Allegory, Allegoresis, and the Deallegorization of Language: The *Roman de la Rose*, the *De planctu naturae*, and the *Parlement of Foules*," in *Allegory, Myth, and Symbol*, ed. Morton Bloomfield (Cambridge: Harvard University Press, 1981), pp. 184–85.

transparent means of revealing an unequivocal truth that, almost by definition, it pretends to be. This new interest in allegory as a rhetorical device, as well as a genre, may provide a means of illuminating the interpretive difficulties presented by *Piers Plowman,* certainly among the most intractable of medieval allegories and what Maureen Quilligan has called "one of the purest examples in the genre."[4] Before turning to a detailed analysis of this poem's allegories, however, I examine in more detail the interrelations between some medieval and postmodern concepts of allegory.

## II

For Augustine, as for most medieval writers, the basis of allegory—the ideal relationship between words and things—is authorized by the Incarnation. In *On Christian Doctrine,* glossing the biblical text "the Word was made flesh," he defines a characteristic Christian perception of the correspondence of language and thought.

> How did He come except that "the Word was made flesh and dwelt among us?" It is as when we speak. In order that what we are thinking may reach the mind of the listener through fleshly ears, that which we have in mind is expressed in words and called speech. But our thought is not transformed into sounds; it remains entire in itself and assumes the form of words by means of which it may reach the ears without suffering any deterioration in itself. In the same way the Word of God was made flesh without change that He might dwell among us. (p. 14)

Augustine here argues that the Incarnation grounds the relationship between signifier and signified and guarantees their correspondence: "our thought is *not* transformed; it remains entire in itself." Like all logocentric thinkers, Augustine privileges speech over writing; he elevates meaning—content or theme—over the language in which it is conveyed. As the Logos becomes flesh through the mystery of the Incarnation, so, through the mysteries of allegory, divine truths are made accessible to human understanding; and as Christ's divine nature remains unchanged when he takes on human form, so the divine truths conveyed through allegory remain unchanged when they are clothed in words. Language, in this passage, becomes for Augustine a trans-

4. Quilligan, *Language of Allegory,* p. 58.

parent medium in and through which meaning, authorized from above, can be read.

But the theory of representation developed in *On Christian Doctrine* contains within itself the possibility of its own undoing. Almost immediately after Augustine states that "the invisible things of God" can be understood by "the things that are made," he questions the basis of representation itself.

> Have we spoken or announced anything worthy of God? Rather I feel that I have done nothing but wish to speak: if I have spoken, I have not said what I wished to say. Whence do I know this except because God is ineffable? If what I said were ineffable, it would not be said. And for this reason God should not be said to be ineffable, for when this is said something is said. And a contradiction in terms is created, since if that is ineffable which cannot be spoken, then that is not ineffable which can be called ineffable. This contradiction is to be passed over in silence rather than resolved verbally. (p. 11)

This passage is a rupture, a seam through which we can read the undoing of Augustine's logocentric concept of representation.[5] Augustine's frustration at the task of representing the divine is evident in the convoluted language of the passage, a language that calls attention to its own hesitancy and cannot say what it means. If God is inconceivable, then we cannot say that he is beyond comprehension, because to say so would be to say something about that of which nothing can be said. Thought cannot assume the form of words, even spoken words, and remain unchanged. Augustine's comparison of the imperfect representations of language to the ideal of the Incarnation can reveal only their irrevocable difference. Because the divine cannot be represented, the contradictions within his theory cannot be verbally—or logically—resolved; they can only be mediated by faith. His silence on this contradiction is finally the silence of faith. For Augustine, this silence becomes

5. For other discussions of Augustine's attitude toward language in *On Christian Doctrine,* see Marcia Colish, *The Mirror of Language: A Study in the Medieval Theory of Knowledge* (Lincoln: University of Nebraska Press, 1983), esp. chap. 1; Eugene Vance, "St. Augustine: Language as Temporality," in *Mimesis: From Mirror to Method, Augustine to Descartes*, ed. John D. Lyons and Stephen Nichols, Jr. (Hanover, N. H.: University Press of New England, 1982), pp. 20–35. Elsewhere in this volume, Peggy Knapp demonstrates how Augustine's assurance of a logocentric language, grounded in the Incarnation, breaks down when confronted by some of the contradictions inherent in language—contradictions created by multiple meanings, translations, and rhetorical obfuscation.

the basis of all allegory—faith in the Incarnation and in representation as a means of transmitting unitary meaning and divine truth.

The contradictions and silences within Augustine's theory of allegory are archetypal and hence may illuminate the Yale Critics' interest in allegory. Hillis Miller suggests that "the possibility that allegorical representation is a human fancy thrown out toward something which is so beyond human comprehension that there is no way to measure the validity of any picture of it is the permanent shadow within the theory" of allegory.[6] Miller and de Man have recognized this shadow within Augustinian and medieval notions of allegorical representation and used it to argue that allegory rather than symbolism best describes the process of a text's "coming into being." Considered by the Romantics and New Critics too prosaic and tendentious to be a conveyor of poetic truth, allegory, in the writings of Miller and de Man, has resurfaced as a critical mode that both confronts and embodies the impenetrability of language and the problematics of interpretation.[7] It is, in this respect, the contradiction that Augustine wishes to pass over in silence that these deconstructive critics wish to foreground.

The concept of allegory that emerges from the critical writings of de Man and Miller destabilizes conventional notions of representation by challenging the one-to-one correspondences between words and things, phenomenon and essence, posited by rhetorical definitions of allegory. Although in this essay I am primarily concerned with allegory's failed attempts to bridge the chasm between human languages and divine presence, the argument can and must be extended to include all human signification. Indeed, the former argument grounds the latter; Logos assures logocentrism. In a passage from *Grammatology* with interesting echoes of Augustine, Jacques Derrida has argued that the history of Western metaphysics documents the search for a transcendental signifier that would legitimate all signs.

6. J. Hillis Miller, "The Two Allegories," in Bloomfield, *Allegory, Myth, and Symbol*, p. 360.

7. See Miller, "The Two Allegories," pp. 355–70; Miller, "Ariadne's Thread: Repetition and the Narrative Line," *Critical Inquiry* 3 (1976), 57–77; Paul de Man, "Pascal's Allegory of Persuasion," in *Allegory and Representation*, ed. Stephen J. Greenblatt (Baltimore: Johns Hopkins University Press, 1981), pp. 1–25, and "The Rhetoric of Temporality," in *Interpretation: Theory and Practice*, ed. Charles Singleton (Baltimore: Johns Hopkins University Press, 1969), pp. 173–209. See also de Man, *Allegories of Reading: Figural Language in Rousseau, Nietzsche, Rilke, and Proust* (New Haven: Yale University Press, 1979), and *Blindness and Insight: Essays in the Rhetoric of Contemporary Criticism* (Minneapolis: University of Minnesota Press, 1971).

> All signifiers, and first and foremost the written signifier, are derivative with regard to what would wed the voice indissolubly to the mind or to the thought of the signified sense, indeed to the thing itself (whether it is done in the Aristotelian manner . . . or in the manner of medieval theology, determining the *res* as a thing created from its *eidos,* from its sense thought in the logos or in the infinite understanding of God).[8]

Allegory, I wish to argue, demonstrates language's inability to guarantee the signified, to wed once and for all word and thing.

In his article "The Two Allegories," Miller quotes Walter Benjamin's aphorism that "allegories are in the realm of thoughts, what ruins are in the realm of things."[9] Allegory, Miller argues, shows the devastating effects of time on thoughts, just as ruins show the devastating effects of time on things. Like ruins, allegories register the gap between past and present, presence and absence. Ruins are the fragments of the past that "represent" a building's or a civilization's past glory by virtue of their difference from a now lost wholeness. Allegories are also fragments; they too direct our gaze backward across a temporal chasm, representing what can no longer be present because of the nature of language. Representation, as Murray Krieger reminds us, must always stress its prefix *re* over its root *present.* The language we use to represent our world is made up of empty and belated markers. Words "seek to refer to what is elsewhere and has occurred earlier."[10] Language, in other words, even as it attempts to recuperate presence, must simultaneously defer it. In this regard, what Coleridge sought to efface by identifying the sign and signified in the symbol, de Man and Miller embrace in allegory—difference, the unbridgeable gap between words and things, between experience and the representation of experience.

This "ruinous" theory of allegory insinuates itself into Augustinian theory (and theology) by reminding us of allegory's difference from the "spirit" it purports to recover. The meaning and truth that allegory seeks to represent are, by the deferred nature of representation, present only as fragments. For Miller, as for de Man, meaning and truth are

8. Jacques Derrida, *Of Grammatology,* trans. Gayatri Chakravorty Spivak (Baltimore: Johns Hopkins University Press, 1976,), p. 11.

9. Miller, "The Two Allegories," pp. 362–63.

10. Murray Krieger, "Presentation and Representation in the Renaissance Lyric: The Net of Words and the Escape of the Gods," in Lyons and Nichols, *Mimesis: From Mirror to Method,* p. 118; see also Krieger, " 'A Waking Dream': The Symbolic Alternative to Allegory," in Bloomfield, *Allegory, Myth, and Symbol,* pp. 1–22.

problematic precisely because "the target toward which signs are turned remains finally unknown":

> Allegory in this view then is quite the opposite of what it often pretends to be: the recovery of the pure visibility of the truth, undisguised by the local and accidental.... But its deeper purpose and its actual effect is to acknowledge the darkness, the arbitrariness, and the void that underlie, and paradoxically make possible, all representations of realms of light, order, and presence.[11]

Allegory, as it tries to incarnate the absent signified that would authorize meaning and truth, testifies to their absence. The more language seeks to clarify (literally to illuminate or free from darkness or gloom) meaning, the more it reveals the void, the darkness of its own reflexivity.

## III

*Piers Plowman,* at times, seems almost an allegory of the impossibility of discovering either significance or truth within language, whether one searches for divine or merely for human significance. Language in the poem, as I have argued elsewhere, becomes "a vehicle for classification (of ways of life, of mental powers), a means of imposing order (the law), [and] a means of disorder and deception. More often than not... one cannot distinguish between these uses of language.... Man's language, although created in the image of the Logos, is capable of only an imperfect parody of it." The more human language strives to represent the world, the more it is trapped and frustrated by its own failure to assure referentiality.[12]

*Piers Plowman*'s resistance to interpretation inheres in its own interpretations of its difficulties. The dreamer's question "How may I save my soul?" leads him to search for Truth (Passus I–VII), for Dowel (Passus VIII–XIV), and finally for Piers himself (Passus XV–XX). These quests become, in one sense, the search for a transcendental signified that would legitimate all the human signs of the mundane world, the

11. Stephen J. Greenblatt, "Preface," in Greenblatt, *Allegory and Representation*, p. vii.

12. See my "Dowel and the Crisis of Faith and Irony in *Piers Plowman*," in *Kierkegaard: Irony, Repetition, and Criticism*, ed. Ronald Schleifer and Robert Markley (Norman: University of Oklahoma Press, 1984), p. 129; there I deal more extensively with the linguistic relativism—the disjunction between human words and earthly things—that infects *Piers Plowman*, particularly in Passus XIX–XX; see pp. 136–37.

world of the "fair field" and the "half acre." Indeed, the promise of a truth in, behind, or beyond the poem's language, and with it the possibility that Will's dreams actually mean "something," is from the beginning of the poem both proffered and withheld. The opening tableau of *Piers Plowman* seems simple enough; Will, the poem's narrator, falls asleep and dreams:

> [Ac] as I biheeld into þe Eest, and heiȝ to þe sonne,
> I seiȝ a tour on a toft treiliche ymaked,
> A deep dale byneþe, a dongeon þerInne
> Wiþ depe diches and derke and dredfull of siȝte.
> A fair feeld ful of folk fond I þer bitwene. (Prologue 13–17)[13]

The dreamer's sight here ("biheeld") is figurative rather than literal. What he sees are not things but representations of things. The dreamscape is composed of signifiers—tower, dungeon, and field—that seem to mean more than the poet tells us about them, that seem to point to other signifiers. The simplicity of the physical scene shades into the ambiguity of interpretation. The reader, like the dreamer, is compelled to ask, "What may it [by]meene?" The scene, in short, demands a gloss, an interpretation, additional text to explain the poetic utterance. The space that exists between the images of the tower, dungeon, and field and what they signify becomes the figural space of interpretation. It can be bridged or filled only by the attempt to understand it, by reading or creating a text that comments upon the text.

In the A and B versions the interpretation of this scene is deferred until Passus I, where the dreamer's first guide, Holi chirche, glosses these images. Of the "tour on þe toft" she tells the dreamer, "truþe is þerInne" (I, 8); in the dungeon, "Wonyeþ a [wye] þat wrong is yhote; / Fader of falsehed" (I, 63–64). The rhetoric of her commentary initially encourages the dreamer to believe that his vision "means" something, that he can pursue a rational account of the allegorical world in which he finds himself, and that the process of interpretation requires simply a translation or a substitution of one set of terms for another. The tower is Truth, the dungeon is Falsehood or Wrong. Holi chirche encourages the dreamer, in this regard, to believe that Truth is some-

13. All quotations from *Piers Plowman* are from *Piers Plowman: The B Version*, ed. George Kane and E. Talbot Donaldson (London: Athlone Press, 1975). All subsequent citations are noted parenthetically in the text.

thing within his reach, a goal, like the tower, at the end of a journey. Truth can be found simply by avoiding *temporalia* or the "tresor" of the world: "þat trusten on his tresor bitraye[d are] sonnest" (I, 70).

The literalness of Will's allegorical thinking, his belief that word and thing can coincide to create meaning, emerges in his request to Holi chirche to "Teche me to no tresor, but tel me þis ilke, / How I may saue my soule" (I, 83–84). But Holi chirche's answer undermines the dreamer's faith in the precision of allegorical language by troping on the very signifier he has rejected as false: "Whan alle tresors arn tried treuþe is þe beste" (I, 85). Neither meaning nor truth, it seems, is as unproblematic as Will had thought, nor the relationships between signs and signifieds nearly as simple or stable. In one instance, treasure is equated with the corruption of falsehood; in another, Truth is described as the best of all treasures. Apparently there are two kinds of treasure: one that is earthly and visible to the dreamer, and one that is invisible and not easily circumscribed by language, even the language of allegory. Each signifier—true treasure, false treasure—defines itself in terms of the other; each, therefore, exists only in opposition to its opposite.

The literal-minded dreamer, however, does not understand Holi chirche's explanation. What he wants is to locate a simple means of identifying truth and to pass in silence over the problematics of representation.

> "Yet haue I no kynde knowying," quod I, "ye mote kenne me bettre
> By what craft in my cors it [truth] comseþ and where." (I, 138–39)

Will is interested in only half of the Augustinian dialectic; for him, allegory is a means of "comprehending the eternal and spiritual" by means of "corporal and temporal things" (*On Christian Doctrine,* p. 10). Holi chirche cannot clarify what truth is, and her inability becomes a measure of the difference or the distance between language and what it represents. The dreamer desires a language that can express experience unequivocally and so allow him to dominate it.[14] However, his guide's response generates not certainties, but more commentary, more opportunities for interpretation.

Holi chirche's response is a *dilatio* on truth. A rhetorical trope of amplification often cited in medieval *ars praedicandi, dilatio,* from the

14. See Hillis Miller's discussion of allegory and narrative in "Ariadne's Thread," p. 72.

Latin *dilatare,* suggests both a deferral and a spreading out.[15] In this respect, Holi chirche's answer simultaneously postpones the dreamer's inquiry and widens its perspective until it encompasses—or attempts to encompass—everything, including the divine.

> For truþe telleþ þat loue is triacle of heuene:
> May no synne be on hym seene þat vseþ þat spice,
> And alle hise werkes he wrouȝte with loue as hym liste;
> And lered it Moyses for þe leueste þyng and moost lik to heuene,
> And [ek] þe pl[ante] of pees, moost precious of vertues.
> For heuene myȝte nat holden it, [so heuy it semed,]
> Til it hadde of þe erþe [y]eten [hitselue].
> And whan it hadde of þis fold flessh and blood taken
> Was neuere leef vpon lynde lighter þerafter,
> And portatif and persaunt as þe point of a nedle
> That myȝte noon Armure it lette ne none heiȝe walles. (I, 148–58)

As this passage suggests, *Piers Plowman*'s poetry is most eloquent—literally, most full of speech—when its language proclaims its own inadequacy. Here it attempts to describe and explain the mysteries of divinity by accumulating a series of highly antithetical images. Yet the allegory circles around the idea of God's highest expression of love and truth—the Incarnation—by calling that love "heuy" and light as "leef vpon linde," "triacle," and "portatif and persaunt," able to pierce any armor or wall. The same phrase, "For heuene myȝte nat holden it," is used to describe both the Incarnation and Lucifer's fall from heaven. This passage is characteristic of the poem as a whole: language does not progress toward an illumination of truth but falls into the deferral of its own rhetoric. Each sign produces the next sign in a repetitive sequence that never arrives at anything but the next trope. The more the poem's language attempts to describe the divine, the less referential—and the more reflexive—it becomes.

I have quoted extensively from the poem's opening episode because it is typical of Langland's double-edged handling of allegory. The complications inherent in Holi chirche's explanation of the opening tableau are paradigmatic of the poem's repetitive, circular structure, its tech-

15. See Lee Patterson's discussion of the *dilatio* in the discourse of La Vieille in Jean de Meun's *Roman de la Rose,* " 'For the Wyves love of Bath': Feminine Rhetoric and Poetic Resolution in the *Roman de la Rose* and the *Canterbury Tales,*" *Speculum* 58 (1983), 669–76.

nique of *dilatio* to defer and expand on the referentiality of its language. Simple, apparently unequivocal figures—Truth and later Dowel and Piers himself—are complicated by the very attempt to define or explicate them. These terms, which de Man might call "primitive words," cannot be defined because their "pretended definitions are infinite regresses of accumulated tautologies";[16] in other words, they can be explained only by recourse to tropes that, like all attempts to represent the unrepresentable, proclaim absence instead of presence, darkness instead of light. Figures—truth is a tower, for instance, or divine love is "triacle"—offer similitudes in the place of definitions, what Derrida calls identity in difference, not the mystical identity that Coleridge located in the symbol.[17]

The need to dilate—to explain, define, and distinguish—in *Piers Plowman* generates the endless monologues so characteristic of all three versions of the poem. These monologues seem to answer every question but the one that Will has asked precisely because it cannot be answered in human terms. His question is Augustine's: How can one distinguish the true or the divine in a fallen world? Yet the more Will seeks to learn (the more questions he asks, the more answers he seeks), the more text is generated and the more complicated the commentary becomes. Each gloss leads not to definitive answers or interpretations but to more glossing. Passus I ends with Holi chirche's reiterating "Whan all tresors ben tried treuþe is þe beste" (I, 207). But the dreamer is no more enlightened than he was before he asked his question. At the opening of Passus II he rephrases his inquiry and asks Holi chirche, "Kenne me by som craft to know þe false" (II, 4). Although the question changes, the rhetorical context does not. Commentary necessitates further commentary. Texts proliferate, but the substance, the thing that Will seeks, remains unattainable.

16. de Man, "Pascal's Allegory of Persuasion," p. 6.

17. For Coleridge, the symbol "always partakes of the reality which it renders intelligible; and while it enunciates the whole, abides itself as a living part in that unity, of which it is representative." Allegory, on the other hand, "is but a translation of abstract notions into a picture-language which is itself nothing but an abstraction from objects of the senses; the principle being more worthless even than its phantom proxy, both alike unsubstantial, and the former shapeless to boot." For a discussion of Coleridge's theory of the symbol and allegory see de Man, "The Rhetoric of Temporality," pp. 177–78, and Krieger, " 'A Waking Dream,' " pp. 4–7 (the quotations are from p. 5).

This "web of words" is the essence of allegory: "a textual plot of another text's tale, a figure of a figure."[18] The nature of allegory, as de Man argues in "The Rhetoric of Temporality," always presents itself as repetition within both the temporal sequence of language—the syntagmatic succession of signs—and the temporal sequence of narrative—the metonymic succession of episodes.[19] The sign always refers to and repeats a previous sign with which it can never coincide. The "meaning" that the allegorical sign constitutes consists only of repetition, which implies, in the Derridean sense of iterability, both identity and difference: "the identity of the *selfsame* [must] be repeatable and identifiable *in, through,* and even *in view of* its alteration."[20] Repetition inscribes in allegory two senses of time: a progression from one manifestation or incident to the next, and a mere iteration of the same. This dual sense of time is what leads Miller to identify the irony of repetition as the trope of all narrative and de Man to privilege allegory as the trope of irony.[21]

The allegorical narrative of *Piers Plowman,* in this respect, operates within two time frames: the temporal narrative of Long Will's quest for Truth (and later for Dowel and Piers), and the atemporal antinarrative of the dream which frustrates the dreamer's attempts to go forward. Dream visions and journeys are commonplace in medieval allegory precisely because they reflect the disjunction within allegory between sign and signified. In *Piers Plowman* these two allegorical strategies are "brought together" in such a way that, more often than not, they work at cross-purposes. The journey is metonymic and sequential; it imparts to the poem a sense of forward movement because it suggests that the signified, like the tower in the Prologue or the King at Westminster who arbitrates the marriage of Meed, may be what the dreamer seeks, even as it displaces his goal beyond wherever he happens to be. The dream, on the other hand, is metaphoric and ahistorical; it frustrates progression by making the goal into something else, by of-

18. Vincent B. Leitch, *Deconstructive Criticism: An Advanced Introduction* (New York: Columbia University Press, 1983), p. 184.

19. de Man, "Rhetoric of Temporality," p. 190.

20. Jacques Derrida, "Limited Inc abc...," trans. Samuel Webster, *Glyph* 2 (1977), 190.

21. J. Hillis Miller, "Narrative Middles: A Preliminary Outline," *Genre* 11 (1978), 386; de Man, "Pascal's Allegory of Persuasion," p. 12.

fering the endlessly referential web of words that lead only into labyrinthine repetition. The narrative pattern of the poem, then, creates a dialectical tension between the journey and the dream which simultaneously asserts and destroys the narrative's claim to linear progression.

The search for Truth which occupies the *Visio* illustrates this disjunction between the narrative's two displacements, the dream and the journey. After witnessing the confessions of the Seven Deadly Sins, the folk on the field set out, at Reason's urging, to "seken Seynt Truth, for he may saue yow alle" (V, 57). Their quest repeats Will's earlier quest for Truth, with a difference but with the same results: the forward impetus of the journey stalls as the dream repeats the symbols of desire. On the pilgrimage the folk encounter two guides, who, like Holi chirche, attempt to gloss the signs. The first is a pilgrim, or at least a "leode" "apparailled . . . in pilgrymes wise." His staff, bowl, and bag, his "Ampulles," "shelles," and "vernycle," are the "signes" of his pilgrimages, his quests for his "soules hele." But as signs they point only to other signs and other journeys: "Syney," the "Sepulchre," "Bethlem," "Alisaundre." He cannot tell the pilgrims the way to Truth, the way to pure signification, because his understanding does not extend beyond the signs themselves: "I [ne] seiȝ neuere Palmere wiþ pyk ne wiþ scrippe / Asken after hym [truth] er now in þis place" (V, 535–36).

The forward progression of the journey is halted; it repeats the sequence with the sudden dreamlike appearance of the second guide, Piers the Plowman, who offers to lead the folk to Truth. He conceives of the way to Truth as a series of signposts pointing the way in a moral landscape: a place called "swere-noȝt-but-it-be-for-nede-and-nameliche-on-idel- þe-name-of-god-almyȝty," for example, or a croft called "Coueite-noȝt-mennes-catel-ne-hire-wyues-ne-noon-of-hire-seruantȝ-þat-noyen-hem-myȝt." This allegorical description (V, 561–82) is no doubt long and dull, but its very lack of poetic immediacy—its plodding, one-to-one correspondence between physical place and spiritual state—comments on the failure of the epistemology of the *Visio,* its search for truth and transcendent meaning. The folk's encounters with the pilgrim and Piers again highlight the disjunction between outward signs and the always elusive inner meaning of truth.

In the last two passus of the *Visio,* Piers attempts to redeem the spiritual signification of the pilgrimage, to close the gap between outward forms and spiritual meaning, by transforming this trope into another trope.

> "And I shal apparaille me" quod Perkyn, "in pilgrymes wise
> And wende wiþ yow [þe wey] til we fynde truþe,"
> [He caste on] his cloþes, yclouted and hole,
> [His] cokeres and [hise] coffes for cold of his mailes,
> And [heng his] hoper at [his] hals in stede of a Scryppe. (VI, 57–61)

In this passage the image of the quest or journey gives way to the repetitive, circular action of plowing as Piers sets the folk to work. The "cokeres," "coffes," and "hoper," the signs of Piers's life of virtuous labor, replace the traditional signs of the pilgrimage: bowl, bag, and scrip. The simple life of labor, Piers assures the folk and the dreamer, will lead them at last to Truth. But all that this plowing of the fields leads them to is yet another dead end that requires more commentary, yet another textual *dilatio,* another attempt to redefine or resignify the *Visio*'s key terms. When the folk cannot persevere in their labor, Truth sends them a pardon, a document that emphasizes metaphorically the disjunction between temporal words and the allegorical incarnation of the spirit. The allegory of Truth's pardon, as I have shown elsewhere, sets the pardon's spiritual significance as a reflection of God's grace against its debasement as an image of ecclesiastical corruption, a popular target of fourteenth-century satire.[22] Piers's tearing of the pardon and his squabbling with the priest mark the end of the dream before the quest to find Truth has reached a satisfactory conclusion.

The interpretive difficulties that the *Visio* creates inhere, in large measure, in the oppositions between the *Visio*'s principal signs—between true treasure and false treasure, true meed and false meed, true pilgrimage and false pilgrimage, true pardon and false pardon. These dialectical oppositions exist symbiotically; each undermines and reinforces its opposite. The language of the poem's allegory is, to borrow Miller's description of Yeats's prose, "always forced to say the opposite of what it seems to want to say, as well as the opposite of that op-

22. Finke, "Dowel and the Crisis of Faith and Irony," pp. 123–27.

posite."[23] This "deconstructive" process of the allegorical text's undoing itself is not, however, nihilistic, nor does it become a simple reversal of dialectical hierarchies that privilege meaninglessness over meaning. The allegory of *Piers Plowman*—its reflexive questioning—is both an attempt to represent what is unrepresentable and an attempt to transcend the mundane world circumscribed by the folk on the field. Its image in the text is the quest, which, precisely because it can never reach a conclusion, must be repeated, for example in the *Vita*'s quest for Dowel and in the quest for Piers with which the poem breaks off. In essence, the rest of the poem unfolds as a repetition of the first two visions, the B and C versions as repetitions with a difference of the A version.

After tearing the pardon and abandoning the life of virtuous labor for that of prayer, Piers all but disappears from the poem until Passus XV, when Anima mentions him as the perfect exemplar of charity. His appearance and transformation at this juncture illuminate the way in which the action of the poem is now generated not by the quest but by language, by puns. This wordplay points to external and material coincidences between signifiers and distorts logocentric fictions about meaning. Piers himself becomes less a "character" than an instance of what happens to a fallen language in its attempts to define its own limitations. As Maureen Quilligan suggests, language becomes a principal actor in the poem—[24] not simply a medium of expression, however imperfect, but an example of what happens to the spirit, to faith, when it is incarnated in the physical world. The actor in Passus XVI–XIX is not Piers the character but "Piers" the signifier, a deferral of the linguistic roots—the puns—that comprise its unstable identity.

When Anima mentions Piers in Passus XV, he is no longer the virtuous laborer who set the folk to work in Passus VI, no longer simply a plowman. His name, inscribed in Anima's phrase "*Petrus id est christus,*" has become a pun that harks back not only to Piers's name-

23. Miller, "Two Allegories," p. 370. Elsewhere Miller has called this phenomenon the *mise en abyme*; contemporary physicists, I have learned, call it a Strange Loop. But whatever we call it, the existence of signs that refer circularly only to their opposite signs undermines the logocentric promise of all language, including scientific language, that signs can point unproblematically to things in the real world. For an illuminating discussion of this phenomenon in contemporary scientific language, see N. Katherine Hayles, *The Cosmic Web: Scientific Field Models and Literary Strategies in the Twentieth Century* (Ithaca: Cornell University Press, 1984), esp. chap. 1, pp. 31–59.

24. Quilligan, "Allegory, Allegoresis, and the Deallegorization of Language," p. 180.

sake St. Peter but also to the etymology of Piers's name, from the Old French *pierre* and the Latin *petrus* for rock, also for foundation or support.[25] Anima's phrase, in this regard, becomes a kind of shorthand for Christ's words to Peter (Matt. 16.18): "*Tu es Petrus, et super hanc petram aedificabo ecclesiam meam*" [You are Peter, and upon this rock I will build my church]. The name Piers is embedded both in the logocentric tradition of etymology, of biblical exegesis, and in the nameless incidence of faith. From a description of the mundane rock, *petrus* achieves a figural significance—the foundation or support for the Church—gathering to itself a tradition of meanings that transcend any one interpretation. The allegorical significance of the name, then, goes beyond what language can possibly describe: the phrase *Petrus id est christus* becomes the incarnation of the divine as a pun on the dual nature of man-as-god.

The pun on Piers's name generates the plot of Passus XVI–XVIII by setting in motion biblical history. The dreamer learns that Piers, no longer a plowman, guards the tree of charity (B XVI). In the course of the dream, the tree becomes an elaborate metonymy for the tree of knowledge (the paradisaical *lignum vitae*) and the tree of the cross, both, as Gerhardt Ladner notes, "part of the metahistorical and historical economy of salvation."[26] The tree is supported by three "piles," props or supports that, with Piers, protect the tree and its fruit from assault by the winds and by demons. The tree's "fruit" is postlapsarian mankind—Adam, Abraham, Isaias, Samson, Samuel, John the Baptist, and the like. When Piers shakes the tree to fetch an "apple" for the dreamer, this "fruit" falls and is gathered up by the Devil, initiating the temporal sequence of biblical history from the Fall to Christ's passion, death, and resurrection. The elaborate and bizarre allegory of the tree of charity, with Piers its gardener, is the first of a series of tropes centered on Piers's name which reenact the history of Christianity. These culminate in the allegory of the Christ-knight in which the Incarnation and Passion are figured as Christ jousting in "Piers armes" (B XVIII, 22) and in the final appearance of Piers in Passus

25. For a seminal article on this passage and on wordplay in *Piers Plowman*, see Bernard Huppé, "*Petrus id est Christus*: Word Play in *Piers Plowman*, the B-text," *Journal of English Literary History* 17 (1950), 163–90.

26. Gerhardt Ladner, "Medieval and Modern Understanding of Symbolism: A Comparison," *Speculum* 54 (1979), 236.

XIX as the Church Militant, the institutional embodiment of faith and spirit as doctrine.

Yet this "sequence" in the poem is itself figural, a representation not of progression but of progressive revelation. Piers does not begin as one kind of signifier and "become" another; his name comprehends multiple meanings, none of which—not even *Petrus id est christus*—is definitive. "Piers" represents not an historical accretion of meaning but the mystery of the unchanging Word that cannot be interpreted, only made manifest. Will's final visions thus unfold in a temporal language that reveals, rather than represents in a more traditional sense, the timeless, ahistorical object of the dreamer's quest for faith. That this revelation can be only obscure and partial, that the essence of what stands behind and gives meaning to the signifier can never be certainly "known," is suggested by the way in which the poem simply breaks off. There is no conclusion, no end to the quest, but only the dreamlike repetition of Will still searching for the absent Piers.

In one sense, *Piers Plowman* becomes what de Man calls an allegory of reading; it explores the process of coming to terms with its own unreadability. Yet allegory—as the failure of literary language to demonstrate a one-to-one correspondence between signs and signifieds—also becomes the mode of faith. *Piers Plowman* does not fool around with literary language but with the inadequacy of theological language; it is an attempt to explore the generic limitations of allegory not simply as a vehicle for truth but as an epistemological exploration of the mysteries of the Incarnation, which, as Augustine suggests, enables truth. Such a reading of *Piers Plowman* posits an alternative to the authoritative procedure sanctioned by Augustinian hermeneutics:

> Whatever appears in the divine Word that does not literally pertain to virtuous behavior or to the truth of faith you must take to be figurative. . . . Scripture teaches nothing but charity, nor condemns anything except cupidity. (*On Christian Doctrine*, p. 88)

This reading of *Piers Plowman* promotes a knowledge—and a transcendence—that, far from enlightening the reader, forces him or her to take a "leap into darkness," a nearly Kierkegaardian leap of faith. The silence that Augustine maintains in the face of the divine, and the silence with which *Piers Plowman* breaks off, may be read as acts of faith as well as the "stillness of metaphysical irony." In this sense, the wandering and the wondering, the quest and the question, are the poem's mechanisms for trying to recover the signified; and the word "recover" suggests paradoxically the hiddenness and the discovery, the absence and the presence, of what lies behind the word.

# *Inter Nocturnas Vigilias:* A Proof Postponed

Louis H. Mackey

> There are metaphors which we can recognize as not wholly arbitrary though that's as far as the line goes. We like to assume that there is somewhere a truth, a description of reality in conformance with reality itself however hard to arrive at or accept the arrival. But even in Shakespeare or the Bible, even in the cosmologies of particle physics, it isn't there. Reality is brought to mind by the inadequacy of any statement of it, the tension of that inadequacy, the direction and force of the statement.
>
> —William Bronk

In the period just before he wrote the *Proslogium,* Anselm was searching for a single argument which all by itself would suffice to show what the *Monologium* had tried to prove by many arguments: God's existence and the supreme perfection of His nature. This argument, which Anselm could neither find nor give up looking for, he finally received as a revelation. The *Proslogium* reports the content of that revelation.

The initial research for this essay was done during 1976–77, when I was on leave of absence from teaching duties. My research was supported by a fellowship from the National Endowment for the Humanities and a supplementary grant from the University Research Institute of the University of Texas at Austin. I am grateful to the Department of Philosophy of the University of Texas, and to N.E.H. and U.R.I., for providing me the opportunity to do this work.

Securely within the Augustinian tradition, the *Proslogium* proof relies like its predecessors on the logic of hierarchy. St. Augustine's demonstration of God's existence defines its object as "that to which none is superior" and builds on the hierarchic principle "that which judges is better than what it judges."[1] The arguments of Anselm's *Monologium* all invoke an asymmetrical relation designated *per* (through) or *propter* (because of), which, though its meaning is never unambiguously explained, generates the hierarchies that enable the proofs to conclude (M I-VII, *passim*). The *Proslogium's* novelty is the realization that the root of all particular and substantive hierarchies is the formal and absolutely general relation of signification: the expression "that than which no greater can be conceived" is taken to be a verbal formula that certifies its own reference. Closing the dichotomy of language and being, it provides in the crucial case a guarantee of the hierarchic ordination of sign to thing signified.

The ordering of word to thing is a condition of the possibility of order in general. Unless we can rely on the bonding of language to reality, none of the other hierarchies we imagine—all of which purport to represent the aggregate of things in an array of words—can be trusted. Given the notoriously linguistic character of the highest abstractions, the relationship of sign to thing signified is even more rudimentary than the priority of being to nonbeing. The suspicion that the achievements of philosophical and theological discourse are nothing but verbal tricks or abuses of language—feats of legerdemain or masturbatory gestures—can be allayed only by the assurance that the founding terms of this discourse cannot fail to signify. The *Proslogium* proof is meant to provide this assurance.

That, I think, is the sense and the import of Anselm's revelation. This conjecture is recommended by (among other things) Anselm's techniques of argumentation. The prominence of grammatical study at Bec is well documented,[2] and it would have been natural for the grammarian's concern with semantics to lead Anselm through the shifting, uncertain, ambiguous, and merely conventional references of ordinary language to a search for the ground of signification as such. A form

1. St. Augustine, *De Libero Arbitrio Voluntatis,* II. vi. 14 and v.12.

2. See R. W. Southern, *Saint Anselm and His Biographer* (London: Cambridge University Press, 1963), esp. chaps. 1 and 2, and Marcia L. Colish, *The Mirror of Language* (New Haven: Yale University Press, 1968), chap. 2.

of words whose reference is self-assured would offer itself to such an inquirer as a divine visitation and an unfailing light of truth.

The (misleadingly) so-called "ontological proof" of God's existence is more aptly described as a proof of the ontological reliability of language. It presumes to locate the moment of linguistic soundness, the plenitude of presence from which other language may deviate but to which (so long as it continues to say "be") it is always bound. "That than which a greater cannot be conceived" expresses the created innocence of language underlying its original guilt—and the point of contact for a redemption of derelict discourse. Anselm's fool personifies fallen but salvageable human reason. The proof is meant to effect his salvation: a restoration of errant thought and speech to their primordial integrity.

Anselm identifies God as "that than which nothing greater can be conceived" (P II).[3] This is something Christians believe, but even an

3. The source of this expression and others like it in the *Proslogium* would seem to be Augustine's phrase "that to which none is superior" (cf. note 1 above). Anselm uses similar expressions in *Monologium* II and IV. In the Introduction to his *Quaestiones Naturales,* two copies of which were in the library at Bec, Seneca characterizes God (i.e., nature) as a magnitude "than which nothing greater can be conceived." Southern, p. 59. In *De Doctrina Christiana,* I. vii, Augustine says that we think of God as "something than which there is nothing better and more sublime."

References to the works of St. Anselm are given parenthetically in the text, by title (abbreviated) plus chapter or paragraph number. *Monologium* = M, *Proslogium* = P, Gaunilon's *Liber pro insipiente* = I, Anselm's *Liber apologeticus* = A. Thus (P XV) = *Proslogium,* Chapter XV.

For the Latin text of St. Anselm I have used *Obras Completas de San Anselmo,* 2 vol. ed. Julian Alameda, O.S.B. (Madrid: La Editorial Catolica, 1952–53). Fr. Alameda reprints the text of the standard critical edition by Dom F. S. Schmitt, *S. Anselmi Cantuariensis Archiepiscopi Opera Omnia,* 6 vol. (Edinburgh: Nelson, 1946–). Translations in the text are my own, but I have made free use of the following editions and translations: M. J. Charlesworth, ed. and trans., *St. Anselm's Proslogion* (London: Oxford University Press, 1965); S. N. Deane, trans., *Saint Anselm: Basic Writings* (La Salle, Ill.: Open Court, 1962); Jasper Hopkins and H. W. Richardson, trans., *Anselm of Canterbury,* 4 vols. (Toronto and New York: Edwin Mellen Press, 1974–76); and Sr. Benedicta Ward, S.L.G., trans., *The Prayers and Meditations of Saint Anselm* (Harmondsworth: Penguin, 1973).

My indebtedness to Anselm scholars is too diffuse to be documented precisely, but I am deeply and extensively influenced by the following: Karl Barth, *Anselm: Fides Quaerens Intellectum* (Richmond: John Knox Press, 1960); Colish, chap. 2; G. R. Evans, *Anselm and a New Generation* (New York: Oxford University Press, 1980); Evans, *Anselm and Talking about God* (New York: Oxford University Press, 1978); Charles Hartshorne, *Anselm's Discovery* (La Salle: Open Court, 1965); Hartshorne, *The Logic of Perfection* (La Salle: Open Court, 1962), chap. 2; Jasper Hopkins, *A* atheist can understand it. To say that he can understand it does not mean that he, or the Christian for that matter, can imagine God or that either of them actually comprehends Him, but only that this formula is coherent and may be thought without contradiction. It is sometimes said that Anselm assumes that the concept of God is the concept of a possible being, leaving it to later thinkers to demonstrate the consistency of this notion.[4] It is true that Anselm never considers the question, Is God's existence possible? But it can (and will) be argued that his proof is so constructed that it disarms the question in advance. For the moment, suppose the concept thinkable, even by an atheist.

Anselm expects the atheist to admit that existence in reality as well as in thought is greater than existence in thought alone. A real being is greater than the mere thought of one. Though often disputed, this should not be troublesome. At stake is the proposition "God exists." The atheist maintains that God does not exist, the believer that he does. Both are occupied with the question of God's real existence, and unless they think real existence "greater" than ideal being, the controversy is vacuous. Few atheists would deny (or care) that people have ideas of God, as long as they do not think them veridical. Therefore, when Anselm says that real existence is greater than mental existence, he is only identifying the condition without which there is no significant difference between believer and unbeliever. It is a presupposition that could be denied only at the cost of trivializing the point at issue.

---

*Companion to the Study of St. Anselm* (Minneapolis: University of Minnesota Press, 1972); Hopkins, *Anselm of Canterbury* (Toronto: Edwin Mellen Press, 1976), vol. 4; Southern, *Saint Anselm*.

Also of interest is Brian Stock's *The Implications of Literacy* (Princeton: Princeton University Press, 1983). Although his problematic differs from mine, Stock's chapter on Anselm (pp. 329–62) certainly bears on the concerns of this discussion. I call attention in particular to his characterization of *exemplum* (example) as "a copy, a transcript," or, in a special sense, a "proof" (332); his definition of Anselmic "understanding" as "to discuss, to comment upon, and to produce a new text" (334); his argument that for Anselm to proceed toward reason is to establish "a text, that is, a discourse modelled on written language" (335); and his distinction between faith, "a received text," and reason, "an established one" (343). For Anselm, as interpreted by Stock, faith is to understanding as the oral is to the written.

4. Leibniz usually gets the credit. Cf. *New Essays Concerning Human Understanding* (La Salle, Ill.: Open Court, 1949), pp. 499–511, 714–15. Long before Leibniz, Duns Scotus had seen and attempted to solve the same problem. His proofs of God's existence always begin by demonstrating that God is possible and then go on to show that God actually exists. Cf. *De Primo Principio,* II and IV. 4.65, and *Opus Oxoniense,* I.2.1.

To say that real existence is "greater than" existence in the mind alone means that the former is *more real than* the latter. Real existence and ideal existence are hierarchically ordered. And that, which is presented as a presupposition of the argument, is the bone of contention. The atheist hears and understands the words "that than which no greater can be conceived," but he does not understand that a being so describable actually exists. The believer argues that if you hear and understand these words, you are obliged thereby to acknowledge the real existence of the being they identify. In this one case word and thing are so ordered that the mere understanding of the words compels recognition of the superior reality of their referent. Therein lies the radical character of the *Proslogium* proof: it presumes to validate its own presupposition by showing that in the critical instance there can be no slippage between language and being, since (at this crux) the thing signified is given along with the sign.

The name of God validates itself. If that can be believed, then the *Proslogium* does provide a single argument which all by itself and without any other, demonstrates the being of God. The expression "that than which no greater can be conceived," which is the proof in a nutshell, guarantees its reference. At the same stroke it legitimates its own presupposition and the supposition of all rational discourse: the order of signification as such. As in the Incarnation, where divinity is veiled by humanity and yet perceptible by anyone who grasps the humanity in its depth, so the being of God is hidden under and yet contained in the words by which we name Him. By which, indeed, He names Himself.

## II

The logical method in which Anselm was trained at Bec was the (grammatically motivated) method of equipollent propositions. By this method the unbeliever's position can be reduced to absurdity and the believer's position confirmed (see Figure 1).

The believer says God is [a being that exists]. The unbeliever says God is [a being that does not exist]. Both agree that God is [a being than which no greater can be conceived]. By substitution of equipollent expressions the believer's assertion becomes: [a being than which no greater can be conceived] is [a being that exists]. And the unbeliever: [a being than which no greater can be conceived] is [a being that does

**FIGURE 1. PROSLOGIUM II AND III**

| | *Believer* | *Fool* |
|---|---|---|
| II | 1. God is [a being that exists]. | 1. God is [a being that does not exist]. |
| | 2. God is [a being than which no greater can be conceived]. | 2. God is [a being than which no greater can be conceived]. |
| | 3. [A being than which no greater can be conceived] is [a being that exists]. 1, 2. | 3. [A being than which no greater can be conceived] is [a being that does not exist]. 1, 2. |
| | 4. [A being that does not exist] is [a being than which a greater can be conceived]. | 4. [A being that does not exist] is [a being than which a greater can be conceived]. |
| | | 5. [A being than which no greater can be conceived] is [a being than which a greater can be conceived]. 3, 4. Since this is necessarily false, "God is [a being that exists]" is necessarily true. |
| III | 1. God is [a being that cannot be conceived not to exist]. | 1. God is [a being that can be conceived not to exist]. |
| | 2. God is [a being than which no greater can be conceived]. | 2. God is [a being than which no greater can be conceived]. |
| | 3. [A being than which no greater can be conceived] is [a being that cannot be conceived not to exist]. 1, 2. | 3. [A being than which no greater can be conceived] is [a being that can be conceived not to exist]. 1, 2. |
| | 4. [A being that can be conceived not to exist] is [a being than which a greater can be conceived]. | 4. [A being that can be conceived not to exist] is [a being than which a greater can be conceived]. |
| | | 5. [A being than which no greater can be conceived] is [a being than which a greater can be conceived]. 3, 4. Since this is necessarily false, "God is [a being that cannot be conceived not to exist]" is necessarily true. |

not exist]. Presumably—for without this presumption the whole debate is pointless—[a being that does not exist] is [a being than which a greater can be conceived]. This granted, the unbeliever's assertion may be transformed by substitution into the following: [a being than which no greater can be conceived] is [a being than which a greater can be conceived]. This is a manifest contradiction and therefore false. Since what the unbeliever says contradicts what the believer says, and since what the unbeliever says is necessarily false, what the believer says is necessarily true. God (necessarily) exists. Because the argument does nothing but unpack the meaning of the phrase "that than which no greater can be conceived," this expression all by itself delivers the reality of that which it purports to name.

That is the argument of Chapter II. Chapter III proposes an intensification of the same point: God cannot be conceived not to exist. That which can be conceived not to exist is less than that which cannot be conceived not to exist. Therefore God ([a being than which no greater can be conceived]) is not [a being that can be conceived not to exist]. He exists so truly that he cannot even be thought not to be. The unbeliever's position is not only false, it is meaningless.

The principle: necessary being is superior to contingent being is just a special form of the principle: being in reality is greater than being in the mind alone, since the inconceivably nonexistent must exist in reality whereas the conceivably nonexistent might exist in the mind alone. It is hard to imagine (if not impossible to conceive) someone who accepts the latter proposition rejecting its modal constriction. With this modification the proof in Chapter III looks just like the proof in II. [A being that can be conceived not to exist] is [a being than which a greater can be conceived]. "God might not exist" means: [a being than which no greater can be conceived] is [a being that can be conceived not to exist]. By substitution of equipollencies: [a being than which no greater can be conceived] is [a being than which a greater can be conceived]. Since this is necessarily false, it is necessarily true that God cannot be conceived not to exist. Anselm adds: if God could be conceived not to exist, then a greater than God could be conceived. But this would mean that the creature could rise above its creator, "which is most absurd."

In Chapter II Anselm says that the words "that than which no greater can be conceived" are intelligible to believer and unbeliever alike. At the beginning of III he says "it is possible to conceive of a being which cannot be conceived not to exist." The possibility of God's existence hangs on the coherence and meaningfulness of these expressions. Anselm does not discuss this problem. But perhaps he does not have to. If God cannot be conceived not to exist, then the mere thought of God entails his necessary existence and the question of his conceivability is foreclosed. What must be conceived and cannot not be conceived can be conceived. What must exist does exist, and what does exist obviously can exist. The possibility of the divine being rests tacitly—and securely—on the ground of its necessity.

It might be objected that Anselm's proof claims necessity for God's *existence,* whereas the prior question concerns the conceivability (in the first place) of that being whose existence the argument is meant (subsequently) to establish. If the concept of God were self-contradictory, it would be simple (though nugatory) to prove his existence. From a self-contradiction all conclusions follow, both "is" and "is not." However—and apart from the fact that it is not easy to see how one could prove that a being than which no greater can be conceived does not exist—the force of Anselm's argument is to insist that in the case of God the gap between concept and existence cannot be opened. If the necessity of God's existence and the impossibility of his nonexistence follow strictly and directly from the divine name, then the question of conceivability is a pseudo-question.

As the certitude of God's existence is confirmed, Anselm is obliged to investigate the possibility of atheism. Where the former is a manifest necessity, the latter begins to look like a mystery. Therefore Chapter IV examines the conditions of unbelief. Anselm contends that the atheist can only say that God does not exist, he cannot mean it. Whoever hears and understands the name of God understands (necessarily) that God (necessarily) exists. The unbeliever obviously does not understand, "because he is stupid and a fool." He hears words: noises at the least and at the most usages. If he understood the meaning of the words—the deep grammar of "God"—he could not persist for a moment in his folly. For the effect of the proof is to show, simply but stupendously, that the words by which God is named guarantee the reality of Him they name.

It is common to complain that Anselm confounds necessities of being with necessities of language. One may not, the objection runs, leap from thought to reality without falling into a category fault. But the objection may not be as devastating as it seems. The *Proslogium* proof relies exclusively on the law of contradiction.[5] Apart from the formula

5. On the understanding of the law of contradiction at Bec, see Southern, *Saint Anselm,* pp. 12–26; also Southern, "Lanfranc of Bec and Berengar of Tours," in *Studies in Medieval History Presented to F. M. Powicke,* ed. R. W. Hunts, W. A. Pantin, and R. W. Southern (London: Oxford University Press, 1948), pp. 27–48.

"that than which . . ." and the assumptions about the superiority of (necessary) existence in reality to (possible) existence in the mind alone, all the statements in the proof are either tautologies (necessary truths) or contradictions (necessary falsehoods). Whether the "name of God" is "correct" is beside the point. Whatever is picked out by the phrase "that than which no greater can be conceived" necessarily exists if the proof is sound.

But the proof not only depends on the law of contradiction, it also tests the application of that law to reality. This may be the final philosophical import of Anselm's proof: if you cannot at the point of contradiction regard necessities of thought as signifying necessities of being, then you cannot credit your thinking with ontic reference at any point. The argument nails down the reference of verbal/conceptual signs to real things by producing the one form of words that cannot be denied to refer.

Of course not everything I think or talk about exists. Anselm knows about falsehoods, fictions, things doubtful, and things uncertain. Certainly nothing exists *because* I think it or name it. Anselm does not claim that God exists because I have to think that He exists. If anything, it's the other way around: Can I deny that what I cannot think without contradiction cannot be? Can I doubt that what I must think on pain of contradiction must be? At this point it is as if reality itself were compelling thought. And that it may not be inappropriate to call a revelation.

If this is so, then it is not gratuitous of Anselm to regard the unbeliever as a fool. If he understands the name of God and still denies that God exists, he is guilty not of a single and superficial error but of a radical and general abstention from rationality. If he refuses to assent to that which reason unconditionally commands him to believe, then he cannot claim rationality for any of his beliefs and he cannot expect to be taken seriously by any rational person on any subject whatever.[6]

"Reason unconditionally commands"—assuming he wants to be rational. This is the point at which (Anselm might be prepared to admit as much) understanding most evidently depends on faith. No one is literally compelled by reason to give real assent to necessities of thought. But such assent is a condition of all further rational intercourse with

6. Aristotle, *Metaphysics,* XI. 5–6.

reality, and to withhold it is not irrationally called folly. As Aristotle noted, few people, and scarcely any fools, having thrown off the chains of consistency, will then be consistent enought to shut up.[7]

Anselm's illumination occurred when he discovered (he would say: was given) a sign that incarnates its meaning. Singularly motivated, its form (signifier) is demanded by its content (signified). The content of this uniquely revelatory sign is the relation of signification itself. "That than which no greater can be conceived" not only establishes the existence of God; at the same stroke it legitimates the claim of signs (as such and in general) to manifest reality. The relation of signification is hierarchic: the sign, which exists for the sake of revealing the thing signified, has its being as sign through or because of the thing signified.[8] The sign *is* (in principle and in the crucial case) the revelation of the signified, so that it is (in principle and in the crucial case) impossible to know what the sign *is* without knowing what it is a sign *of*. Ends are superior to means,[9] and Anselm's argument, by grounding signification (the sign exists in order to reveal the signified), warrants its own presupposition (existence in reality is superior to existence in the intellect alone).

The *Proslogium* formula, a signifier perfectly persuaded by its signified, perfectly exposes their hierarchic order. It illumines as a window illumines: it lets you see things through it, provided there is light on the other side. In this case the light and the thing seen are one. "If you say that it is not understood and is not in the understanding because it is not fully understood, then you must say that one who cannot gaze into the purest light of the sun does not see the daylight, which is nothing but the light of the sun" (A II). If Anselm infers realities from thoughts and from language, it is only because he believes that being itself has revealed to him the words in which it names itself and elicited within him the thoughts by which it makes itself known. "He himself has given your reason the ability to think so devoutly and so truly about him."[10]

## III

Occasional misunderstandings aside,[11] Gaunilon speaking on behalf of the fool attacks Anselm's argument at its root. The nub of the proof

7. Ibid., IV. 4.
8. Cf. *Monologium* I–VII and p. 70 above.
9. St. Augustine, *De Magistro,* IX.
10. St. Augustine, *De Libero Arbitrio Voluntatis,* II.vi.14. Augustine is commending Evodius for describing God as "that to which none is superior."
11. For example, Gaunilon replaces "that than which no greater can be conceived"

is a verbal formula which, understood, communicates the existence of its referent. Gaunilon's strategy is to drive wedges into the structure of the argument so as to break down the unity of word-thought-thing on which its soundness depends.

He distinguishes, for example, conceiving from understanding (I, 2, 7). To conceive a thing is to think it, but what is thought may or may not exist. To understand a thing is to comprehend its real existence. From the fact that God's existence is conceived, it does not follow that He exists. Unless His nonexistence is conceivable, Anselm's dispute with the atheist is nothing but shadowboxing. If His existence is to be understood and not just conceived, this should be proven. If it be granted that God cannot be understood not to exist, it must also be admitted that I cannot understand myself—or any real thing—not to exist. But by the same token, if I can conceive myself not to exist, I can also conceive God not to exist. Opening the gap between thought and reality, Gaunilon protests that without independent argument, no concept proves the existence of its putative referent. However tight the unity of signified and signifier, no sign infallibly delivers the thing it purports to stand for. If this be true, Anselm's demonstration is demolished.

Gaunilon attempts an analogous division of words and thoughts (I,4). When the atheist hears "that than which nothing greater can be

---

with "greater than all." This substitution causes him to mistake the point of the argument and allows him to formulate the misconceived and quite irrelevant example of the lost island (I 6 and *passim*). Again, he mistakes Anselm's vignette of the painter and his picture, which is intended only as an example of the relation of real existence and mental existence, for an integral part of the argument (I 2, 3). In this connection, however, Gaunilon makes a significant allusion. "For as St. Augustine says: When a craftsman is about to make a chest, he first has it in his art. The chest which is produced is not alive; but the chest which is in the art is alive because the soul of the craftsman is alive, and in it exist all those artefacts before they are produced. [*On the Gospel of John,* I, 17] For why are these artefacts alive in the living soul of the craftsman except because they are nothing other than his soul's knowledge and understanding?" (I 3). Recalling the Augustinian hierarchy of being, life, and intelligence (*De Libero Arbitrio Voluntatis,* II.iii), this passage makes the startling suggestion (on the authority of Augustine himself) that perhaps existence in reality is not always superior to existence in the mind. Gaunilon does not develop the implications of this suggestion, but the perturbation of hierarchic order it implies points in the direction of his principal objection to the *Proslogium* proof. It also points toward the Bonaventurian schema: things exist in three modes—in their own kind, in the mind, in the eternal art—and existence in the mind is superior to existence in their own kind or in matter. (*Christus unus omnium magister,* 7; *De scientia Christi 4 corpus; Collationes in Hexaemeron,* III.8.) Bonaventure gets it from Hugh of St. Victor, *Didascalicon,* Appendix C.

conceived," does he hear noises or significant noises? If the former, nothing follows. If the latter, then it remains to be determined whether God is understood or only conceived by these words. And we are back where we were. Like Gaunilon's first objection, this is potentially devastating. If Anselm's formula is just noises unaccompanied by conception or by understanding, it proves nothing. If it is noise plus understanding, no argument is necessary. And if it signifies a conception, we still want a proof to show that God exists.

In the *Monologium* (M X–XI), Anselm makes the following distinctions:

| | (corresponding to Gaunilon's |
|---|---|
| the divine Word | God |
| created words (things) | understanding |
| [B] | |
| mental words (concepts) | conceiving |
| [A] | |
| spoken or written words | words as mere noises). |

Anselm thinks of this as a tightly linked hierarchic chain. Words spoken or written are intelligible only by reference to concepts, concepts by reference to things, and things by reference to the divine Word. Given this scheme, it is difficult for Anselm to avoid claiming too much or too little. Either one gets the divine Word along with the verbal noises, in which case the proof of God's existence is superfluous, or one has nothing but the noises, in which case proof is impossible. Appealing to concepts to mediate between word and Word escalates the dilemma but does nothing to resolve it.

If the Word is really present in all the words by which it is expressed, then it does not need proving.

If Gaunilon can break the chain at points [A] and [B], the game is up. Anselm's world view, Augustinian in origin and inspiration, presumes the fundamental identity of meaning and being. Once the integrity of the significative relation is broken, the cosmos itself is shattered and nothing remains but disjunct fragments of word and thought and thing.

If the Word is absolutely absent from the words by which we disturb the air and deface the surface of the world, neither the existence of God nor anything else can be demonstrated.

Gaunilon's refutation draws its strength from the weakness intrinsic to Anselm's position. Allowing his distinctions makes Anselm's proof impossible; refusing them makes it fatuous. If Gaunilon is right, what Anselm takes to be the condition of rationality is the confounding of reason. Who then is the fool? In his rebuttal Anselm restates the argument of *Proslogium* II and III in such a way as to underscore its force against the atheist. The demonstration of God's existence is an example of the method of equipollency, but the assault on atheism is a case of *redarguitio elenchica*. Its grammar concludes to the being of God, but its rhetoric exposes the atheist's folly by showing that the principles he holds are incompatible with the acts by which he enunciates them.[12]

Anselm accepts Gaunilon's distinction between conception and understanding: what is conceived is possible, what is understood is actual. But he adds a third term: what cannot not be conceived is necessary. Nothing actual can be understood not to exist; God cannot even be conceived not to exist and therefore necessarily does exist (A IV). At the limit of necessity, conception entails being and prevents the sundering of possibility and act.

There is a fault in Gaunilon's use of "understand." On the one hand he says that falsehoods can be understood, whence he concludes that God's existence does not follow from the understanding of His name. On the other hand he says that to understand a thing is to understand its existence, whence he infers that God cannot be understood not to be. Anselm prefers to keep the notion of understanding fluid. He begins with a form of words which we can understand but which we may not

12. In this connection, see the discussion of "pragmatic paradox" in Henry W. Johnstone, Jr., *Philosophy and Argument* (State College: Pennsylvania State University Press, 1965), p. 71. The method of equipollency, or equipollent propositions, was a kind of grammatical logic taught by Lanfranc at Bec. It is a technique by which one may transform a given proposition into another logically equivalent proposition by substituting for expressions in the first proposition expressions that are grammatically of equal weight and value. For further details, cf. the references in note 3 of this essay. *Redarguitio elenchica* is a refutative technique: it consists in showing that *what* your opponent asserts is inconsistent with the *fact* of his asserting it. For example, a determinist cannot believe that he is *obliged* to be a determinist, because his determinism disallows the free will that is a necessary condition of obligation.

understand to represent a real entity. When we come to understand it in depth (so the argument goes), we understand that a being so named and so conceived must exist (A VI).

When Anselm complicates the distinction between conceiving and understanding and finds a contradiction in Gaunilon's use of "understand," he approaches the main point of his rebuttal. Gaunilon had argued: when one hears the words "that than which no greater can be conceived," either (1) he understands the reality they stand for, or (2) he hears only the words, or (3) he conceives but does not understand the sense of the words. If (1), no proof of God's existence is needed. If (2), no proof is possible. If (3), a proof might be offered but Anselm has not offered it. A sign is intelligible only if one first knows the reality it signifies.[13] If one knows what "God" means, one knows God. If one does not know what "God" means, there is no way, merely by thinking and speaking, to find out. The proof of God's existence, in Anselm's terms, is either impossible or unnecessary. And the proof that might be given is not even proposed.

Anselm's response (A IX) is to turn the horns of the dilemma against Gaunilon by pointing out a fatal incoherence in the atheist's view. When the atheist says that God does not exist, he is foolish. For if he understands "that than which no greater can be conceived," he also understands that it exists. And if he denies that he understands it, he is shameless, for the denial makes his atheism meaningless. His refusal to acknowledge the existence of God is either illogical or vacuous. Gaunilon wants to sever word, thought, and thing. Not a difficult task, given Anselm's epistemology. But to do so would not only destroy belief in God, it would dismantle the conditions of all rational belief.

It is easy to understand Anselm's impatience with Gaunilon's attempt to insert the concept as a wedge between word and thing. That complicates the problem (whether we are assured of the existence of God by the mere understanding of His name) but does nothing to solve it one way or the other. Instead it raises the new and (to Anselm's mind) unprofitable question of the relation between word and concept (meaning). A signifier without its signified is not yet a sign, so that to manipulate noises without meanings is not to use words at all. As Anselm says (P IV), the unbeliever "uses" words only in the Pickwickian sense

13. St. Augustine, *De Magistro,* X.33, XI.36.

that he utters sounds without understanding or with an improper understanding. Gaunilon's distinction makes no difference. Far from strengthening the atheist's case, it only makes his folly more obvious.

This is another place at which the need for faith is evident. It is always possible for an infidel reason to separate signifier, signified, and referent, leaving a debris of hidden realities, drifting concepts, and opaque symbols. But to do so is to forfeit the intelligibility that resides in the connection of word, thought, and thing. It was the necessity of that connectedness that was given to Anselm as an illumination. Like any revelation, it had to be received in faith. In his own words—neglected by philosophical critics from Gaunilon to the present day—the purpose of Anselm's proof is to bring this faith to understanding. That is why Anselm, responding to Gaunilon, replies to the Catholic rather than the fool and calls upon his faith and conscience to retract his defense of unbelief (A I).

And that in no narrow theological sense, but generally. The atheist refuses to admit that the words "that than which . . . " refer to the Being whose existence they imply. But the same person confidently uses ordinary language every day of his life. He banks on its reference to extramental realities. Yet the connection of sign and referent is, in ordinary language, conventional and contingent. In the case of God the reference is necessary and natural. If the unbeliever trusts ordinary language and does not credit the reference of this unique form of words, he is perverse. If the atheist understands the name of God, he is bound by logic and by honor to acknowledge God's existence. If he does not understand the divine name, his atheism is a piece of impudent folly.

In either case, when the unbeliever says "God does not exist," the meaningfulness of his utterance, as a verbal act, is undercut by the meaninglessness he tacitly affirms. Conversely, the faith which (in Anselm's argument) seeks enlightenment is simply fidelity to the conditions and implications of linguistic performance that will not be shaken by the theoretical possibility of meaninglessness and is therefore rewarded with understanding. Atheism is not credal recalcitrance but verbal nihilism, its opposite (theism) a surrender to the terms of linguistic and personal coherence that includes but far exceeds particular theological commitments.

IV

Though virtually all its interpreters have supposed otherwise, the *Proslogium* proof does not end with Chapter IV. The *Proslogium* proof is the *Proslogium,* and neither its logic nor its import is clear until the argument is seen in this larger view. Even in the more restricted view the proof extends from Chapters II–IV, through V, XII, and XV, to Chapter XXII. The proof in this narrow sense is grammatical: a string of equipollent substitutions. But the *Proslogium* as a whole is a rhetorical text. Its title, *Proslogium id est alloquium* (P Preface), and the pervasive presence of the second person singular identify it as an address to God: a prayer.[14]

As the use of language to persuade, rhetoric posits a hierarchic relation between persuader and persuadee: the persuader locates himself (at least verbally) beneath the persuadee.[15] In prayer the worshiper abases himself absolutely before God, who is absolutely elevated. *Proslogium* I describes the situation of the persona who is seeking to understand God. By means of paradox, antithesis, and other techniques of verbal self-effacement, the seeker is humbled and God exalted.

The rhetorical act then proposes to reduce this distance. Its aim, as persuasion, is the communion of persuader and persuadee. So the worshiper desires to achieve reconciliation with God through forgiveness, sacramental communion, or spiritual excess. The *Proslogium* wants to uplift the lowly believer to union with God through intimate cognition.

From the point of view of a rhetoric that reflects on its own presuppositions, the difference underlying all differences is the space between itself and reality opened up by language. The use of language posits an ontic and epistemic difference between word and thing: words, which exist for the purpose of signifying things, are to that end necessarily distinct from and inferior to the things themselves. Rhetoric, tensed toward closure (overcoming the difference it starts with), will have as its transcendental goal closing the gap between language and

14. See *The Life of St. Anselm Archbishop of Canterbury by Eadmer*, ed. and trans. R. W. Southern (London: Oxford University Press, 1972), p. 31.

15. For my understanding of rhetoric I am indebted to Kenneth Burke, *A Rhetoric of Motives* (Berkeley: University of California Press, 1969), esp. pp. 49–55, 137–42, and 267-333. For the metarhetorical extension of Burke's doctrines, and for any distortions thereby occasioned, I alone am to blame.

being. Reflexively, rhetoric is the endeavor by means of language to repair the breach with reality effected by language. Prayer is quintessentially the expression of this linguistic principle: alienation from being struggling to negate itself.

Anselm's *Proslogium* is at once an act of piety linking man to God and a reconciliation of words and things. It projects the immolation of the sign in the thing signified, symbolized by the rapture of the human into the divine. At the ideal limit the dual motives of Anselm's text—grammar and rhetoric, devotion and reason, confession and argument, faith and understanding—are one.

But, like language itself (itself language), the *Proslogium* is never yet at the limit, but always only straining toward it. It remains amid the hierarchies it longs to transcend. Remains (in other words) in mystery. Beyond the divergence of language and being, thing and sign are one: God *is* the Word that expresses Him. Short of that identity, word and thing are both joined and sundered by the dialectic of difference and participation that constitutes hierarchic order. When Anselm writes that "if any mind could conceive something better than thee, the creature would rise above the creator and judge the creator, which is most absurd" (P III), this is not a pious intrusion on the argument but a necessary condition of signification. If it were possible to conceive something superior to that being of which conception is the sign, the order of signification would be confounded. "Which is most absurd": being in its alterity always exceeds its signs. Never contained in, with, or under the sign, being is that into which the sign desires to pass as into its death and larger life.

Anselm's remark does, however, locate the rationale of piety by exposing its impatience with the mediations, displacements, and postponements inherent in the hierarchy of signification. Viewed from above, every hierarchy is an intelligible order available for understanding; seen from below, it is a mystery accessible only to faith.[16] "Faith seeking understanding" is the apprehension of mystery as order, the apprehension of order through mystery, and the transformation through elevation of the latter into the former. Almost. No longer just faith, never quite understanding, Anselm's argument ("in the person of one striving... and seeking") is never more (and never less) than a

16. Ibid., pp. 114–27, 137–42, 174–80, and 301–13.

FIGURE 2

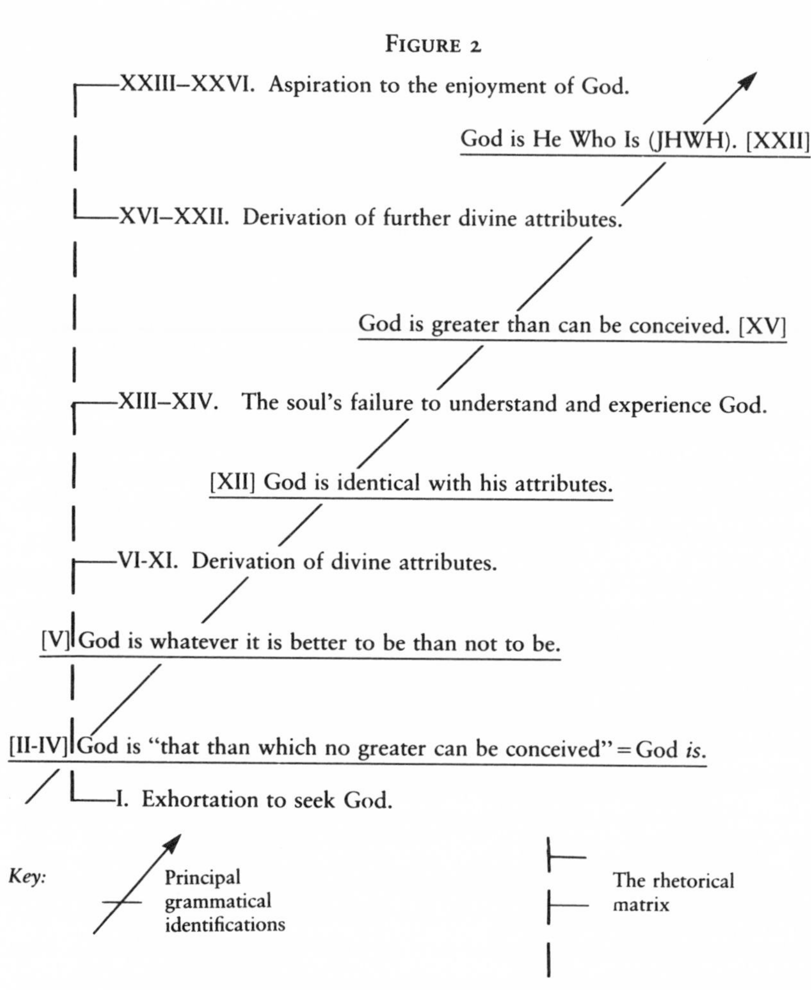


seeking, destined to live and move and have its being within the unfathomable mystery ("inaccessible light") it seeks unceasingly to fathom.

Designed to arouse the mind to the contemplation of God (P I), Anselm's argument is a grammatical exercise embedded in a rhetorical matrix of prayer (see Figure 2). Critics of the proof, ignoring its rhetorical setting and concentrating exclusively on its dialectic, have almost unanimously supposed it a real or purported tautology. "Exists" is already contained in "God," so that to conclude that "God exists" tells us nothing we did not know to begin with. Or (the other way around) "exists" cannot be the predicate of a tautological proposition about God because it is not a predicate at all. Or (a variant of the same thing) the argument slips surreptitiously from the conceived existence included in the subject to the real existence affirmed by the predicate, so that the identity which would make the proof valid (but question-begging) is dissolved. The proof is either a genuine tautology and therefore uninformative or a specious tautology and therefore inconclusive.

The critics are right: the argument is tautological. A sequence of equipollent propositions set in the context of prayer, Anselm's proof is a commentary on the divine name. Mounting the steps of a grammatical logic, it approaches an understanding of the tetragrammaton. Everything in the *Proslogium,* including the reaffirmation of the name of God in Chapter XXII ("Therefore, O Lord, thou alone art what thou art, and thou art who thou art") is already implicit in the formula "that than which no greater can be conceived." It is evident that the divine name revealed to Moses recommended the choice of that formula in the first place. Faith at the end elicits from this form of words the understanding that informed it in the beginning: the argument (a tautology sprung from a *petitio*) is just this movement from a faith imbued with understanding to an understanding empowered by faith.

From the formula "that than which no greater can be conceived" Anselm first concludes, by the method of substitution, that God necessarily exists. From the same formula it may be inferred (P V) that God is "the highest of all beings, the only being that exists through itself, and makes all other things out of nothing, supremely good, just, truthful, blessed," and so forth. Whatever was not these would not be "that than which a greater cannot be conceived." God is (the principle from which all His attributes may be derived) "whatever it is better to be than not to be." Taking "better" as equivalent to "greater" (M II), this follows directly from the name of God. If God is not whatever it is better/greater to be than not to be, He is not that than which no greater can be conceived.

The principle formulated in Chapter V enables Anselm to resolve a number of theological paradoxes: God is sensible but not corporeal, compassionate but impassible, omnipotent but incapable of many things (P VI–VIII). Faced with the question How can God be both just and merciful without contradiction (P IX–XI)? Anselm replies:

> Truly, then, all the ways of the Lord are mercy and truth, and yet the Lord is just in all his ways. And assuredly these two statements are not incompatible, because it is not just that those whom You will to punish should be saved, nor just that those whom You will to spare should be condemned. For only what You will is just, and only what You do not will is not just. (P IX)

Obscurantist as it may appear, the rule here invoked—"that alone is just which thou dost will, and unjust what thou dost not will"—is implicit in the divine name. If God were compelled to submit to a standard of rectitude superior to Himself, He would not be that than which no greater can be conceived.

Analogously, God is the life by which He lives, the wisdom by which He is wise, the goodness by which He is good, and so on through all the predicates of divinity (P XII). His attributes are identical with His substance, so that all theological propositions are tautologies. Since that which is substance through and through is greater than that which is subject to accident (P XIII), if God's attributes were not identical with God, He would not be that than which no greater can be conceived.

This conclusion leads to another: God is greater than anything that can be conceived (P XV). A further inference from the name of God, this proposition reminds us that were He not "greater than can be conceived," God would not be "that than which a greater cannot be conceived." This is not to suggest that the human mind can conceive the inconceivable, but rather to acknowledge the fact that divinity surpasses conception. God is (this we can and must conceive) beyond conceiving. In the previous chapter (P XIV) Anselm's persona complained that, though he had learned many things about God, he did not enjoy intimacy with Him. The proof that God is "greater than can be conceived" provides a necessary reason for this testimony of experience and leads (P XVI) to the ecstatic realization that God, though everywhere present, dwells in unapproachable light. From this point on, the tone of the *Proslogium* becomes more intensely personal and more deeply devotional. Formerly concerned with understanding God, it now moves through understanding toward communion.

After deducing some additional divine attributes (P XVII–XXI), Anselm states his final conclusion: "Therefore, O Lord, thou alone art what thou art, and thou art who thou art... Thou art truly what thou art.... And thou art who, properly and absolutely, thou art" (P XXII).[17] Though followed by trinitarian reflections (P XXIII) and aspirations toward heaven (P XXIV–XXVI)—a denouement of sorts—this is the climactic moment of the *Proslogium*. It derives, through Chapters II–IV, V, XII, and XV, from the formula with which the work began. From Gaunilon on identified with the demonstration of God's existence in Chapters II–IV, the *Proslogium* argument is not really complete until Chapter XXII. The goal of the proof as a whole, attained in this chapter, is to show that "that than which a greater cannot be conceived" is equivalent to the tetragrammaton: "I am who am." The name of God proposed by (given to) Anselm is identical with the name entrusted to Moses.[18] Beginning with "that than which no greater can be conceived," which believers believe and even fools can understand, we come at last to this sublime truth of revelation: He is who is. By faith and by a reason empowered by faith, it is possible to arrive at that which is beyond faith and reason and may be received only in its self-bestowing. Thus Anselm's illumination resumes in faith and in reason confirms the revelation contained in Holy Scripture.

God exists. That is: theological discourse is about something. But this is only the first and minimal inference from the name of God. More ambitiously, the *Proslogium* articulates the mystery of the Name by working out its grammar: the equipollencies that enable us to rise from what we call Him to what He calls Himself. From beginning to end it frames a vast tautology: God [that than which no greater can be conceived] is [He who *is*], so that the conclusion of Chapter XXII is an emphatic iteration of the conclusion of Chapters II–IV. "God is He who is" is the infinitely potentiated equivalent of "God is." That, plus Anselm's incorporation of the fool into the ambience of his proof (by making God's existence a condition of the intelligibility of atheism),

17. The simplicity of the language in this passage—most of the words are monosyllables, and the grammar is elementary—echoes the simplicity of the divine nature as Anselm sees it.

18. Exod. 3.14.

and his insistence that the controversy with Gaunilon be included as an integral part of the published text, make the *Proslogium* a tautological cycle of terms for order:[19] the textual representation of that circle God is said to be, whose center is everywhere and whose circumference nowhere. Representation: that is, recuperation. The *Proslogium* is also a rhetorical performance. Presuming the extremest difference—the distance between "slight man" and a God whose dwelling place is unapproachable light, the contrast between the "is not" of the fool and the believer's "is"—Anselm's *alloquium* assumes the atheist's abstention into the theist's creed and adumbrates the heavenly reconciliation of God and man. The grammarian's concern for reference and the rhetorician's passion for reunion are both expressions of the desire of language to repair its alienation from being. The language of the *Proslogium* exhibits God as the always other who contains in His perfect self-sameness everything He surpasses, so that (both theologically and linguistically) the absolutely different is encompassed within the circle of the same.

V

But we began with a revelation. Do we end (so soon) with vision? Anselm began with a revelation: an experience of illumination and joy (P Preface). Eadmer describes it as a matutinal moment ("on a certain night during matins") in which the grace of God dawned in his heart.[20] Anselm wrote the *Proslogium* not only to share the joy of his experience with others but also to recover and retain for himself this moment filled with the presence of God. In his Preface he tells us how he sought earnestly and often to find a single argument that would demonstrate the being of God, how the argument again and again eluded him, how he tried (and failed) to give up the search (which was distracting him from his duties), and how the proof he had despaired of finally offered itself to his eager embrace. The Word itself enters his mind, enlightens it, and takes possession of it. Doubts and uncertainties forgotten, his soul's dissension repaired, Anselm is filled with confidence, light, and joy.

19. See Kenneth Burke, *The Rhetoric of Religion* (Boston: Beacon, 1961), pp. 183–96.

20. Southern, *Life of St. Anselm*, p. 30.

The experience narrated by Eadmer and recalled in Anselm's Preface is a necessary condition of the work it inspires. Without it the *Proslogium* had never been written. Indeed, the project of Anselm's text is just the recuperation of the moment of presence that made it possible. But it is not clear that the experience of presence—the gift of full and intimate cognition—can be recaptured by its textual repetition. The possibility of a true writing—a writing that preserves and transmits presence—does not follow from the luminous moment, the evanescence of which is the exigence of its inscription.

Fore and aft, the *Proslogium* is beset by problems of writing. There was, to begin with, some difficulty getting the revelation recorded.[21] Immediately after the proof had offered itself, Anselm wrote it down on wax tablets and gave them to a monk for safekeeping. When he asked for them a few days later, the tablets had disappeared and could not be found. Thereupon Anselm wrote another draft on new tablets and entrusted them to the same monk, who hid them in a cupboard near his bed. The next morning he awoke to find the tablets broken into bits and strewn about the floor of the dormitory. Anselm pieced together the fragments and "recovered the writing, though with difficulty."[22] This reconstructed text Anselm ordered "in the name of the Lord" to be transferred to parchment.

Between the experience itself and its first inscription there is (even though it was performed "at once") a difference, however minimal, of time and memory. Between the first and second sets of tablets there is the (now considerable) difference of time and memory (twice removed) and . . . the second draft.[23] Finally there is the broken and scattered text, with difficulty reassembled and committed to parchment, which copy presumably is the eventual source of the work we now have. Is there anywhere in this history an authentic text or a definitive edition of Anselm's revelation? He was hard-pressed even to get a permanent record of the proof, and the text that has managed to endure is more than several removes from its origin in Anselm's experience.

As the origin of the *Proslogium* recedes, its termination is postponed. To the parchment record, which we assume (without sufficient reason)[24]

21. Ibid., pp. 30–31.
22. Ibid., p. 31.
23. Ibid., p. 30.
24. This seems to be the implication of what Eadmer says at ibid., p. 31 (see note

contained the substance of Chapters II–IV, Anselm added some further considerations (P Preface). Eadmer says that "from" the parchment version Anselm composed a "little volume" which he called the *Proslogium.*[25] After he had read Gaunilon's critique and written his reply, Anselm requested that both refutation and rebuttal be included in any further copies of the work. The chapters (some twenty of them) added by Anselm to the "first" inscription of his experience, plus the revisions occasioned by his controversy with Gaunilon, supplement their founding revelation. Anselm's inclusion of Gaunilon's "on behalf of the fool" and his own response in the published text of his work serves not to expose and to silence his critic but rather to underscore the essential incompletion of the "original" work. The recuperation of presence, its origin forever lost, progresses through a chain of supplementations without end. Is there any reason why the whole history of criticism and commentary since Anselm's day should not, like the debate with Gaunilon, be incorporated into the text of the *Proslogium?*

The moment of presence is never recovered, but ever distanced and deferred, by writing. A necessary condition of the text it elicits, the enjoyment of the presence of God now (always) past is postponed (by that text) until (always) later. The *Proslogium* is a failed project of recuperation, inhabiting the interim between a before that is no longer and an after that is not yet. The immediacy that calls for inscription is forfeit by the act that would preserve it.

Always already forfeit. For what we have—what Anselm had—is not the moment itself but never more than the writing of the moment. Describing his illumination, Anselm says that "*what I had despaired of finding* offered itself" and that "I embraced *the thought I had been rejecting*" (P Preface). What is given him is not an unpremeditated immediacy, but rather the very argument he had been seeking. What he receives is *already interpreted,* an immediacy mediated before its advent. Repeated in advance, its subsequent repetition evacuates its plentitude: the spacing that is a condition of writing and the absence marked by every grapheme infect the inscribed along with the inscription. Insofar as it wanted to be written, Anselm's experience was not an experience of presence but already a representation: the inscription

---

25 below), but of course we do not know exactly what was contained in the parchment draft.

25. Ibid., p. 31.

of presence, on the soul and (at length) on parchment. Presence itself is always already lost—there is difference and deferment from the start—and never to be recovered. The always already lost presence was not first possessed and subsequently misplaced (like wax tablets), but ever and only: missing. What was never possessed is forever lacking, and therefore never lost. The "moment of presence," an original absence aboriginally written, is not reclaimed by writing, but quoted and requoted in the text it evokes. From this point of view the *Proslogium* is not (even the project of) the recuperation of a remote origin but the iteration of an original nostalgia.

Anselm says (P Preface) that the *Monologium* was composed "in the person of" one investigating matters of which he is ignorant and the *Proslogium* "in the person of" one striving to lift his mind to the contemplation of God and seeking to understand what he believes. In addition to the differences already noted, both within and without Anselm's experience, there is the difference between Anselm and his persona. Anselm has already received the knowledge of God as a revelation, while his persona is still straining toward contemplation and trying to understand what he believes. By differentiating himself from his persona Anselm transforms himself from person into mask. The possibility of prosopopoeia, once imagined and grafted upon the text, changes all persons (including the author) into fictions. The *Proslogium* is distanced not only from the moment but also from the subject of its origin.

To these remarks about his rhetorical strategy Anselm adds that in his opinion neither the *Monologium* nor the *Proslogium* deserves to be called a book; and that neither would bear a title save for reasons of convenience (the short titles) and to entice readers (the long titles: "an example of meditation on the grounds of faith" and "faith seeking understanding"). Neither text would bear the name of its author had not a number of people (especially Hugh, archbishop of Lyons and apostolic delegate in Gaul) urged him to sign them. This because (when the Preface was written) the texts had already been copied (and corrupted) many times. Someone, under authority, had to assume responsibility for all these citations and disseminations (P Preface).

The differences that punctuate the production of the text are reproduced within the structure of the *Proslogium.* Chapter I, which magnifies the distance between God and the believer, also opens the space of signification. The pilgrim's return from exile to the fatherland, foreshadowed in Anselm's exordium, will also be the return (reference) of the signifier to its proper signified. But the breach, which is the effect of writing, is never closed by inscription. Chapter XXVI anticipates a plentitude of joy not yet enjoyed, and concludes: meanwhile let my mind meditate on this joy, let my tongue speak of it, let my heart love it, let my mouth talk of it (a double entry for language), let my soul hunger for it, let my flesh thirst for it, let my whole being desire it until I enter into the joy of the Lord. But the accumulation of subjunctives—let it meditate, let it speak, let it love, let it preach, let it hunger, let it thirst, let it desire—never adds up to the simple indicative "Is" which is the name of the living God. Anselm's terminal *intrem* (enter) is only a paragram of his earlier *interim* (meanwhile), the flow of signifiers into the abyss could go on forever, and the pilgrim's progress is endlessly inhibited.

The attributes of God (P VI–VIII) are all difference and negation. Different from the homonymous human attributes, and their negative counterparts: God's perception is not a perceiving, his omnipotence proscribes many actions, and his compassion is not a passion. "We feel the effect of mercy, but you do not feel the affect" (P VIII), and this effect of the unaffected is the whole of his mercy. God's mercy ("according to us, not according to you") is his justice ("according to you, not according to us") (P X). That all his attributes are identical with his substance (P XII) means that they are not (in any sense we may conceive) attributes. Whatever God is is "not-____ ," where "____" is the place of the alienated signifier, and the "not-" revokes the mortal word to the heavenly logos. The paradoxes of the human condition (P I) are not resolved, but rehearsed and reenforced, as we approach God.[26]

It is for this reason that the soul (P XIV) seeking divinity as light and truth sees therein only its own darkness. For this reason also God is greater than anything that can be conceived (P XV). That than which no greater can be conceived is necessarily beyond conceiving, and this inconceivability of God is the light in which He lives. We do not see the light, but through it we see whatever we do see (P XVI). The immeasurable excess of divinity releases the intelligibility of finite being:

26. Cf. Alan of Lille, *Anticlaudianus,* trans. James J. Sheridan (Toronto: Pontifical Institute of Medieval Studies, 1973), esp. Book V, where the language becomes increasingly paradoxical as the poet and his persona (Prudence) approach (the description of) God.

the infinitely inconceivable is the limit of the finite, which by limiting it makes it conceivable. The horizon of our comprehension is the uncomprehended that comprehends us, and our enclosure within our own darkness (P XVII), which is our distance from ourselves, is our inclusion in God, the ever self-same light who uncontained contains all things (P XVIII–XIX) and unseen makes all things visible.

The creature's exile—a distance yearning to be traversed—is represented as an epistemological paradox: God is the unknowable condition of the possibility of knowledge. It is also an ontological paradox: the creature is the different that differs both from itself and from its creator, while God in His perfect self-identity embraces every difference. Including His own. For, as Anselm's trinitarian chapter (P XXIII) suggests, God in His unity differs from Himself. The chain of representations and reflections is inaugurated at the heart of being. Even the uncreated good is defined exclusively (P XXIV) by its difference from created goods.

All these differences, through which the creature (as other than God) is given by God (as other than the creature) being, intelligibility, and value, are alembications of the fundamental impasse of signification. Never a signifier, God is the transcendent signified intended in every sign, by whom our signifiers are fulfilled and empowered to signify. He is at the same time and by virtue of the same difference the unsignifiable who exceeds every sign and frustrates signification, who is (as Gaunilon saw) drawn into the web of signifiers by every attempt to conceive Him. It is this paradox that defines the impossibility of Anselm's project, which impossibility his text faithfully and with the acutest understanding transcribes.

Sensitive to this double bind, Anselm's persona (P XIV) breaks off his prayer and turns to address his soul. You were seeking God, he says. Have you now found Him? His soul replies that while she has conceived and known with certainty many things about God, she does not feel what she has found. Knowledge—even certain knowledge—does not coincide with the known. The difference necessary to cognition precludes the experience of presence. Ten chapters further on (P XXIV), the seeker again addresses his soul and exhorts her to rouse herself so that she may conceive the supreme good. But what she is offered is a repetition of Chapter I: an intenser vision of the difference between the divine and the human. And in the expansive chapter that follows (P XXV) the soul is referred to the future along the trajectory of desire:

love and desire the supreme good, and it shall be yours. All the important verbs in this chapter are futures, and as the chapter progresses the future becomes increasingly subjunctive (if you . . . then you will . . . ) until the end, which announces that even the greatest love of which the heart is capable will not be able to contain the joy with which it shall be filled.

The final chapters of the *Proslogium* ironically counterweight Chapter I. The end is to the beginning as the not quite negation of a negation. A double negation deferred, the conclusion just fails to conclude. The difference between seeker and sought remains, a parenthesis approaching but never achieving closure in the reconciliation of God and man. Their repletion with the signified indefinitely postponed, the signifiers of Anselm's text begin to stutter. In Chapter XXVI his persona turns back to God and resumes the prayer of Chapter I: speak, Lord, and show yourself, show me the joy you have promised to the saints. But his prayer is not yet answered. "I have not yet said or conceived, then, Lord, how greatly your blessed will rejoice. . . . Certainly neither eye has seen, nor ear heard, nor has it entered the heart of man in this life how much they will know you and love you in that life" (P XXVI). After his confession of failure the seeker plainly puts off his enjoyment of God. The experience which it was the project of this text to recover must wait until later. The concluding paragraph of the *Proslogium*, filled with contrasts of "here" and "there," ends with a "meanwhile" and a string of subjunctive exhortations to the soul to desire the still outstanding fullness of joy.

The elusive signified slips through the signifying differences and escapes signification. The experience of presence cannot be contained by the text that presupposes it and proposes to (re)capture it. It is possible (if at all) only as an excess of the text: a moment lost before the moment of its first inscription and never recovered in the writing but always projected beyond it. There is nothing outside the text, and that nothing is what the text is all about. Is, as an interim, within. Anselm's text can only enact—can only be—this interminable meanwhile: the peregrination of the soul in the kingdom of difference,[27] which is language. The patria of presence, before and after the text, is never departed

27. The expression "land of unlikeness," is from St. Augustine, *Confessiones*, VII. 10.

from and never returned to. Always already lost and so never lost, it is never yet regained.

And so always possessed? Anselm writes:

> Lord, if you are not here, where shall I seek you absent? But if you are everywhere, why do I not see you present? Surely you dwell in unapproachable light. But where is unapproachable light? Or how shall I come to unapproachable light? Or who shall lead me to this light and into it, that I may see you in it? And then, by what signs and in what form shall I seek you? (P I)

In Chapter XVI, after he has shown that God is beyond conceiving, Anselm says:

> Truly, Lord, this is the unapproachable light in which you dwell.... Truly I do not see this light, because it is too much for me, and yet whatever I see I see through it, just as the weak eye sees what it sees through the light of the sun which it cannot look at in the sun itself. (P XVI)

And finally, in his response to Gaunilon:

> But if you say that it ["That than which..."] is not understood and is not in the understanding because it is not completely understood, then you must say that one who cannot look into the purest light of the sun does not see daylight, which is nothing but the light of the sun. (A I)

How much weight will the figure bear? Will it bear the whole weight of the *Proslogium?* There is always a sun... and a flower that perishes in the attempt to track the central brilliance. A dried flower in a book.[28]

"By what signs... shall I seek thee?" In the formula "that than which a greater cannot be conceived" Anselm('s persona) claims to have found a sign that guarantees its own signification. The *Proslogium,* as prayer and as argument, tries to enforce this claim. Both rhetoric (prayer) and reference (grammar) are essays in the recuperation of being by the sign. Yet the rhetoric and the grammar of this text work against each other even in their collaboration. Anselm's grammatical logic sponsors a firm

28. Cf. Jacques Derrida, "White Mythology: Metaphor in the Text of Philosophy," *New Literary History* 6 (Autumn 1974), 74.

and final conclusion, but the effect of his rhetoric is to defer the full appropriation of this conclusion indefinitely. And the *Proslogium*, caught in the middest, can only prolong the interval between a paradise (always already) lost and paradise (never yet) regained. Faith no longer, not yet understanding, the argument as a "seeking" remains an unfulfilled signification: a discourse in the hiatus between signifier and signified. Walking the line and breaching the boundary, the *Proslogium* is a perpetual pilgrimage through the differences of language that sunder sign from being and delay until eternity (P XXVI) the advent of presence.

> I would be the last to reject a criticism under the pretext that it is metaphoric or metonymic or both at the same time. Every reading is so, in one way or another, and the partition does not pass between a figurative reading and an appropriate or literal, correct or true reading, but between capacities of tropes.[29]

Language is a self-proliferating nonsystem of tropes. The radical of language is catechresis, by which the (properly?) nameless receives a(n improper) name. Every trope, from the boldest metaphoric identification (=) through synecdoche and analogy and simile down to the merest metonymic juxtaposition (; ),[30] is a devolution from that original catachresis. There is no literal language and no proper speech. Every attempt to tell it like it is gets lost in the intricate evasions of as. Yet every trope is (also) the (impossible) *project* of repossessing (an always already unlost because never possessed) immediacy. Every trope is apotropaic: turning away from propriety to figuration, it turns away from its turning. Moving to close the gap between word and thing, it stammers (in) the difference.

And knows this. The mark of a perfectly (but the appearance of the mark shows that it never is) sophisticated and self-conscious language is that it is at once and without mediation ironic and committed. It sees through its own commitments and remains detached from them, marking all the positions it does not take as well as the position it

29. Jacques Derrida, "The *Retrait* of Metaphor," *Enclitic* 2 (Fall 1978), 16.

30. For the forms of metaphor, see Northrop Frye, *Anatomy of Criticism* (Princeton: Princeton University Press, 1957), pp. 122–25; cf. also Louis Mackey, "Anatomical Curiosities: Northrop Frye's Theory of Criticism," *Texas Studies in Literature and Language* 23 (Fall 1981), 442–69.

occupies. Simultaneously it takes a stand and makes itself responsible for affirmations that trangress its own disengagement. It always knows better than to trust itself, and it always trusts itself beyond its knowledge. Continually deconstructing and reconstructing itself, only a discourse at odds with itself is (and only in this sense is it) reconciled to itself.

Only a text so constituted can read the text of (purported) revelation without deceiving itself. In this respect as in others a paradigm of medieval philosophical and theological writing, Anselm's *Proslogium* marshals prayer and argument in an effort to lay hold on divinity... and knows that it doesn't do it. Knows that every such endeavor necessarily fails by reason of the incommensurable transcendence of God and the invincible incapacity of language to contain him. This solicitous self-knowledge is the source of the ambivalence of Anselm's text. Is its conjunction of inference and invocation just another attempt to appropriate the alterity of the Other? Or does it express the composure which, patient and self-possessed, awaits the arrival of the Other as a gift? The ambiguity does not escape Anselm's awareness, but is inscribed (redemptively?) in the text of the *Proslogium.* By postponing the enjoyment of presence until forever, by allowing the advocate of folly to speak within its precincts, and by insisting that whatever understanding it achieves depends upon and may not dispense with the faith that both inspires and qualifies its seeking, the *Proslogium* deconstructs, even as it celebrates them, the radiant certainties that have incensed its critics. Marking thereby its necessary failure, it also secures its only possible—and most ambiguous—success.

# PART II

# *Intertextuality*

# Gawain in Wace and Laȝamon: A Case of Metahistorical Evolution

MARTIN B. SHICHTMAN

Among historians who see the ultimate goal of historical discourse as the conveyance of "truth," historical writings of the Middle Ages have been often found suspect, even ignored, because of their tendency toward literariness.[1] Contemporary historiographical theory argues, however, that the search for objective historical truth is a delusion. Historical writing is, it suggests, subject to the same forces that give form to all narrative. This position, with its insistence that, in Hayden White's words, "*historical* inquiry is born less of the necessity to establish *that* certain events occurred than of the desire to determine what certain events might *mean* for a given group, society, or culture's conception of its present tasks and future prospects," presents a context for a reevaluation of the histories produced during the Middle Ages.[2]

1. A case in point involves the work of William of Malmesbury, a medieval historian who took great pride in the accuracy of his investigations and the laboriousness of his research, a medieval historian quick to condemn colleagues for excessive literariness. William has been criticized for the lack of objectivity in his historical method. Antonia Gransden, a scholar generally sympathetic to William's efforts, argues in *Historical Writing in England c. 550 to c. 1307* (Ithaca: Cornell University Press, 1974), p. 176: "He had a great gift of imagination, which appears in his numerous excellent stories. ... But sometimes this led him to extremes. One slender fact or unauthenticated rumor could rouse the story-teller in him."

2. Hayden White, "Historical Pluralism," *Critical Inquiry* 12 (1986), 487.

Many medieval historians seem to have been aware of, and intent upon making use of, the literary/historical tension in their endeavors. As early as the seventh century Isidore of Seville, influenced by the work of Latin grammarians, wrote that "Historia est narratio rei gestae per quam ea quae in praeterito facta sunt, dignoscuntur" [History is the narration of events by which those things which were done in the past are sorted out].[3] Amid the intellectual upheaval of the twelfth century, Hugh of Saint Victor created a controversy by reasserting Isidore's position and arguing for a narrative view of history: "Historia est rerum gestarum narratio" [History is the narration of events].[4] For Hugh, as M. D. Chenu notes, "the term *historia*... embraced the same ambiguity which it retains in our modern languages, where it designates at the same time the facts, as the stuff of history (objective sense), and the intellectual discipline which treats these facts (subjective sense)."[5] Like Isidore, Hugh recognized the medieval historian as a literary stylist, a writer of narratives who, in sorting out the facts of history, was given a chance to demonstrate both his individuality and his artistry.

According to Northrop Frye, "most historians would prefer to believe... that history is one thing and poetry another."[6] Such historians see their discipline as the objective, undistorted reporting of "reality"; they believe their prose directly imitates actions, reproducing what has actually occurred. Frye casts some doubt on the notion that history can be perfectly imitative of reality, suggesting instead that "when a historian's scheme gets to a certain point of comprehensiveness it becomes mythical in shape, and so approaches the poetic in nature";[7] at this point history becomes metahistory. Hayden White even more specifically denies the possibility of a "scientific knowledge" of history. In fact, he insists on history as metahistory, on the historical text as literary artifact. White maintains that historical narratives are "verbal

3. Isidore of Seville, *Etymologiarum*, in *Patrologiae cursus completus, series latina*, 82, ed. J. P. Migne (Paris, 1850), p. 122. The translation is from M. D. Chenu, *Nature, Man and Society in the Twelfth Century: Essays on New Theological Perspectives in the Latin West*, ed. and trans. Jerome Taylor and Lester K. Little (Chicago: University of Chicago Press, 1968), p. 167.

4. Hugh of Saint Victor, *De sacramentis fidei Christianae*, in *Patrologiae cursus completus, series latina*, 176, ed. J. P. Migne (Paris, 1880), p. 184. The translation is from Chenu, *Nature, Man and Society*, p. 167.

5. Chenu, *Nature, Man and Society*, p. 166.

6. Northrop Frye, *Fables of Identity: Studies in Poetic Mythology* (New York: Harcourt, Brace & World, 1963), p. 55.

7. Ibid., pp. 53-54.

fictions, the contents of which are as much *invented* as *found* and the forms of which have as much in common with their counterparts in literature [as] they have with those in the sciences."[8] For White, the historical narrative reveals as much about the process of writing history as it does information concerning past events.

Like Frye and White, Michel Foucault writes of the historian as structuring received materials. Commenting on a recent shift to a "new form of historical study," Foucault focuses on the notion of discontinuity:

> And the great problem presented by such historical analysis is not how continuities are established, how a single pattern is formed and preserved, how for so many different, successive minds there is a single horizon, what mode of action and what substructure is implied by the interplay of transmissions, assumptions, disappearances, and repetitions, how the origin may extend its sway well beyond itself to that conclusion that is never given—the problem is no longer one of tradition, of tracing a line, but one of division, of limits; it is no longer one of lasting foundations, but one of transformations that serve as new foundations, the rebuilding of foundations.[9]

Foucault claims that the "new history" challenges earlier principles of cohesion "when it speaks of series, divisions, limits, differences of level, shifts, chronological specificities, particular forms of rehandling, possible types of relations."[10] It provides for a way of reseeing history and ultimately liberates the historian from the continuous tracing back to origins. As White notes, for Foucault "events gain the status of 'facts' by virtue of their susceptibility to inclusion within the set of lexical lists and analysis by the syntactical strategies sanctioned by the modes of representation prevailing at a given time and place."[11] The writing

8. Hayden White, *Tropics of Discourse: Essays in Cultural Criticism* (Baltimore: Johns Hopkins University Press, 1978), p. 82.

9. Michel Foucault, *The Archaeology of Knowledge,* trans. A. M. Sheridan Smith (New York: Harper & Row, 1972), p. 5.

10. Ibid., p. 10.

11. White, p. 257. Also see Claude Lévi-Strauss, *The Savage Mind,* trans. George Weidenfield (Chicago: University of Chicago Press, 1966), pp. 257–58. Lévi-Strauss similarly claims: "What makes History possible is that a sub-set of events is found, for a given period, to have approximately the same significance for a contingent of individuals who have not necessarily experienced the events and may even consider them at an interval of several centuries. History is therefore never history, but history-for. It is partial in the sense of being biased even when it claims not to be."

of history is thus the transcribing of the illusions of an age. The "new historian" recognizes these illusions, recognizes that traditional historiography is continuously frustrated in its efforts to comprehend similitudes, and therefore searches for the differences in things.

For many historians during the Middle Ages, and particularly from the twelfth century onward, the writing of history involved the revision of materials received, the perception of data from new perspectives. These historians emphasized not similitude, not their ability to reproduce precisely events that had already taken place, but rather differences, their purpose being to retell history in a new manner. As Raymond Klibansky notes of the twelfth-century cleric Peter Abelard, "In the *Historia clamitatum* he portrays himself as a man with singular powers, able to rely on his genius (*ingenium*) when others depend on laboriously acquired learning. In each field of knowledge he can, trusting in his own powers, penetrate more deeply than others who, not daring to challenge accepted doctrines, have become slaves to tradition."[12] Robert W. Hanning maintains that "Abelard's exaltation of *ingenium* puts him firmly in touch with that main current of twelfth-century culture that stressed the manipulation of institutions and situations to impose a favorable order on them."[13] Abelard voiced the attitudes of an emerging group of medieval historians who refused to subordinate their individuality and cultural identity to their discipline, refused to privilege solely the historical "facts" that they had inherited. For these historians, historical discovery and invention merged as their narratives took shape.

Most writers of twelfth-century Arthurian chronicles either directly or indirectly followed Geoffrey of Monmouth's *Historia regum Britanniae,* but efforts were made to undermine its authority. According to Robert Huntington Fletcher, "the history of the Arthurian material in the chronicles after Geoffrey is the history of the treatment to which Geoffrey's version of the story was subjected by later writers."[14] For Geoffrey's followers, his text functioned as the "story," a "primitive" element in the ongoing conceptualization of the historical work. White

12. Raymond Klibansky, "Peter Abailard and Bernard of Clairvaux: A Letter by Abailard," *Medieval and Renaissance Studies* 1 (1961), 21.

13. Robert W. Hanning, *The Individual in Twelfth-Century Romance* (New Haven: Yale University Press, 1977), p. 30.

14. Robert Huntington Fletcher, *The Arthurian Material in the Chronicles* (1906; rpt. New York: Franklin, 1966), p. 116.

suggests that "when a given set of events has been motifically encoded, the reader has been provided with a story; the chronicle of events has been transformed into a *completed* diachronic process, about which one can then ask questions as if he were dealing with a *synchronic structure* of relationships."[15] The questions that the historian asks of the story give direction to his discourse. The answers that he discovers, or perhaps even invents (and White admits that discovery and invention are often difficult to tell apart), allow for an explanation by emplotment, the creation of a newly formed narrative.

Both Wace and Laȝamon were indebted to Geoffrey of Monmouth for the information appearing in their chronicles: Wace followed Geoffrey, Laȝamon followed Wace. But neither was a slavish imitator. Both chronicled the Matter of Britain poetically (Wace in octosyllabic couplets, Laȝamon in alliterative lines), yet it seems doubtful that either writer would have described himself as strictly a poet or a historian. More likely, they would have seen themselves as historians who used vernacular language and popular poetic forms to make their histories accessible to audiences with very specific—and different—demands and agendas, historians who emplotted their received materials to create new narratives differing from those of their predecessors. The achievements of Wace and Laȝamon are not to be found solely in their skills as poets or as historians, therefore, but in their abilities to present history literarily, to write metahistory.

Geoffrey's discussion of Gawain's career, though sketchy, demonstrates the author's skill in the creation of historical biography, and it forms the story on which successors based their modes of emplotment. What Geoffrey learned about Gawain from Celtic sources is impossible to determine; his Latin sources say little about the knight. Geoffrey might have been responsible for making Gawain an important Arthurian figure, creating for him a personal history highlighting important moments in the knight's life. Gawain's being born to Loth, duke of Lothian, and Anna, sister of Arthur, is recorded for the first time in the *Historia.* At the age of twelve Gawain is sent by Arthur into the service of Pope Sulpicius, from whom he eventually receives his arms. As a young man Gawain becomes Arthur's ambassador to the court of Lucius Hiberius, emperor of Rome. Still impressionable, he is influ-

15. Hayden White, *Metahistory: The Historical Imagination in Nineteenth-Century Europe* (Baltimore: Johns Hopkins University Press, 1973), p. 6.

enced by youthful comrades to create an incident that will bring the already feuding nations of Britain and Rome to war. In fact Gawain murders Lucius's nephew, Gaius Quintillianus, during his visit to the court—an act of aggression that Geoffrey appears to endorse. Gawain proves himself a great knight and leader of men in the conflict that follows. When several of his fellow commanders are killed in battle, Gawain rallies their retreating troops and routs the Roman forces. He also engages Lucius in single combat, fighting him to a draw. At the height of his career, however, Gawain learns that his brother, Mordred, has treasonously usurped Arthur's throne. He returns home to fight in the war against Mordred and becomes an early casualty.[16]

A study of Gawain's characterization in Wace's *Roman de Brut* and Laȝamon's *Brut* indicates the directions that these works take as metahistories. The changes that Wace and Laȝamon make in their received Gawains, and in their received histories in general, are small, but they are sufficient to individualize their works. In transforming Geoffrey's *Historia,* both authors re-view history and demonstrate their poetic artistry. Wace's *Roman de Brut* is emplotted as a romance, as the type of history that according to White "is fundamentally a drama of self-identification symbolized by the hero's transcendence of the world of experience."[17] Wace's Gawain, while living in a brutal world, is witty and charming, endowed with an urbane sophistication reflecting the attitudes of the author's twelfth-century, courtly Norman audience. Laȝamon's *Brut* is emplotted as a tragedy, demonstrating the "resignation of men to the conditions under which they must labor in the world . . . conditions . . . asserted to be unalterable and eternal, and the implication is that men cannot change them but must work within them."[18] Laȝamon's Gawain is dark and brooding; he stoically endures a savagely cruel existence. He is a hero for a defeated English people, a people who, though they must struggle to retain even their national language, persist in producing a poetry filled with intensity. Wace's mode of emplotment offers a powerful legitimation of the ruling-class's deeds and aspirations; this is history written for winners. Laȝamon presents explanations for those who have lost.

Wace selected his mode of historical emplotment to appeal to the

16. On Gawain's role in the *Historia,* see Geoffrey of Monmouth, *Historia regum Britanniae,* ed. Acton Griscom (London: Longman, Green, 1929), pp. 444–97.
17. White, *Metahistory,* p. 8.
18. Ibid., p. 9.

tastes of twelfth-century Norman nobility. Certainly the *Roman de Brut,* completed in 1155, was a departure from his earlier religious writings. As Urban Tigner Holmes, Jr., claims, "it is surprising that Wace even undertook the *Brut,* for he was undoubtedly a sober man, a hardheaded moralist."[19] Between the years 1140 and 1150 Wace composed at least three saints' lives: a *Life of Saint Nicholas,* a *Conception Nostre Dame,* and fragments of a *Life of Saint Marguerite* (he may also have been responsible for a *Life of Saint George,* though there is little evidence attesting to his authorship). But Wace found the writing of secular history more rewarding than hagiography; in an autobiographical section of the *Roman de Rou,* Wace would later admit that he specifically directed his discourse toward

> la riche gent,
> ki unt les rentes e le argent,
> kar pur eus sunt li livre fait
> e bon dit fait e bien retrait.
>
> rich folk who possess revenues and silver, since for them books are made and good works are composed and well set forth.[20]

The return that Wace received for writing the *Roman de Brut* was considerable. According to Laȝamon, Wace presented a copy of the *Roman de Brut* to Eleanor, the new queen of England.[21] In 1160 Henry II, Eleanor's husband, commissioned Wace, then a clerk at Caen, to compose a chronicle of the dukes of Normandy, the *Roman de Rou.* By 1169 Wace had been awarded the canonry at Bayeux. Eugene Vance suggests that "the late twelfth century was a period when even the upper class was preoccupied with the order of discourse as a matter

19. Urban Tigner Holmes, Jr., "Norman Literature and Wace," in *Medieval Secular Literature,* ed. William Matthews (Berkeley: University of California Press, 1965), p. 62.

20. Wace, *Le Roman de Rou,* ed. A. J. Holden (Paris: A. & J. Picard, 1970), I, 167. The translation is from Charles Foulon, "Wace," in *Arthurian Literature of the Middle Ages,* ed. Roger Sherman Loomis (London: Oxford University Press, 1959), p. 94.

21. See Laȝamon, *Brut,* ed. G. L. Brook and R. F. Leslie, EETS, O.S. 250 and 277 (London: Oxford University Press, 1963 and 1978). In citing his sources, Laȝamon claims: "Boc he nom þe þridde leide þer amidden. / þa makede a Frenchis clerc. / Wace wes ihoten þe wel couþe writen. / [and] he hoe ȝef þare æðelen Ælienor. / þe wes Henries quene þes heȝes kinges" [He took the third book and laid it there among the others. It was made by a French clerk named Wace, who knew how to write well, and who gave it to Eleanor, queen to the high king, Henry] (19–23). All further quotations from the *Brut* are cited in the text. All translations from the *Brut* are my own.

of status."[22] Wace clearly appreciated the power of historical writing and understood that his role as historian involved favoring the positions of an influential audience.

In the *Roman de Brut,* Wace continuously colors received material with the prevailing attitudes of Norman France. He transforms Geoffrey's story—the *Roman de Brut* was primarily influenced by two versions of the *Historia regum Britanniae,* the so-called Vulgate and the abbreviated Variant—into a romantic history suited to an audience familiar with the marvelous tales of *conteurs* and partial to narratives concerning chivalry, lady love, and the glorification of the individual. He also transforms Geoffrey's story into a romantic history suited to an audience anxious that its own status should be endorsed. For the Norman nobility, the twelfth century was both a time of culture, during which the pleasures of *courtoisie* might be pursued, and a time for expanded military adventurism.[23] Henry II and Eleanor were characteristic of a new aristocracy that was literate, interested in reading, and willing to patronize poets who wrote in the vernacular of such matters as would validate the assumptions and ambitions of their society. In the *Roman de Brut,* Wace took upon himself the challenge of producing a history that would not only be faithful to the "facts" of his sources but also present them in a manner appreciated in an age of romantic vision, an age when the possibility for human achievement seemed boundless.

Wace transforms Geoffrey's Gawain into an articulate spokesman for the new romantic age. Wace first mentions Gawain's greatness at the time of Arthur's birth, that is, before Gawain himself is even born. He tells the reader that Gawain, a knight known for his prowess, will be the son of Anna (Arthur's sister) and her husband, King Lot. Like Geoffrey, Wace mentions that Gawain is sent to Pope Sulpicius to be trained, but Wace elaborates on Gawain's education by describing the young man as he returns to Arthur's court. Garbed in a mantle bestowed on him by Pope Sulpicius, Gawain "Preuz fu et de molt grant mesure, / D'orguel ne de sorfet n'ot cure. / Plus volt fere que il ne dist, / Et plus doner qu'il ne promist" [was valiant and endowed with great moderation, concerned with neither pride nor excessiveness. He did

22. Eugene Vance, "Love's Concordance: The Poetics of Desire and the Joy of the Text," *Diacritics* 5 (1975), 47.

23. On the varied concerns of the Norman nobility, see J. S. P. Tatlock, *The Legendary History of Britain* (Berkeley: University of California Press, 1950), p. 465.

more than he said he would and gave more than he promised] (1317-20).[24] Although he has not yet actually proved himself, Gawain is presented as both the perfect Christian and courtly knight. His birth, training, dress, and demeanor are the best that Arthurian society can offer. The suggestion is that this young knight represents the future, and an exceptional one it is.

Wace adds some material that changes Gawain from the unwavering, unthinking warrior of the *Historia* to a more civilized French knight. When Arthur's council meets to discuss a response to Lucius's demand for tribute, Cador, an elder of the court, urges war, arguing that his countrymen have grown soft from an extended peacetime. Gawain tempers Cador's inflammatory remarks with the good-natured statement:

> Bone est la pes anprés la guerre,
> Plus bele et miaudre an est la terre.
> Molt sont bones les gaberies
> Et bones sont les drueries.
> Por amistiez et por amies
> Font chevalier chevaleries.
>
> Good is peace after war; the land is much more beautiful and better for it. Very good are the pleasantries, and good are the amorous pleasures. For love and ladies knights perform chivalrous deeds. (2219–24)

Wace sides with Gawain's position in this dialogue, and by doing so he simultaneously endorses the romantic emplotment of history and sets his text apart from Geoffrey's story. In the exchange Wace's Gawain becomes the youthful romance hero confronting and ultimately overcoming the advocate of tradition.[25] Gawain now clearly represents an emerging order in both Arthur's society and Norman society. He belongs to a generation that has learned the pleasures of courtly living. Cador's attitude would have appealed to Geoffrey and to the audience of the *Historia regum Britanniae:* Cador loves war for its own sake. Gawain, who, significantly, is the final speaker to address Arthur's

24. Wace, *La partie arthurienne du Roman de Brut,* ed. I. D. O. Arnold and M. M. Pelan (Paris: Klincksieck, 1962). All further quotations from the *Roman de Brut* are cited in the text. All translations from the *Roman de Brut* are my own.

25. In his discussion of Jules Michelet, the nineteenth-century writer of romantic historiography, White maintains that "Michelet *emplotted* his histories as dramas of disclosure, of the liberation of a spiritual power fighting to free itself from the forces of darkness." *Metahistory,* p. 152.

council, sets the tone for a new code of knightly behavior, one that Wace's readers would have found comforting: he relishes thoughts of battle because he enjoys the delights of victory. Gawain voices, for the first time in French literature, the notion that knightly deeds are performed at least in part to gain the appreciation of women, and thus he distances himself from the vulgar spokesman of an older, fading point of view.

In the *Roman de Brut,* Gawain is again made an ambassador to Lucius's court in Rome, but Wace supplies a reason for the knight's appointment. According to Wace, Gawain "a Rome ot longues esté" [had been in Rome a long time] (3104), and like his fellow emissaries, Guerin and Boso, he was "bien prisié, / Bien coneü, bien anseignié" [well-praised, well-known, and well-educated] (3105–6). The delegation sent by Wace's Arthur is not only forceful but diplomatic; Gawain is chosen because, despite his tender years, he has already gained respect in Rome. Following Geoffrey, Wace depicts the young men of Arthur's court attempting to convince Gawain that he should incite a war, but this time their arguments seem ineffective. When Gawain, Guerin, and Boso arrive in Rome, it is Gawain who takes charge of the mission. Demonstrating the maturity of an experienced statesman, Gawain presents Arthur's position to Lucius and the Roman council. For both Arthur's society and Norman society, he is a model of ambassadorial decorum. Only after Lucius's nephew, Quintilian, remarks that Britons are a vainglorious people does Gawain resort to violence. Michael Herzog notes that "in Geoffrey's *Historia,* Gawain was goaded into a hostility towards the Romans that he may or may not have felt. In Wace's *Brut,* [he] is the willing, self-motivated voice of his young companions."[26] Wace's Gawain is aware of his position and the implications of his actions—Wace even seems to emphasize the knight's initial restraint. Gawain kills Quintilian because the Roman has behaved badly and broken the protocol of diplomacy. Quintilian disrupts the negotiations; he, like Cador, prefers war to more civilized forms of intercourse. Gawain puts Quintilian's argument to rest in a manner that Wace's audience would have applauded; from its own situation, this audience would have understood that at times the maintenance of

26. Michael Herzog, "The Development of Sir Gawain as a Literary Figure in Medieval German and English Arthurian Romances" (diss., University of Washington, 1971), p. 19.

authority (and, ultimately, the status quo) demands that appropriate steps be taken to destroy the unruly.

Wace follows Geoffrey's *Historia* in his discussion of Gawain's involvement in the war against Lucius. He eschews Geoffrey's restrained approach, however, enlarging upon the single combat between Gawain and Lucius. Wace focuses on the possibilities for individual glorification, closely describing and admiring each of the combatants. War becomes a courtly spectator sport as Gawain and Lucius engage in an evenly matched contest that in some ways resembles the tournaments of later Arthurian romances. Margaret Houck maintains that Wace "seems to dislike the expression of barbarous feelings, and he usually abridges or omits passages which indicate motives for cruelty."[27] But Wace seems more purposeful than squeamish in softening Geoffrey's violence. Wace isolates Gawain in the battle with Lucius from the remainder of the Arthurian forces and thus shows him to be a new type of fighting man: Gawain is raised up above the fray, presented not as a rude warrior but as a chivalric knight. By conquering Rome, the Arthurian empire reaches its apogee, and its success is, in part, attributable to men like Gawain, civilized heroes of the new romantic order who have refined war, transmuting its ugliness and horror to a form of art. The portrayal of Wace's Gawain makes imperialism seem respectable—the beautiful and rightful activity of those with romantic vision—to an audience itself bent on empire.[28]

As Geoffrey concludes the Arthurian section of the *Historia,* Gawain's is just another name in a catalogue of the dead; but Wace takes special care to elaborate on Gawain's demise. Having elevated Gawain to the status of a hero, Wace allows him to die like one. Killed by an unknown assailant at the beginning of the war against his brother Mordred, Gawain is mourned by Arthur, "Car il n'amoit nul home tant" [for he loved no other man so much] (4536). Following Gawain's burial, Arthur "Son mautalant torna et s'ire / Sor Mordret, molt bee a l'ocirre" [turned his wrath on Mordred; much he desired to kill him] (4581-82). In the *Roman de Brut,* Gawain's murder is the rallying point for those who desire Mordred's ruin. Gawain simultaneously

27. Margaret Houck, "Sources of the *Roman de Brut* of Wace," *University of California Publications in English* 5 (1940–44), 185.

28. On Arthurian romance as a literary basis for imperialism, see Charles Homer Haskins, *The Renaissance of the 12th Century* (New York: New American Library, 1927), p. 260.

transcends and lends inspiration to Arthurian society. He becomes more than a knight; he becomes a symbol. Wace specifically notes that Gawain's burial site remains unknown, and in the context of Wace's romantic history this "factual" remark takes on added significance. For those who succeed and admire him, Gawain is more than a man whose remains can be exhumed, examined, and verified. He is the eternal, living spirit of the romantic dream. For Wace and his audience, Gawain is proof that "historical" man can aspire to the romantic ideal.

Laȝamon claims that his *Brut,* written in England at the beginning of the thirteenth century, was influenced by Wace's *Roman de Brut,* Alfred's English translation of Bede's *Historia ecclesiastica gentis anglorum,* and a book written in Latin by Saints Augustine and Albin. In fact, Laȝamon relied almost entirely on Wace for his "historical" material, which he augmented by an imaginative emplotment that both expanded and radically altered Wace's story. If Wace emplots Arthurian history as romance to celebrate the values of the Norman aristocracy, Laȝamon's history is tragedy, consolation to a conquered people. White, at least in part, defines a tragic conception of history as one in which "man springs from nature, creates a society adequate to his immediate needs out of his reason and will, and then engages in a fatal combat with this, his own creation, to provide the drama of historical change."[29] The *Brut* contains none of the celebration of courtly values so central to Wace's work, primarily because these values would have close associations with French (especially Norman) culture. According to J. S. P. Tatlock, when Laȝamon "ignores French culture, we may attribute this not only to his inexperience of the great world but to his poetic tact in adapting to an audience which would have found it unintelligible and disturbing."[30] Laȝamon was a priest to a vanquished people; he wrote to an audience that had to tolerate but never fully accepted the authority and enthusiams of its French conquerors. He wrote in English, making his work accessible to those who persisted in rejecting French as the official language of their land. For Laȝamon and his audience, daily witnesses to the effects of foreign occupation, the Arthurian legend held little hope. Whereas Wace describes the glorious emergence of an assertive, glittering, courtly society, Laȝamon captures the elegiac strain of his Anglo-Saxon ancestors. He

29. White, *Metahistory,* p. 226.
30. Tatlock, *Legendary History of Britain,* p. 489.

produces a tragic history, cognizant of the smallness of all men, even the greatest, in a world that is fallen, transitory, meaningless. In Laȝamon's hands the Arthurian story is turned into a somber history lesson demonstrating the futility of all human gestures to improve earthly existence: "Nu bidde[ð] Laȝamon alcne æðele mon. / for þene almiten Godd. / þet þeos boc rede [and] leornia þeos runan" [Now Laȝamon asks each noble man, for Almighty God, that he read this book and learn this counsel] (29–31).

Wace depicts Gawain as a good-humored young man; Laȝamon focuses on the solemn side of his personality. When Laȝamon's Gawain responds to Cador's war-affirming speech, there are changes both in the mood of the incident and in the knight's remarks. Rather than providing amusing repartee, Laȝamon's Gawain is angered and insists:

> Cador þu ært a riche mon þine ræddes ne beo[ð] noht idon.
> for god is grið and god is frið þe freoliche þer haldeð wið.
> and Godd sulf hit makede þurh his Godd-cunde.
> for grið makeð godne mon gode workes wurchen.
> for alle monnen bið þa bet þat lond bið þa murgre.

> Cador, you are a powerful man, but your counsels are not good. Good is peace and good is concord to the one who freely holds with it. And God Himself made it through His Divinity. For peace makes a good man perform good works; and all men are better and the land is happier. (12454–58)

These are not the words of a romance hero. The confident assertiveness of Wace's Gawain is gone, and in its place are the more resigned perceptions of a man who recognizes his insignificance in the universe, a man who does the best he can with what he has. Laȝamon's Gawain understands how tenuously his society is held together, and he becomes the voice of religious pacificism in an attempt to strengthen social bonds. But even Gawain cannot long live by his words, for religious ideals and earthly exigencies are no more compatible in Gawain's world than they are in Laȝamon's Britain. Despite his eloquence in rebuking Cador, Gawain soon assumes the role of the traditional Anglo-Saxon warrior; he becomes like Cador, and his pacificism gives way to rash, proud, brutal action. Laȝamon modifies the incident involving Gawain's ambassadorial mission to Lucius, emphasizing the knight's helplessness to alter the conditions that he endures. Gawain demonstrates a fiery temper from the very onset of his negotiations with the Roman emperor. No sooner does he meet Lucius than the two men begin exchanging boasts and threats; there is an ever-present atmosphere of conflict. In Wace's text, Quintilian's insults undermine a tense dialogue; Laȝamon presents these remarks as the logical extension of an already heated debate. It is as if, for Laȝamon, the skirmish that breaks out was always unavoidable.

This sense of inevitability dominates Laȝamon's *Brut*. There is consolation in tragedy, as the audience, which has never known a society of its own, is constantly apprised of the inadequacy of secular institutions to relieve suffering. Perhaps Laȝamon's most significant addition to Gawain's characterization is his strengthening of the bond between the knight and his evil brother, Mordred. Gawain is portrayed as a man torn in two directions. On the one hand he is responsible to his community and the dream of King Arthur; on the other hand are the loyalties of kinship owed to his demonic, destructive brother. Despite the noblest of human intentions, Laȝamon's Gawain cannot reconcile the forces that divide him. While he struggles to maintain that vision of society through which he defines himself as a person, his efforts are confused and undermined by devotion to Mordred.[31] From Gawain's introduction into the *Brut,* he appears burdened by Mordred. Unlike Wace, who makes predictions about Gawain's future achievements, Laȝamon first presents him as only a "lute child" [little child] (11082). He chooses instead to dwell on Gawain's brother, warning his audience: "Wale þat Moddræd wes ibore muchel hærm com þerfore" [Alas that Mordred was born; much harm came from that] (11084). Laȝamon hints at Gawain's coming sufferings, not his triumphs. He hints at the disappointment entailed in Gawain's failure to build and be part of a thriving, uplifting Arthurian society.

Laȝamon's readers no doubt felt betrayed by the turn of events that had allowed the French to overrun their land. Even after 150 years, they must have resented being deprived of the rich legacy that was

31. White points to Alexis de Tocqueville, the nineteenth-century author of *Democracy in America* and *The Old Regime and the Revolution,* to demonstrate how a tragic vision of history functions: "Man remains as Tocqueville put it, 'on the verge between two abysses,' the one comprised of that social order without which he cannot be man, the other comprised of that demonic nature within him which prevents his ever becoming fully human. It is the consciousness of this existence 'on the verge between two abysses' that man constantly returns at the end of every effort to raise himself above the animal and to make thrive the 'angel' which resides within him, suppressed, tethered, and unable to gain ascendency in the species." White, *Metahistory,* p. 193.

rightfully theirs. But it is the nature of earthly society, Laȝamon insists, to betray those who put their greatest faith in it, and the tragedy of Gawain makes his point. The military career of Laȝamon's Gawain corresponds to that of Wace's Gawain. He proves himself a capable leader of men and distinguishes himself in a closely contested single combat with Lucius (from which neither of the well-praised participants emerges victorious). But Gawain's sterling reputation, both on and off the battlefield, proves, in some sense, a liability in Laȝamon's *Brut*. Mordred's treason goes unsuspected because

> Ah al hit wes stille in hirede and in halle.
> for na man hit ne wende þat hit sculde iwurðe.
> ah men to soðe i-wenden for Walwain wes his broðer.
> þe alre treoweste gume þe tuhte to þan hirede.
> þurh Walwain wes Modræd monnen þe leouere.
>
> It was all secret in court and hall, for no man believed that it should be. In truth, men believed him, for Gawain, the truest of all men who came to the court, was his brother. Because of Gawain, Mordred was more believed by men. (12717–21)

Laȝamon is the first writer to stress Gawain's close family ties. Thus it is a particularly intense moment when Gawain learns of Mordred's treachery. Asked to choose between his brother and Arthur, Gawain dramatically declares, in a speech original to Layamon, "to-dæi ich at-sake hine here biuoren þissere duȝeðe, / and ich hine for-demen wulle mid Drihtenes wille" [today I forsake him here before this assembly, and, with the Lord's will, I will destroy him] (14080–81). The choice is not an easy one, because Gawain obviously loves his brother, but responsibilities to society come first. Order must be protected from constantly encroaching evil. However, Gawain and his society are as much doomed by the tragic progression of history as they are by Mordred's scheming. Mordred is simply that irrational force, relentless in its efforts, which even the most organized social institutions cannot completely control. In terms of Laȝamon's overall historical vision, Mordred represents the inherent evil that undermines all gestures of fallen mankind.

To Wace's narrative Laȝamon adds Arthur's allegorical dream concerning Mordred's uprising. In his dream Arthur sees himself raised up on a hall, with Gawain sitting before him; Gawain is armed with Arthur's sword. Mordred then destroys Arthur's hall and breaks Gawain's arms. In this dream not only is Gawain recognized as Arthur's main line of defense, he almost comes to represent the doomed Arthurian society. Secure in his victories against foreign foes, Gawain is blind to the enemy that lurks at home. Both Gawain and the Arthurian community, once vital and triumphant, are easy victims of Mordred's undetected corruption. When Gawain is killed in the war against Mordred, Arthur laments, "wa is me þat ich was mon iborn" [woe is me that I was born a man] (14147). The king realizes that he must continue the struggle in order to defeat Mordred; the impulse to bring order to chaos persists in him. But he also understands that the Arthurian dream has died with Gawain. By showing the tragic fall of the Arthurian court, Laȝamon brings into focus the hopelessness of all secular human endeavor. For Laȝamon, history bears out the theological position that the things of this world are the temporal reflections of human vanity. In Laȝamon's *Brut,* those living in historical time, those committed to earthly institutions, those who have not performed the necessary ceremonies returning them eternally to what Mircea Eliade refers as "mythical time"—when celebrants enjoy the "continual reactualization . . . [of an] atemporal mythical instant"[32]—are, like Gawain, tragically destined to fail. Laȝamon, the stern priest of western Britain, presents his history to demonstrate that there is no hope in history, there is salvation only in God. To Laȝamon's audience, already betrayed by the course of history, the alternative, the spiritual life, may have been a reasonable one.

Contemporary historiographical theory allows us to regard the historian in a new light, not as an objective communicator of "truth" but rather as a writer whose reliability is necessarily compromised by the nature of discourse itself. This theory clouds the differentiation between history and fiction; it suggests that all histories are fictive, controlled in part by literary modes of emplotment and all that gives rise to these modes. Contemporary historiographical theory may, therefore, allow us to see medieval historians much as they might have seen themselves, not as scholars committed to an illusory scientific method but rather as writers who appreciated and made use of the literariness of their productions. The real value of history, according to Friedrich

32. Mircea Eliade, *The Myth of the Eternal Return; or, Cosmos and History,* trans. Willard R. Trask, Bollingen Series 46 (Princeton: Princeton University Press, 1954), p. 76.

Nietzsche, lies "in inventing ingenious variations on a commonplace theme, in raising the popular melody to a universal symbol and showing what a world of depth, power, and beauty exists in it."[33] To judge properly the *Roman de Brut* and the *Brut* one cannot think of them as failed histories, tarnished by their literariness, or as fictions weakly disguised as histories. Such judgments are too easy and ultimately inappropriate. Interest in the *Roman de Brut* and the *Brut* must be directed not at the historical information they include but at how the writers handled this information. Wace and Laȝamon re-viewed the materials they inherited and reshaped them into new narrative forms. In emplotting their histories to meet the demands of their audiences, Wace and Laȝamon created individual works that comment on the practice of historical writing. For Wace, living in the affluence of Norman France, history was a means to show the infinitude of human potential. For Laȝamon, living in Norman-occupied Britain, history was a means of showing his audience the way to God.

33. The translation is from White, *Tropics of Discourse,* p. 54.

# Absolute Reflexivity: Geoffroi de Vinsauf

ALEXANDRE LEUPIN

> Trahit ars ab utroque facetum
> Principium, ludit quasi quaedam praestigiatrix
> Et facit ut fiat res postera prima, futura
> Praesans, transversa directa, remota propinqua;
> Rustica sic fiunt urbana, vestuta novella,
> Publica privata, nigra candida, vilia cara.

> Art can draw a pleasant beginning out of either [the end or the middle of a work]. It plays about almost like a magician, and brings it about that the last becomes the first, the future the present, the oblique direct, the remote near; thus rustic matters become polished, old becomes new, public private, black white, and vile precious.[1]

At the beginning of the thirteenth century Geoffroi de Vinsauf announces a monumental project, an undertaking implied in the very title of his *Poetria Nova:* the development and writing of a new poetics. Ernst Robert Curtius has keenly observed this essential dimension: "So Geoffrey of Vinsauf, author of the *Poetria nova* (*ca.* 1210), intends no

1. Ernest Gallo, *The Poetria Nova and Its Sources in Early Rhetorical Doctrine* (The Hague: Mouton, 1971), lines 120–25. All quotations from the *Poetria Nova* are cited within this essay. I am following Gallo's scrupulous translation.

more by his title than to say that he is putting forth a new poetics."[2] However, it appears that Curtius's fertile remark has not yet been echoed in critical commentary.

Considering the magnitude of Geoffroi's project, it would be reductive to discuss his text with an exclusive view toward its pedagogic thrust (the text is also a manual for beginning or advanced poets). This is the effect of a reading such as Faral's or Baldwin's, critics who focus on the issues of technique, "formula writing," and scholarly transmission while dismissing the question of modernity.[3] Though it contains an evident wealth of technical instruction, the *Poetria Nova* actually transforms its own doctrine into a metaphoric veil for the speculative and specular enterprise that is its true aim.

My intention, then, is to restore the problem of *modernitas* to Geoffroi's work, to follow the developments of this problem, and to grasp its relation to history; while demonstrating the pertinence of this issue in a thirteenth-century context, I shall also stress its importance for our own age, a period that traces its "modernity" only as far back as the romantic era.

## *Theory and Practice*

First, it is important to examine the discursive status that the *Poetria Nova* claims for itself. Because the text overturns all attempts at rigid classification, it is impossible to refer here to a preestablished theory of genres. In fact a modern reader, accustomed to thinking along the lines of clear-cut categories (criticism/theory on the one hand, writing/creation on the other), can be only baffled by a treatise that submits its doctrinal content to the perfectly controlled metrics of poetic form. Moreover, in the theoretical division of his tract, Geoffroi does not hesitate to practice the instruction given to his readers or pupils: his

2. Ernst Robert Curtius, *European Literature in the Latin Middle Ages,* trans. Willard R. Trask, Bollingen Series no. 36 (New York, 1953; rpt. Princeton: Princeton University Press, 1973), p. 153. See also the remarks on p. 100 n. 33 (on Geoffroi de Vinsauf and the "puer senex") and p. 255 n. 23 (on Walter Map's awareness of his own modernity); and the important chapter "The 'Ancients' and the 'Moderns,' " pp. 251–55.

3. See Edmond Faral, *Les arts poétiques du XIIe et XIIIe siècles: Recherches et documents sur la technique littéraire du moyen âge* (1924; rpt. Paris: Champion, 1962), and Charles Sears Baldwin, *Medieval Rhetoric and Poetic (to 1400)* (New York: Macmillan, 1928).

precepts (paranomasia, alliteration, various tropes) are applied and abundantly illustrated in his own discourse. This is a characteristic frequently found in other theoretical writings of the twelfth century (e.g., Alain de Lille's *De planctu naturae*): theory is subsumed in the poetic practice of language.

Inversely, yet correlatively, the examples Geoffroi de Vinsauf gives to illustrate his theory constitute a recitative allegory of the theoretical, emerging as they do to strike up doctrinal discussion in the chasms of their textuality. This occurs despite any generic differences: in fact, the *Poetria Nova* borrows indiscriminately from mythology, the ancients, biblical narrative, fables—and when these traditional sources falter, the text is quick to invent illustrations for its purpose. Geoffroi's theory is thus reflected in the example, and the example glistens in doctrine. Because of this interplay, the examples have much more than a purely illustrative status: they must be considered in terms of a dynamic movement necessarily evolving from the discursive elaboration of Geoffroi's doctrine.

This dynamic force functions reflexively to collapse or otherwise blur the distinction between the text's writing and its "content." The reflexive movements of this specular dynamism are not truly separable; however, for the sake of clarity we may think of them in two distinct steps, using two different "examples" from Geoffroi's text to demonstrate their respective effects. The first example shows us how the text's writing obeys the doctrinal instruction that it communicates. In this passage Geoffroi de Vinsauf recommends *brevitas,* a widespread prescription in medieval poetics, and distinguishes it with a positive allusion to its modernity:

> Sic breve splendet opus: nihil exprimit aut magis aequo
> Aut minus. Iste novae brevitatis acutior usus.
>
> Thus will a brief work shine forth; it expresses nothing more or less than is fitting. This latter kind of brevity is sharper. (735–36)

The emphasis here is not only on brevity but on a *new* ("novae") kind of brevity that lends itself to greater precision. Geoffroi very consciously applies this precept to his own treatise and claims that adherence to the rule gives his work a singular force.

> Accipe magne
> Hoc opus exiguum, breve corpore, viribus amplum.

> Accept, O great one, this poor work, short in body but great in strength. (41–42)

By submitting its own script to the lesson of *brevitas,* the *Poetria Nova* manages to erase the boundary between doctrinal "content" and the practice of writing.

Our second example is the converse of the first since it shows how the text's illustrations regularly allegorize its own writing. This example, a fabliau known as *L'enfant qui fut remis au soleil,*[4] is presented in a profoundly specular structure that brilliantly reflects the substance of Geoffroi's subject matter. The mirror effects of this tale are internally lodged in an echoic pattern between images of the snow's luster and the sun's radiance. Moreover, Geoffroi cites the fabliau twice, thus multiplying its mirror effects through repetition. Here is the second version of the tale which, according to the *Poetria,* exemplifies a more polished form of *brevitas:*

> De nive conceptum quem mater adultera fingit
> Sponsus cum vendens liquefactum sole refingit.
> Vir, quia quem peperit genitum nive femina fingit
> Vendit et a simili liquefactum sole refingit.
>
> The child which the adulterous mother feigned was conceived of snow the father sold, similarly pretending that the sun had melted it. Because his wife pretended that the son she bore was engendered of snow, the husband sold it and similarly pretended it had been melted by the sun. (738–41)

It is clear that the second version is much more than a simple repetition of the first: this passage not only replicates a tale previously cited in the *Poetria* but goes even further by repeating the account internally. Thus, the minimal narrative unit of the fabliau is endlessly reproduced. In its bottomless specularity, the example offers the reader no less than a parable of fiction's beginnings. This notion of birth, emblematized by the child, is reinforced by the text's insistence on the radical *fingere,* the etymon of "fiction." As we know, this paradigm has innumerable applications in medieval prose romance, the most notable example being King Arthur's adulterine origin. In addition, the child in the

4. The French version appears in Anatole de Montaiglon and Gaston Raynaud, *Recueil général et complet des fabliaux des XIIIe et XIVe siècles* (Paris: Librairie des Bibliophiles, 1872–90), I:162.

*Poetria*'s illustration, though engendered by the blackness of adultery, is born in a pristine and originary whiteness symbolized fleetingly by the snow. This blank, this founding emptiness is also widely echoed elsewhere and everywhere in medieval narrative.[5] We shall probe the incidence of this vacuous and originary space later in relation to the *Poetria*'s own specular problematic.

The discursive blending of theory with its corroborative examples—a mingling that annuls their differences—may be noted on still another level: the graphic aspect of writing as it appears in the manuscripts of Geoffroi's tract. Graphically speaking, nothing separates one discursive type from the other. The italics used in Faral's and Gallo's editions to indicate the examples are the diacritical legacy of modern printing and in no way reflect the actual graphics of the manuscripts. This fact in itself leads us to question the status and parameters of the two "genres":[6] as a matter of fact, the text's graphics and scriptural practice turn illustration and theory into two barely distinct vectors of the same poetic discourse.

So Geoffroi actually exemplifies the utopic dissolution or fusion of theorist and writer promoted by Roland Barthes more than seven centuries after the *Poetria Nova*. Moreover, the text inscribes itself beautifully, with an incomparable "gratia linguae" (14), in medieval writing's general tendency to combine theoretical reflection with refined fictional elaboration. As a result, medieval discourse—whether poetic, romantic, epic, or didactic—bears in itself all of the premises and conclusions necessary to its own theory.

## *Modernity and the Obsolete [Caduc]*

The old or, even better, the obsolete [*caduc*][7] is understood within various categories. Here it is associated with the unpolished, the rude, whatever has not been elaborated by new art:

5. See in this regard Roger Dragonetti's commentary on the white depth of writing in "L'enjeu et l'événement: Entretien avec Roger Dragonetti, Alexandre Leupin, et Charles Méla," *L'Esprit créateur* 23 (1983), 12–13.

6. The parameters are contestable. Gallo, *The Poetria Nova,* p. 108, may therefore find himself opposing Faral.

7. See in this regard Charles Méla on the old as that which no longer speaks and Dragonetti on the modern as that which is always present: "L'enjeu et l'événement," pp. 7 and 9.

> Thematis haec rudis est facies: ego rem sceleratam
> Consilio feci. Faciem sic innovo verbi:
>
> The appearance of this theme is unpolished: I did a wicked thing through advice. Thus I renew the appearance of the words. (1690–91)

The crux of this is that there is no wording that isn't obsolete unless it has been submitted to a reactualization that transforms it (we shall scrutinize the modalities of such an operation later). The *Poetria* thus theorizes the act of writing as a constant and endless transformation of the obsolete, a perpetual relaunching of the old.

Considered as unfinished matter, the obsolete has many of the attributes of *Natura;* here it is more specifically formulated in terms of the *raw,* the *arid,* the *hirsute,* the *uncultured,* and the *rural* (see *rudis et veteranus,* 1028):

> Sermonem discute quis sit virtus
> Crudus an excoctus, succosus an aridus, hirtus
> An comptus, rudis an excultus, inops an opimus.
>
> Consider whether your discourse is raw or well done; juicy or arid; shaggy or combed; rude or cultivated; poor or rich. (915–17)

In this regard, art is understood as the perpetual transcendence of unpolished matter; and this unpolished matter is viewed as the first element of a comparative function in which the comparing term is always superior to the compared.

Two remarks are in order concerning Nature's role in the *Poetria Nova* as well as in the more general context of medieval culture. First, Nature belongs to neither a factual nor an objectivistic order, but rather assembles and "metaphorizes" all of the *topoi* bequeathed by ancient literature, Christian and pagan alike. *Nature is first and foremost a text*—it is always an articulation—and poetry functions to transform one articulation into another (as with those examples used as foils in the comparisons).

Next, it is important to point out that although "brute," Nature or the obsolete is never considered a negative category. So when Geoffroi de Vinsauf cites Sidonius Appolinarius and Seneca to illustrate his theory of nominal determinations, he is careful to emphasize his predecessors' excellence: "Dignus uterque tamen titulo" [Both are worthy of honor] (1842). Ancient texts thus constitute the necessary (and in a certain sense, unexcelled) repository from which the new poetics draws the material to be rewritten. Once again, the obsolete is the condition of this sublation or *Aufhebung*. A radical demand for newness thus emerges in the form of a negative from the rewriting of ancient texts:

> sed utram sequar? Istum
> Aut illum? Novitas quia plus juvat et modus idem
> Nos satiat, nec ero velut hic, nec vero velut ille.
>
> But which shall I follow, the one or the other? Since the novelty pleases us, and restraint likewise satisfies us, I will copy neither. (1842–44)

Such a "modernist" position (radical, though nuanced) should lead us to a thorough re-evaluation of the medieval writer's attitude toward his legacy of innovation and tradition, especially since Geoffroi de Vinsauf's taste for *novitas* was prevalent in other poetic writings of the period. Medieval writers show neither idolatrous respect for a tradition they would complacently repeat, nor the anguish of innovation conceived as rupture: at every turn the old is rejuvenated within the new, and the new is the incessant transformation of a textual "already there." This could well be a lesson for "modernists," writers as well as critics, who follow the romantic train of thought in thinking of the commonplace as dead repetition and of novelty as a radical break with the past.

The question of modernity has all the earmarks of an obsession for Geoffroi de Vinsauf. It revolves around the sememes of *novitas* and *rejuvenatio*; according to Geoffroi, these functions constitute the ultimate goal of artistic activity, and there can be no texts or writings without them:

> Si vetus est verbum, sis physicus et veteranum
> Redde novum...
> Et placeat novitate sua. Si conficis istud
> Antidotum, verbis facies juvenescere vultum.
>
> If the words are old, be a physician and rejuvenate them. ...And let it please by its novelty. If you prepare this remedy, you will rejuvenate the face of the word. (762–69)

The goal of the operation is pleasure, *delectatio*. The old does indeed have its delights, but the work of youthful writing procures a supplement, a premium of pleasure: "Novitas . . . plus juvat" [Novelty . . . pleases more] (1843). And elsewhere: "Et fricat interius nova delectatio mentem" [And a new enjoyment inwardly stimulates the mind] (956).

It is not excessive, then, to say that Geoffroi de Vinsauf chisels the theory and practice of literature's perpetual renovation, the terms of medieval writing's explicit or implicit creed. This rejuvenation functions not at all on the level of content, ideas, or the signified, but rather, as the *Poetria* frequently insists, on the level of the word or language in a more general sense. Take, for example, Villon, the Arthurian *Vulgate* romances, or the poetry of the troubadours and trouvères: all of these texts involve a rewriting of older material, and all of them show how this operation brings something new to the model text while surpassing it in the same stroke. The *Poetria* thus specifies the generalized practice of medieval *rewriting* by formulating its most pertinent and comprehensive definition.

Now we shall isolate the modalities and emblems of this highly self-conscious modernity. In principle, all work upon figures of style, tropes, or figures of diction, *ornatus gravis* and *ornatus levis* alike, involves the rejuvenation of those *topoi* bequeathed by the ancient authors. In Geoffroi's rhetorical arsenal, however, one figure stands out among the rest: *transsumptio* or conversion. Its importance is emphasized, for example, in lines 941 through 953, where its sememe *transumo* (or *transfertur*) is mentioned five times. As an approximation of metaphor, *transsumptio* is the genus including the species constituted by the ten flowers of rhetoric (the tropes):

> Genus omnibus unum:
> Scilicet improprium vocum status et peregrina
> Sumptio verborum.
>
> This is the common genus—that is, the changed meaning
> of the words and their wandering application. (967–69)

Gallo has accurately remarked that conversion "is not a specific figure, but it is a method applicable to all tropes and figures" (209). Let us specify even further: in conformity with the obliteration of the distinction between theory and writing practice in the *Poetria, transsumptio* is simultaneously a concept, a method, and a usage halfway between the pragmatic and the doctrinal.

Etymologically, *transsumptio* is an ambivalent term: it designates both the act of taking *and* the act of receiving something from another text, so that it subsumes in one term the notions of borrowing, stealing, and giving. Quintilian proposes a fascinating theory about this equivocation: as a *metalepsis, transsumptio* performs a displacement of meaning from one alien base to another, so that the concept of proper location or property is nowhere implied. The originary locus of the figure and its displaced site are both radically other:

> Superest ex his, quae aliter significant metalimpsis,
> id est transumptio, quae ex alio tropo in aliam viam praestat.
>
> There is but one of the tropes involving change in meaning which remains to be discussed, namely, *metalepsis* or *transumption,* which provides a transition from one *trope* to another.[8]

In the figure's movement, then, proper meaning, linguistic propriety, and sameness never truly appear. It is always the other (place) that beckons in what Geoffroi will later call *translatio* or *peregrinatio*. The operation of *transsumptio* never actually passes through proper meaning; it is an empty space "signifying nothing in itself," as Quintilian says, that merely enables the dynamics of transference:

> Est enim haec in metalepsi natura, ut inter id quod transfertur et in quod transfertur sit medius quidam gradus, nihil ipse significans sed praebens transitum.
>
> It is the nature of *metalepsis* to form a kind of intermediate step between the term transferred and the thing to which it is transferred, having no meaning in itself, but merely providing a transition.[9]

For Geoffroi, on the other hand, proper meaning does indeed exist in conversion, but only as the exact analogue of the commonplace. As such, it has been so often appropriated and reworked in an intertextual network that its propriety is irretrievably lost behind a massive accumulation of metaphors. But even considering that proper meaning does exist, its sole purpose for Geoffroi is to be surpassed, to serve as the basis of a transcending displacement:

> Semper noli concedere verbo
> In proprio residere loco.

8. Quintilian, *Institutio oratoria,* Loeb Classical Library (Cambridge: Harvard University Press, and London: William Heinemann, 1953), 8.6.37. Translations are from this edition.

9. Ibid., 8.6.38.

> Do not always allow a word to reside in its usual place.
> (763–64)

This *sumptio verborum* (969) is accompanied by a certain violence suggested once again by its etymology (*sumptio:* capture). The writing practice espousing it is comprised of both tradition's resistance and modernity's otherness, and functions to plunder or otherwise violate the wording of ancient texts. The subject of writing is then recognized only against the background of an otherness construed in purely linguistic terms:

> Quando tuum proprium transsumis, plus sapit istud
> Quod venit ex proprio. Talis transsumptio verbi
> Est tibi pro speculo: quia te specularis in illo
> Et proprias cognoscis oves in rure alieno.

> It is more pleasing to apply human characteristics in such a way. Such a metaphorical use of words serves you like a mirror, for you can see yourself in it, and recognize your own sheep in a strange countryside. (801–4)

Newness thus emerges in a never-ending peregrination from the other to the other, without ever stopping to rest in proper meaning—the only chance that sameness would have to be recognized:

> loca propria vitet
> Et peregrinatur alibi sedemque placetens
> Fundet in alterius fundo: sit ibi novus hopes
> Et placeat novitate sua.

> let it [a word] avoid its proper place and wander elsewhere, to find a pleasing seat in another's ground: let it be a new sojourner and please by its novelty. (765–68)[10]

Geoffroi gives an impressive series of names to the writer who employs *transsumptio:* among others, he is an architect (43), a tailor (60), a hairdresser (63), a gem-cutter (66, 1029), a magician (121), a walker (205), a cook (266), a doctor (762), a weaver (772), a gardener of the flowers of rhetoric (1230), a banquet host of language (266, 1960), and a blacksmith (813, 1620). It is as though the entire range of human activities, particularly those activities relating to what the Middle Ages called the practical arts, could be summoned as metaphorical desig-

10. Roger Dragonetti has astutely discussed this movement of estrangement in "Le Contredit de François Villon," *Modern Language Notes* 98 (1983), 598 n. 10.

nations for the alchemical labor of the poet who transforms lead into gold—the obsolete [*caduc*] into the modern.[11]

In similar fashion the *Poetria* offers several models of art's prestidigitation. The first of these, of course, is the one to whom the tract is dedicated, Pope Innocent III. The *Poetria* transforms this eminently "political" pope into the absolute symbol of Geoffroi's poetics (we shall later discuss this mutation, in itself a highly provocative example of *transsumptio*). The pontiff is actually portrayed in the text as a *puer senex*.[12] This is a commonplace that functions in a reversible manner: the *puer senex* or "old youth" is first of all the one who renews the obsolete by giving it a previously unheard inflection or an unprecedented appearance (the pontiff himself is young in physical appearance). Next, the *puer senex* conserves the wisdom of his cultural tradition in the transference of modernity. For these reasons, Innocent III is a perfect emblem of the doctrine proposed by Geoffroi:

> Ubi corpus ista juventus
> Tam grandis senii, vel corpus tanta senectute
> Insita tam juvenis? Quam mira rebellio rerum
> Ecce senex juvenis!
>
> Where else is such bodily youth engrafted on such noble old age, or where else does a heart so old dwell in one so young? What a wonderful paradox of nature: behold the old young man! (20–23)

The Pope embodies a revolt (*rebellio*) against the natural order of things because his youthful physique hides an extremely ancient wisdom. The *topos* thus enables us to situate the specific sites of antiquity and newness: oldness is located in the heart or the spirit, and novelty in the physical aspect of the body or, as Pauline terminology would claim, of the letter. However, in Geoffroi's practice of scriptural renovation the letter is implicitly linked to life and the spirit to death, unlike the spirit of biblical commentary. Contrary to the well-known biblical wisdom, then, the *Poetria*'s doctrine proposes that Ancient tradition relives only in its rewriting: this is how medieval literature in general reverses the tenets of theology.

11. See Gallo's remark in *The Poetria Nova*, p. 208 n. 157.

12. See the detailed study by Curtius, *European Literature and the Latin Middle Ages*, pp. 98–101.

The *puer senex* is one of the treatise's most frequent commonplaces. Here it is prominently featured in an exemplum dedicated to Androgeus, son of Minos and Pasiphae:

> Androgei Livor animum speculatus et annos
> Hinc puerum videt, inde senem, quia mente senili
> Nil redolet puerile puer.
>
> Even Envy of Androgeus admits that he is a boy in years but an old man in mind, for in his mature mind the boy was not at all childish. (174–76)

As might be expected, all of the examples illustrating *oppositio* (679–94) or antithesis stem from the same commonplace. This fact leads us to note another dimension of Geoffroi's poetics: one of the most prominent rhetorical forms of his tract is the *oxymoron,* a figure translating in one linguistic unit a fusion of opposites that assume their reciprocal meaning only by being united. Therefore, the relation between the obsolete and the modern may be viewed both as a dialectic between *sic* and *non* and as a conjunction lending new meaning to the terms of the antithesis.

The most ample and pertinent example of *metalepsis* or *transsumptio* is probably the Christ, who is represented on earth by Innocent III; Geoffroi specifies the pope's relation to Christ by calling him "Christ's vicar": "Pater ergo, vicarie Christi" (2079). The *Poetria* lends to the biblical example a functionality that transforms it into an integral part of the new poetics.

First, there is the paradigm constructed by the personification of the Holy Cross, a prosopopoeia explicitly cited as an example of modernity ("exemplum novitas" [467]). The Cross has been subjected to the violence of theft and *peregrinatio,* figures designating the underlying operations of *sumptio* and *translatio* from the old (Jerusalem, the crucifix's proper site) to the new:

> Crux ego rapta queror, vi rapta manuque canina
> . . . Sum rapta pudenter
> A veteri
>
> I, the ravished cross, lament being snatched away by the force of rabid hands . . . I was shamefully taken away long ago. (469–71)

And:

> ...pudit minus in peregrinus
> Quam castris sordere meis.
>
> it is less shameful to be reviled in a foreign land than in my own home. (478–79)

The transformation and redemption of the old by the new is brilliantly allegorized by Christ's own figure in the text. It is not only a symbol of *conversio,* in all senses of the term, but also conforms to the method favored by medieval exegesis; it functions as a *concors discordia* (848) between the Old and New Testaments, the Fall and the Redemption. Christ has transformed ancient darkness into new light: "Convertit tenebras luctus in gaudia lucis" [He transformed the darkness of sorrow into the joys of light] (1530).

Christ finds his own place then by abandoning human flesh to transfigure it, through the Resurrection, into the Glorious Body; though not exclusively or simply rhetorical, this movement has a rhetorical significance within the context of Geoffroi's treatise: the *sumptio* of the body is enhanced in the text by the sparkle of a *resumptio*—a moral, religious, and poetic redemption:

> Rupit enim vitam moriens, mortemque resurgens,
> Nec praesumpta suos, sed vita resumpta redemit.
>
> For he broke the bonds of life by dying; and by rising again, the bonds of death; not by adopting human life, but by losing it, did he his own redeem. (1172–73)

The new spirit of Christ ("Spiritus emissus, noves hospes," [1215]) thus becomes the *analogon* of Geoffroi's poetics, or vice versa. Further, the assimilation smacks of a certain perversity: though the *Poetria* has assumed an eschatological tone here, its primary intention is to resuscitate ancient textuality rather than to save souls. We may recall that this principle was assiduously upheld by those who wrote in the vernacular: the "romans d'antiquité" (*Aeneas,* etc.) and Christianized versions of Classical authors such as the *Ovide moralisé* exemplify the vernacular writer's taste for reanimating old texts.

Continuing now with the biblical example, we shall focus briefly on Adam's role: in Geoffroi's text, Adam's fall is presented as the primary cause of the Redemption. But this fall also has a grammatical aspect because the term *casus* indicates both "fall" and the "case" of the Latin noun. The *Poetria* elsewhere (1685–89) develops a theory of nominal conversion based on case declension: a technique called *adnominatio* submits the noun's essence and its nominative form (*casus rectus*) to misappropriated and highly conventional declensions, and so moves the noun away from its most essential property. Like Dante's Babel, then, the Fall has relatively little to do with theology, even though Christ is used as the symbol of its redemption; in the *Poetria* the Fall is presented as the opportunity to resuscitate old men and redeem ancient literature with the new poetics.

The poet and his body are not exempt from the *conversio* that turns all the text's elements into emblems of transference. Geoffroi points this out by using a topographical symbology: "Jam mare transcurri, Gades in littore fixi" [Now I have crossed the sea, I have settled on the shores of Thule] (2071). During his peregrination, the author/narrator acquires his "vestments of light" and finds Lost Paradise once more:

> Me transtulit Anglia Romam
> Tanquam de terris ad caelum, transtulit ad vos
> De tenebris velut ad lucem.
>
> Coming from England to Rome was like going from earth to heaven; I came to you as from darkness to light. (31–33)

Cast in analogy to the profiles of Innocent III and Christ, the poet's biography is thus absorbed by his text's rhetorical operation. But from a theological standpoint, this analogy has a perverse tincture: by assimilating the kingdom of heaven to the realm of modern language, the analogy suggests easy access to the Divine, and depicts Lost Paradise as something within reach *hic et nunc*. Rarely are poets more deviant than when they claim to imitate theology merely to construct an earthly paradise within the realm of literature's pleasures.

## *"History"*

We have just shown how the text swarms with referentiable figures and how it includes the figure of Christ in that count. These references are so numerous that they allow us to date the tract with some degree of certainty,[13] a rare matter for a manuscript of the Middle Ages. What

13. See Faral, *Les arts poétiques*, pp. 28ff.

concerns us here, however, is determining the status of the historical reference in the *Poetria,* not the specific problem of manuscript dating.

The insertion of history into a doctrinal treatise, or of poetics into historical discourse, might seem curious to a "modern" mind accustomed to separating the genres; but here we have only another example of the typological jumbling that medieval writers practiced freely, with no compunction. Even speaking of discursive jumbling is questionable because generic distinctions scarcely existed; further, the medieval literary text was always quick to seize upon the gamut of possibilities offered by all established fields of knowledge.

In this light Richard the Lionheart's figural inclusion in the *Poetria* is more easily understood. The text pays tribute to his historical influence by presenting him as the mirror and model for the English people: "Rex tuus est speculum, quo te speculata superbis" [Your king is a mirror: you are proud of being seen in him] (330). But within the text, the king's image is used primarily to reflect and resonate with the *Poetria*'s own specularity, for he is appositively called a paragon of rhetoric: "dulcor in aure" [sweetness to the ear] (390).

However, the *translatio* affecting the text's historical discourse is most finely emblematized in the figure of Pope Innocent III. Geoffroi especially celebrates the pontiff's eloquence, which he considers superior even to the oratory of the Church Fathers—Saint Augustine, Saint Gregory, Saint John (the poet is a little shameless in his effusion). Innocent III is heralded as a new Chrysostom whose dazzling language sparkles with golden reflections:

> Superest de dotibus una,
> Quam nulli fas est attingere: gratia linguae. . . .
> Esto quod in verbis aut hic aut ille sit ore
> Aureus et totus resplendeat: os tamen ejus
> Impar est, orisque tui praejudicat aurum.

> One of your gifts stands out, which no one else is permitted to rival: your eloquence. . . . Let this or that one be completely resplendent in golden-tongued eloquence: his is not to equal yours; the gold of your eloquence surpasses him. (13–19)

So whatever the historical "reality" might have been, the pontiff seems a particularly apt choice to receive the dedication of the new poetics. Following an often used topic in medieval literature, the praise addressed to Innocent III actually flashes back, mirrorlike, on the poet himself; in this way Geoffroi subtly introduces his own *laudatio* and transforms the pope/dedicatee into a pawn of his own poetic game.

Geoffroi's strategy of self-celebration is nowhere more obvious than in the *Poetria*'s somewhat violent treatment of the pope's proper name. According to an old Cratylist tradition that the poet adopts here, the pontiff's name should be the *analogon* of his being and should properly designate his essence: "Nomen tibi vult similari" [Your name is meant to be similar to you] (3).[14] But the first line of the tract submits the pope's name (and thus, his being) to the rigor of a poetic meter that cuts it in two. Here Geoffroi is using an apheresis, a specific figure of *ornatus levis*:

> Papa stupor mundi, si dixero Papa Nocenti
> Acephalum nomen tribuam; sed si caput addam
> Hostis erit metri.
>
> Pope, marvel of the world, if I were to call you "Pope Nocent," I would be giving you a headless name; but if I add the prefix, it would spoil the meter. (1–3)

Like his decapitated name, the pope then becomes the very antithesis of those virtues that Geoffroi later attributes to him (*nocens* = harmful). The *Poetria* here demonstrates through emulation the powers of rhetoric bearing on one of language's sensitive points, the proper name—the element that should represent being in its individual integrality. Moreover, the *Poetria begins* in the strictest sense with the name's alienation, with an improper cut that simultaneously designates the text's autonomy in relation to its exteriority (e.g., power) and problematizes the text's origin in terms of a fissure or division.

However, the name's integrality is reestablished further on in what seems to be a compromise providing for both the rigors of prosody and the sovereign pontiff's susceptibility:

> Nec nomen metro, nec vult tua maxima virtus
> Claudi mensura.
>
> Neither must the name be imprisoned by the meter, nor your great virtue restricted by any measure. (4–5)

14. The *adequatio* of the name and the thing is one of the elements of Geoffroi's doctrine: "Si bene dicta notes et rebus verba coaptes / Sic proprie dices" [If you are careful about your expression and fit the words to the subject, you will discourse well] (1847–48).

But Geoffroi subtly returns to the principle of division he had applied at the very beginning of the text, and argues that the name *must* be split up because the pope's virtue supercedes all human computation:

> Divide sic nomen: "In" praefer, et adde "nocenti,"
> Efficiturque comes metri.
>
> Rather, divide the name thus: set down "in," and add "nocent," and thus it will fit the meter. (7–8)

The division then seems to serve the purposes of *laudatio*, because the fracture of the proper name merely points up the name's inadequacy in relation to the person's grandeur. Still, a certain ontological fragility is revealed in the fact that the name is subject to such great distortion; the name should indeed resemble the thing (*rem*), but the *Poetria* shows only how this old Platonic dream meets with impossibility.

What the distorted name suggests is that Innocent III is not viewed in the text through a proper historical dimension external to the text's writing. In fact, the opposite is true: in the course of Geoffroi's un-"innocent" name game, the pope loses his autonomy as a figure outside the text and becomes (through *transsumptio*) an example of the poet's doctrinal and poetic demonstration. Villon, among others, later takes this lesson to heart by constantly changing "historical" onomastic terms into pawns for his literary chessboard.

In Geoffroi's tract, then, the historical reference and its poetic function are absolutely interchangeable: each is the *analogon* of the other, and there is no discernible priority between them. The poet theorizes this reversibility as a *permutatio,* an allegorical subcategory of metaphor; further, one primary articulation provides for reversibility in the *Poetria,* and that condition is an absence, a blank alien to both terms of the *permutatio.*

## *Representations of the Mirror*

In the *Poetria Nova* there are several criteria of aesthetic judgment: the sense of smell, which distinguishes the metaphorical perfumes of the flowers of rhetoric (1591); usage (1958, 1971); the ear, responsible for *ornatus levis* (1965, 1972); the spirit and the heart, which examine the word's soul (744, 971); and finally the eye, which is somewhat privileged in the text: "Certior aure / Arbiter est oculus" [The eye is a surer judge than the ear] (272–73). To stress the importance of sight in aesthetic judgment the poet refers to two mythological figures worthy of imitation. There is Janus—"Aemula Janus: retro speculeris et ante" [Imitate Janus: look before and after] (281)—and of course Argus, who saw everything because he had one hundred eyes:

> Sed in his quae dixero esto
> Argus et argutis oculis circumspice verba
> In re proposita.
>
> But be like Argus in choosing your words: with an acute eye look over the words of the subject set out before you. (754–56)

Sight is relatively favored in the *Poetria Nova* because the text's axis (which cannot be located) is pivoted by a specular metaphor that subtends and organizes all of the tract's elements (historical, mythological, doctrinal). As we have seen, the text offers several relevant paradigms of this specularity: Innocent III, Richard the Lionheart, and the reflexive relation between doctrine and example are only a few cases in point. The fabliau entitled *L'enfant qui fu remis au soleil* is even explicitly presented as theory's *speculum,* the mirror in which the text's principle functions most brilliantly: "Ecce rei speculum: res tota illucet in illo" [Here is a mirror of the subject: the entire matter shines out from it] (717). This specularity is never purely reducible to either an illustrative or a prescriptive content; rather, the treatise assumes it as a fundamental rule, as the reflection in which poetry reveals those laws intended for poets:

> Ipsa poesis
> Spectet in hoc speculo quae lex sit danda poetis.
>
> In this mirror let poetry itself see what law must be given to poets. (48–49)

The specular principle is compared to a comb with which shaggy discourse may control its hair and check to see that it is well-groomed:

> Ecce dedi pecten, quo si sint pexa relucent
> Carmina tam prosae quam metra. Sed an bene pectas
> Hoc speculo poteris plene discernere formam.
>
> Behold, I have provided a comb which, if used, can make both prose and verse resplendent. Whether you have combed well, you will fully discern in this mirror. (48–49)

The act of combing (*pectere*) is also phonetically allied to the activity of looking (*spectare*) that enables aesthetic discernment. In a like manner, vision is linked to the speculative dimension (*speculare*) that the mirror introduces into the artistic fabric; the text is then set within the temporal limits and distance of a *review*, a revised form prescribed by a second or *other* look. This absent, other look imposing reflexive transformation is the mirror's gaze.

*Transsumptio* or metalepsis is not excluded from the text's generalized specularity:

> Talis transsumptio verbi
> Est tibi pro speculo: quia te specularis in illo.
>
> Such a metaphorical use of words serves you like a mirror,
> for you can see yourself in it. (802–3)

Yet even in an instance of pure reflexivity where the subject of writing may recognize himself, that subject cannot be grasped in his own proper identity or sameness any more than he can attain the proper essence of his own writing's object. Though the outside (history, world, texts, writer) may admire its own reflections in the swiveling glass, the *speculum* in itself is no more than an absence. During the second half of the nineteenth century, Mallarmé evoked this specular vacancy in his sonnet entitled "Sonnet allégorique de lui-même" (a superscript found in one manuscript: the poem's definitive version is untitled): "En l'obscurissement de la glace, décor / de l'absence, sinon que sur la glace encor / De scintillation le septuor se fixe." As the blank depth of writing, the mirror has no meaning per se, but by its very vacuity allows objects (the two terms of a comparison, poetry and history, etc.) to reveal what is radically *other* in each of them. In the locus of this absence, then, alterities are assembled under the cloak of a reflection deceptively identical to itself; this deception is indubitably why Mallarmé's looking glass is the site of darkness rather than light.

One of the text's many examples of this covert function is the comparison (*collatio*), a subclass of metalepsis; according to Geoffroi this figure operates furtively, screening its proper face in order to promote a certain kind of novelty. The comparison's newness does not emerge from an order of sameness (identification and projection), but from a reappraisal or re-cognition of its own alterity:

> Quae fit in occulto nullo venit indice signo
> Non venit in vulto proprio, sed dissimulato

> Et quasi non sit ibi collatio sed nova quaedam
> Insita mirifice transsumptio.
>
> No such telltale signs occur in the covert Comparison, which does not show its own face but wears a mask, as if no Comparison were actually taking place there but rather a sort of new changeover, marvelously engrafted. (247–50)

Thus, modernity and the mirror enabling its emergence are not attributable to the imaginary; rather, they are the site where the symbolic, the Other, is both revealed and reflected in a new strangeness.

The profound originality of Geoffroi de Vinsauf's specular concept must be stressed here, especially considering that the medieval *speculum* constitutes one of the period's most prominent literary genres. As the mirror of princes, of history (e.g., the *Speculum historiale* of Vincent de Beauvais), or of sainthood (*La vie de Saint Alexis*), the specular text in the Middle Ages claims to be no more than the faithful reflection of another space or another text. This claim applies even if a particular writing purports only to imitate Nature, because Nature itself is viewed as a text, the mirror of divine intention.

The *Poetria Nova* subverts this mimetic principle governing the strict reproduction of cosmological, historical, and divine orders by turning the mirror into a space free of mimetism's constraints; in this text the mirror becomes the absent locus of poetic language's transformational power and autonomy.

Geoffroi de Vinsauf's *speculum* also differs radically from the specular narrative as Lucien Dällenbach has defined it within a corpus of nineteenth- and twentieth-century literary texts.[15] In these so-called "modern" novels the *mise en abyme* of writing— its miniaturized representation—is always enclosed in the general frame of the narrative. Though the embedded image of writing may clarify a specific function of the overall work, it does not withold the text's unique condition, its sine qua non; the *mise en abyme* can reflect no more than its text's own virtualities and cannot withdraw from its text's economy as an autonomous absence, a pure virtuality reflecting nothing. On the other hand, Geoffroi's mirror is the symbol *and* organizing principle of a general economy of writing; more specifically, the specular image in his treatise both represents and provides for the text's construction.

15. Lucien Dällenbach, *Le récit spéculaire: Essai sur la mise en abyme* (Paris: Seuil, 1977).

Neither can the *Poetria* be read within the registers of analytic specularity, particularly as elaborated by Jacques Lacan. The "Stade du Miroir,"[16] an often read and even more frequently misconstrued work, as well as the texts in the first seminar[17] focusing on the mirror, repeatedly stress the imaginary dimension of narcissistic specularity. Contrary to Lacan's view, Geoffroi de Vinsauf theorizes the *speculum* as that which reveals alterity in and of itself; if there absolutely had to be an equivalent in Lacanian discourse, it would be the symbolic, language, the Other.

Returning now to the *Poetria,* we shall conclude by scrutinizing a selection of the text's mirror emblems; among these, Geoffroi seems to privilege the figures of polishing as metaphors of poetic production: "Est modus iste mihi sudanti verba polire" [It is my practice to laboriously polish my words] (1955).[18] This refining labor is characterized by the transformation of brute, unpolished material: as a kind of artistic reworking, polishing makes the natural (the obsolete or ancient text) strange unto itself and forever capable of reflecting whoever peers into it.

By extension, there is no beauty possible without a mirror or, even further, there is no simple essence of beauty: to obtain its glow, beauty must necessarily be submitted to the *speculum*'s empty space and be affected by an "originary" displacement conformable to the *Poetria*'s organized prescriptions. Moreover, natural material, or the face of beauty, is *already* a mirror; even before art intervenes, it has undergone the polishing indispensable to its reflective capacity. As a result, the material to be transformed loses its nature as raw, primary matter and is inscribed in the secondariness of reflection:

> Mentumque polito
> Marmore plus poliat Natura potentior arte.
> Succuba sit capitis pretiosa colore columna
> Lactea, quae speculum vultus supportet in altum.
>
> Let Nature, more powerful than art, polish the chin smoother than marble. Let the milky supporting column of the head, of exquisite color, raise the mirror of the face on high. (583–86)

16. Jacques Lacan, *Ecrits* (Paris: Seuil, 1966), pp. 93–100.
17. Jacques Lacan, *Le séminaire de Jacques Lacan,* I: *Les écrits techniques de Freud,* ed. Jacques-Alain Miller (Paris: Seuil, 1975), pp. 87–103, 125–47, 185–98.
18. See also lines 66 and 1029.

All of the metaphors of brilliance and luminosity strewn throughout the treatise are thus only repetitions of the incidences of specularity. Examples of this reflected radiance abound in the text: the luminous jewels used to adorn womanly beauty (605ff.); the golden cups refurbishing Bacchus's powers to the state of poetic ebriety so dear to Plato (631ff.); the stars and their counterpart, the sun, that melts the snow-child (717ff.). And the poet/narrator himself is not exempt from this reflexive brilliance: as we have seen (31–33), his *peregrinatio* from England to Rome is also a voyage from obscurity toward light.

The *Poetria* appears, then, as a triumphant manifesto. Here the ancient or the obsolete takes on a new sparkle, and the Lost Paradise of old poetic words is recuperated in modernity's most dazzling mirror. While magically transforming black into white, negative into positive, and tarnish into luster, Geoffroi de Vinsauf turns theology's malediction into the metaphorical and improper fount of his new poetics.

—Translated by Kate Cooper

# Wandrynge by the Weye: On Alisoun and Augustine

PEGGY A. KNAPP

*mulier garrula et vaga.*—Prov. 7.11

Alisoun of Bathe's doctrinal vagaries, her wandrynges by the wey, have attracted almost as much attention from Chaucer's readers as her sexual peregrinations. Her arguments against patristic readings of Scripture—glossing—early in her Prologue pose very pointedly the problem of controlling biblical interpretation in an age of increasing lay literacy. Later in the Prologue, moreover, she speaks of herself as a text to be glossed. In this essay I use Alisoun's *cas* to pose some questions about textual glossing. I make four related assertions: 1) Alisoun's allusions to glossing may be unpacked to show her as not only an interpreter of texts but a theorist of interpretation; 2) Saint Augustine's *On Christian Doctrine,* which was and is taken to be the origin of the interpretive system the Wife attacks, cannot be said to authorize that system unequivocally; 3) gradual historical accretions closed Augustine's allegorical system and fused it with institutional authority, but eventually social and intellectual pressures reopened it; 4) these issues bear directly on the interpretation of the figure of Alisoun herself. The discussion is posed in terms of some of the directions taken in Jacques Derrida's critique of language and by M. M. Bakhtin's analysis of narrative voice.

## *Alisoun on Glossing*

When Alisoun describes the relish with which her fifth husband read aloud to her the story of Clytemnestra's lechery and murder, she locates his pleasure in the decisive role that authoritative texts, classical and biblical, have been made to play in their domestic marriage-debate. The climactic episode of that debate is the physical tussle in which the Wife tears a page from the sacred book and endures the blow that renders her "somedel deaf" ever afterward. In her view, Jankyn uses texts not in the interest of educating or reforming her but in the interest of consolidating his *cas* against her and her *secte*. The "ful good devocioun" he displays in his reading is, therefore, manipulative and malicious.

Alisoun sees this domestic case as part of a general configuration of interpretive strategies. She forcefully rejects the idea of disinterested truths embodied in unassailable textual bulwarks, asserting that the Bible itself (the true authority) has been consistently misinterpreted through the bad offices of the clerks entrusted with that duty. The *interest* on behalf of which these errors—or worse—are committed is the war against women.

> The clerk [in general], when he is oold and may noght do
> Of Venus werkes worth his olde sho,
> Thanne sit he doun and writ in his dotage
> That wommen kan nat kepe hir mariage. (III, 707–10)[1]

The authoritative texts of the glossing tradition are linked from the start with malice toward women and deserve no great authority as direct formulations of the truth.

The Wife refers directly to glossing three times in her Prologue. The first instance is her rejection of the indecisive debate about the number of allowable remarriages ("this nombre diffinicioun") in favor of the "gentil text" that people should "wexe and multiplye." Her reference to glossing, "Men may devyne and glosen up and doun" (III, 26), on the remarriage question is clearly dismissive, and she contrasts that interpretive game with the clearer directive to multiply and to leave

1. *The Complete Poetry and Prose of Geoffrey Chaucer*, ed. John H. Fisher (New York: Holt, Rinehart & Winston, 1977).

one's parents in order to marry. Implied are two principles: first, that glossing attaches allegorical, debatable ("up and doun") layers of significance to the Bible's plain sense (here the literal visit of Christ to only one wedding is taken allegorically to restrict Christians' entering into more than one marriage); second, that an allegorical statement in one part of the Bible will be reinforced by plainly stated passages elsewhere.

Alisoun's second explicit mention of glossing concerns debates about the purpose of the sexual organs: "Glose whoso will and seye both up and doun / That they were maked for purgacioun" (III, 119–20). Again there is the suggestion of unresolvable debate, but this time concerning traditional interpretations of Nature, God's other great book. Alisoun assumes that Nature and Scripture will provide the same lessons, that in creating the world as He did God was not working at cross-purposes with His directives for moral life. In this way she brings her *experience* of the created world into conflict with traditional *auctoritas* but not, as she sees it, with the congruence between God's world and his Word.

During her fifth marriage, Alisoun sees her own clerk as a clever appropriator of the glossing tradition. Her third direct mention of glossing reads:"And therwithal so wel koud he me glose" (III, 509). This seems a more complicated use of the term, one that links glossing with more than convoluted or "academic" reasoning. In this one telling line coexist at least four potential implications: 1) Jankyn could beguile or cajole his wife into good humor and sexual pleasure even though, as the passage goes on to say, he had beaten her on every bone; 2) Jankyn could interpret ("glose"—provide an interpretive commentary on) Alisoun so well that he could get his way and yet retain her love; 3) Jankyn could interpret his authorities so well that Alisoun was weakened in their domestic debate; 4) taking "therwithal" to refer directly to Jankyn's powers abed, alluded to in the preceding line, Jankyn gave Alisoun so much pleasure—a somewhat metaphoric use of *glose* as brighten, gloss over, flatter, as in the Manciple's refusal to please the Cook (IX, 34)—that she loved him in spite of what she saw as his bad treatment of her. In this last case the aura of *lie* hovers conspicuously over the word *glose,* as it does in a neat irony over the *glose* that the Summoner's fictional Friar offers Thomas—biblical commentary but also lie, trick (III, 1920)—and the clearly malicious lying *glose* that Fortune offers man to lure him to destruction in the *Monk's Tale* (VII, 2140). It makes a good deal of difference to our reading of

Alisoun's situation whether Jankyn is glossing in the tradition of the Fathers (and whether or not that would be a good thing) or flattering his wife, selfishly lying to her, and using his clerkly training to do so.

The Wife sees textual production and interpretation as deeply aligned with institutional interests, here the church and more distantly the court, and with personal intentions. Words and fictions are presented not primarily as statements of the truth about God, people, and Nature but as instantiations of power, in this case conservative power. As she insists throughout her Prologue on her right to interpret, Alisoun participates in and prefigures a historical shift to a less "centered," more open, style of exegesis.

Contemporary theorists might even see Alisoun's protest against her era's accepted way of reading as movement away from "logocentrism," as Jacques Derrida calls the West's unhealthy fascination with the authoritative word, and toward a heady delight in textual play.[2] Her Prologue certainly indulges in such play, demonstrating over and over how hallowed scriptural passages may be turned against their traditional interpretations and made to point to something outrageous (or worse still, something logical but heterodox). Alisoun also treats language playfully in reporting the details of her life, with the result that readers disagree widely about her faithfulness to her marriage vows, her children or lack of them, her sexual powers, her complicity in the death of her fourth husband, and the like. In addition to her vigor in diverting linguistic systems to her own uses, moreover, she remains a polemicist, often frustrated by her continual war with tradition.

If insistence on linguistic play and textual openness links Alisoun's position with Derrida's attack on logocentrism, the Wife's insistence that institutional and personal affiliations rather than revealed truth or disinterested reason control the textual tradition links it with the analysis of M. M. Bakhtin. What Alisoun objects to is a way of reading which treats the word as binding "quite independent of any power it might have to persuade us internally," a word "with its authority

2. Derrida's position is that the repeated mistake of Western metaphysics is the identification of the word with some originary, authorizing presence. In his analysis the word is never transparently related to a nonlinguistic item but is infinitely referrable back through a linguistic chain. Words merely stand in for other words, apart from any grounding in reality, a mere play (patterned motion, theater) of differences. See *Of Grammatology*, trans. Gayatri Chakravorty Spivak (Baltimore: Johns Hopkins University Press, 1974), and *Dissemination*, trans. Barbara Johnson (Chicago: University of Chicago Press, 1981), p. 206.

already fused to it." She aligns herself with what Bakhtin calls the "internally persuasive" and experience-generated word, which "is denied all privilege, backed by no authority at all."[3] Bakhtin's work shows the two kinds of discourse in dialogue within the narratives of the post-epic world.

Perhaps those who regard Alisoun as a "hopelessly carnal and literal" exegete will agree that she has an affinity with these more recent commentators on discourse—that is just what is wrong with her. She has set herself against her own intellectual world, the fountainhead of which is Saint Augustine. It is worth inquiring, therefore, to what extent Augustine's *On Christian Doctrine* unambiguously authorizes the reading practices that Alisoun finds so frustrating.

## *Augustine on Glossing*

When Augustine of Hippo wrote *On Christian Doctrine,* Catholic Christianity needed to stabilize a reading of its two texts, the Bible and the natural world, to avoid the present danger of becoming a series of sects without a unifying doctrinal system. With incalculable intellectual force, Augustine focused early Christian thought and transformed a potpourri of sometimes unconnected, even contradictory, stories into a body of doctrine. He did so not primarily by asserting *what* the Bible meant but by asserting *how* it conveyed its meaning. To perform such a task, Augustine had to valorize language and connect its signifying power with God's plan for salvation. The surface and usual reading of Augustine's text, therefore, is that it establishes logocentrism, in Derrida's sense (the Word underwritten by the presence of God), for the Christian tradition.

Augustine established the connection between language and God's will through an analogy to the Incarnation. When we speak, our minds' thought is changed to words: "But our thought is not transformed into sounds; it remains entire in itself and assumes the form of words by means of which it may reach the ears without suffering any deterioration in itself. In the same way the Word of God was made flesh without change that He might dwell among us."[4] Jesus, unchanged in

3. M. M. Bakhtin, *The Dialogic Imagination,* ed. Michael Holquist, trans. Caryl Emerson and Michael Holquist (Austin: University of Texas Press, 1981), p. 342.

4. Saint Augustine, *On Christian Doctrine,* trans. D. W. Robertson, Jr. (Indianapolis: Bobbs-Merrill, 1958), I.13.12.

substance by his emergence into the time-bound world, is, as the Word, a figure of truth unchanged as it assumes changing expression in human language.[5] Although conventional, signs (here words), properly interpreted, are taken to be reliable guides to faith and conduct.

Proper interpretation must distinguish between literal and figurative signification; it requires diligence, humility, and erudition. Nonetheless Augustine's teaching leaves open some unexpected interpretive spaces for anachronistic and idiosyncratic readings.[6] *On Christian Doctrine* expresses a distinct preference for the figurative: literal reading of a nonliteral surface is "slavish." The *Confessions* reveals that Augustine's own salvation hinged on the way Ambrose opened the truth of the Bible to him through allegorical readings:

> I was glad when I often heard Ambrose speaking in his sermons to the people as though he most earnestly commended it as a rule that "the letter kills, but the spirit quickens." For he would draw aside the veil of mystery and spiritually lay open things that interpreted literally seemed to teach unsound doctrine.[7]

In *On Christian Doctrine,* Augustine devises a test to determine which passages are not literal, a test based on a theme, *the* theme, he says, of the whole scriptural text: "This method consists in this: that whatever appears in the divine Word that does not literally pertain to virtuous behavior or to the truth of faith you must take to be figurative" (III.10.14). And conversely, "what is read should be subjected to diligent

5. Marcia Colish finds that in Augustine, words are both "authentic, sensible signs of knowable realities" and "an adequate means to the knowledge of God": *The Mirror of Language* (New Haven: Yale University Press, 1968), p. 55. For another view see Margaret W. Ferguson, "Saint Augustine's Region of Unlikeness: The Crossing of Exile and Language," *Georgia Review* 29 (1975), 842–64. Ferguson argues that in the *Confessions,* "all language is a metaphorical detour in the road to God because no sequence of words, even 'proper' words, can adequately represent an atemporal and holistic significance" (p. 576). Colish's view accounts for Augustine's overt aims, Ferguson's for the implications that the text reveals inadvertently.

6. He freely allows anachronistic interpretation, since the Author-God is not subject to created time. See Augustine's *Confessions,* Book 11. Old Testament events have New Testament applications, as well as intimations about the postapocalyptic world still (from our point of view) to come. Augustine even suggests that some passages mean many things and that an idiosyncratic reading not contrary to faith "may have been" seen by the human author and was "certainly" seen by the Spirit of God, who "undoubtedly foresaw that this meaning would occur to the reader or listener" (III.28.38).

7. *The Confessions of Saint Augustine,* trans. John K. Ryan (New York: Image, 1960), 6.4.6.

scrutiny until an interpretation contributing to the reign of charity is produced. If this result appears literally in the text, the expression being considered is not figurative" (III.15.23). *Caritas* is the love of God and the use of everything else in order to come to that love. *Cupiditas* is the love of anything other than God for its own sake.[8] Whoever finds these ideas in a scriptural passage, even if the interpretation is wrong in some detail, is like one who leaves the road but arrives at his destination by going through a field. A teacher of exegesis would not want to encourage such a procedure "lest the habit of deviating force him to take a crossroad or a perverse way," but the student has succeeded in achieving his goal (I.36.41). Furthermore, "hardly anything may be found in these obscure places which is not found plainly said elsewhere" (2.6.8). Note the affinity between this and Alisoun's desire for plainness in line 26 of her Prologue. Whether her Prologue and Tale eventually arrive at a mode of *caritas* is in question, but her exegetical methods are not entirely alien to Augustine's scheme.

Augustine decides the composition of the canonical Bible by appealing to authority of the church:

> In the matter of canonical Scriptures he [the biblical exegete] should follow the authority of the greater number of catholic Churches, among which are those which have deserved to have apostolic seats and to receive epistles. . . . He will prefer those accepted by all catholic Churches to those which some do not accept; among those which are not accepted by all, he should prefer those which are accepted by the largest number of important Churches to those held by a few minor Churches of less authority. (II.8.12)

In choosing a translation Augustine puts forward the Septuagint as the best, even an inspired, translation of the Old Testament into Greek: "In all the more learned churches it is now said" that without consulting one another, all of the translators produced the same words in the same order. No one, however learned, should set himself against "the consensus of so many older and more learned men" (II.15.22). Again the appeal is openly to institutional prestige. Augustine recognizes the openness of biblical meaning to interpretive disagreement, but he also recognizes the need to establish stable doctrine, especially in meeting the threat of division from Donatists, Pelegians, and Arians (and Do-

8. I use the Latin *caritas* throughout my discussion to distinguish Augustine's broad term from the more limited *charity* of modern English.

natist believers were at times more numerous than Catholics in Africa). In *On Christian Doctrine* Augustine not only appeals to ecclesiastical authority to achieve that stability, he later invites the intervention of civil authorities to use legal constraints against schism. Alisoun's intuition about the alliance between biblical and institutional authorities has some justification from this early date.

Augustine's position is appealing and appealingly stated, and he demonstrates how it works in many powerful readings of difficult scriptural passages. Nonetheless, the logical circularity of his reasoning is obvious. Words are reliable and capable of conveying truth because they resemble the Incarnation of Christ, which is predicated in the Bible. The Bible must be believed because the will of God is expressed in it in true ("proper") words. The stability of the word is therefore linked to the authorship of the unchanging God, who wills only *caritas*, the theme of the whole text, available either literally or figuratively in its every part. To avoid mistakes and settle disputes the Scripture's central thematic sense—the rule of *caritas*—must be invoked. But the privilege that *caritas* enjoys in Augustine's argument is established through his *prior* interpretive act, which has assigned importance, meaning, and connectedness to the diverse events and formulations of a still-fluid biblical canon.

The mutual dependency of Bible and institutional church weakens the sense that the word alone is the center of the Augustinian system,[9] but other matters on the surface of *On Christian Doctrine* also undermine it. Augustine acknowledges that the familiar Latin text is already mediated by its translation from Greek and Hebrew, both difficult languages. Difficulties in interpretation can arise from unknown signs, the remedy for which is the study of languages; from unknown things, remedied by the study of nature and culture; and from ambiguous signs. Augustine's advice about managing these problems is sensible, useful, and wise, but it undercuts the absoluteness and stability of the received word, deferring to language study, judgment, likelihood, comparison, and human authority.

The right interpretation of figurative signs constructed on the basis of the properties of animals, stones, or plants requires the exegete to

9. *On Christian Doctrine* is, of course, addressed to those who already believe. The rule of faith is, for them, *"a thing which teaches itself,"* as Mark Jordan puts it. See his "Words and Word: *De Doctrina Christiana,*" *Augustinian Studies* 11 (1980), 191.

rightly understand those properties. (Here we might remember Alisoun's interest in the link between Nature and Scripture.) Augustine does not allege that there exists a general, consistent key to the figurative terms of Scripture (as some latter-day defenders of medieval allegory appear to do). He argues that even important, frequently occurring figures such as leven, bread, lion, and serpent have several possible interpretations, some clear from context, some not. Sometimes the various meanings are contradictory, sometimes merely different (III.25.35–37). Figurative language uses the conventional tropes of the grammarian, too, which must be understood in order to apprehend the expression rightly (III.29.40-41). When numerology, history, practical arts, or logic enter divine discourse, they must be interpreted according to a knowledge of those pursuits.[10] Even philosophical arguments, associated for Augustine as for most Christians of his day with the pagan Greeks, may be mastered to enlighten Bible reading, just as the Israelites took gold from Egypt to transform it to better uses (II.40.60). Although taking figurative language as literal is a serious interpretive error, the freedom that Christians enjoy in being empowered to pass beyond the signified to its spiritual reference is nonetheless hedged about with warnings. Even for an exegete guided by the rule of *caritas* it is easy to err, on account of variability in customs in biblical times, mixed expressions containing both literal and figurative elements, and passages not intended to apply to every believer. All these hedgings-about may be read as signs pointing not to the clear, readable, fixed discourse of a firm logocentrism but to the mixed, obscure, shifting nature of discourse in dialogue with its reader.

Augustine ends Book III by denying that any system of interpretive rules will fully and accurately guide interpretation. He seems unexpectedly generous toward the exegetical manual of Tyconius, a Donatist, drawing from it many commendable insights and condemning it primarily for promising too much reliability. Tyconius's rules, for example, cannot guide the choice between a literal and a figurative promise that the Israelites would be gathered together and brought into their own land. Are these the hereditary Hebrews or the saved of the new dispensation? are they promised a geographical space or a spiritual identity? No rule suffices, although Augustine confidently chooses the spiritual over the literal reading:

10. For music: II.16.25; for history: II.28.42; for practical arts: II.30.47; and for logic: II.31.49.

> But the high prophetic style, when it speaks to the carnal Israel or about it, *secretly* moves to the spiritual, and when it speaks now of one and now of the other, it seems to be confusing them, not that it envies us an understanding of the Scriptures, but in order to provide a medicinal exercise. (III.34.49)

No rule will ever suffice, for it is the intention of the Holy Spirit to keep meaning partly hidden, to call forth the deductive and intuitive powers of readers in the interest of their edification, making them accomplices in the meaning-building process. Unless they transgress the rule of *caritas*, many readers' interpretations are within the wide arc of God's intention: "For what could God have more generously and abundantly provided in the divine writings than that the same words might be understood in various ways" (III.27.38). To close scriptural interpretation through skills of translation, judgments of context, knowledge of created things, of history, numerology, music, and tropes, is ultimately to open it. It is to render meaning internally persuasive rather than to place it in an isolated, eternal haven of logocentric authority. There is no infallible, direct way through our mediated linguistic realm to God's unmediated domain; there is always some wandering by the way. Augustine's own espousal of *caritas* and his own humility let him glimpse the richness and profligacy of language and keep open any closure beyond the injunction to *caritas* which his exegetical system might have threatened to imply.

## *Closing and Reopening*

What Augustine's interpretive system left open to new knowledge, however, subsequent history pushed toward elaboration and closure. The allegorical method, reserved by Augustine for reading Scripture, especially for seeing the lessons of the New Testament in the Old, was applied more and more widely to the reading of texts and natural phenomena. What kept the multitude of semblances provided as interpretive guides from flying off in all directions was not close observation of the behavior of serpents or the properties of brown diamonds but the interest of institutions that sponsor discourse about things, those forces, as Bakhtin would say, which "unite and centralize verbal-ideological thought" (p. 271). For Bakhtin, emerging or insurrectionary forces constantly push discourse toward variety and change, while institutional forces for centralization operate to contain and stabilize it.

The practice of monastic copying, in which extant texts were readily included in later ones as a series of glosses—Augustine on Genesis, Peter Lombard on Augustine on Genesis—tended to standardize interpretations of things and scriptural reading from one scholarly text to another. Preaching manuals, in turn, disseminated standard readings for use in the popular pulpit, from which "information" about Nature and Scripture drifted down toward the aphorisms and folklore of ordinary people. By the late Middle Ages this array of correspondences had come to constitute an elaborate discursive code, enduring both because it could master so many linguistic formulations and because it was productive of new textual discourse. (The Wife of Bath says matter-of-factly and without stopping to explain herself: "For blood bitokeneth gold, as me was taught" [III. 581].) Glossing had come to show that "centripetal" tendency toward standardization described by Bakhtin as binding its readers by being fused to social authority (p. 342). The authority of the patristic glosses prevented a chaotic proliferation of biblical readings but at the cost, as Alisoun notes, of much investigative freedom, especially that which relies on experience for its persuasiveness.

Yet at every stage there was disparity too, as in all "languages," disparity about the common signification of things and disparity in readings of the biblical passages in which they were invoked. These codes were also manipulable, able to accommodate particular personal and ideological attempts to appropriate the Scripture's prestige, as Jankyn's case shows. From a Derridean standpoint, this unraveling is implicit in the slippery connection between all language and what it signifies.

In the case of patristic *glossing,* however, more concrete social explanations are available. Bakhtin's emphasis on language as a social construction and his contention that words always exist in a "dialogically agitated and tension-filled environment" (p. 276) turn inquiry toward the social world surrounding the *Canterbury Tales.* One tension-filled environment in which glossing figures is fourteenth-century England's wide dispersion of social power and literacy, which may account in part for the fictional case of Alisoun, whose situation seems to rest on a new kind of social self-awareness. Another is the influence of Lollardy, which has a direct bearing on the authority of patristic glosses.

The Lollards wrote and preached that the plain truths of "goddis word" had been obscured by centuries of commentary and that the time had come to deliver the unencumbered Scripture in English to lay people. John Wyclif himself denied neither the need for interpretation of the Bible, including figurative interpretation,[11] nor the wisdom of much patristic commentary—he is remembered as an extreme Augustinian realist—but he does seriously undercut the authority of the traditional glosses. The preaching style practiced by the Lollard "poor priest" was a severe textual commentary followed by moral instruction. That style became known as "gospel glossing," which explains one pilgrim's objection when the Host asks the Parson to preach: "He schal no gospel glosen here ne teche" (Epilogue, *Man of Law's Tale,* II.1180).[12]

The "gospel glosen" associated with Lollardy did not, of course, immediately cause the patristic glosses to lose currency, but Wyclif's attack on the system's authority and attempted substitution of a "gloss" with different underpinnings made the ideology that sustained it *visible.* Ideology works best not when it is an idea being argued for but when it is the ground on which other ideas are argued: it cannot become fully visible without losing some of its privilege. The Lollards accused users of patristic glosses of obscuring the truth of the Bible, and ecclesiastical authorities accused Lollards of the same thing. In these controversies both sides used the word *glose* to mean "specious or sophistical interpretation" *(Middle English Dictionary)* alongside its positive meanings. In short, "gloss" had become by the fourteenth century, in Bakhtin's phrase, "an active participant in social dialogue" (p. 276). Once a "lying gloss" is conceived of, the patristic tradition takes its place, important but not alone, among other interpretive sys-

11. John Wyclif, *Select English Works,* ed. Thomas Arnold (Oxford: Oxford University Press, 1869–71), 1.30 and 2.277–78.

12. The Squire, Summoner, and Shipman are credited with the line in various manuscripts, and Fisher's edition emends the speaker's name to "the Wif of Bath" to make the passage serve as a link to Part III of the *Tales,* arguing that this change may represent Chaucer's earlier draft. If Alisoun was intended to have said this, it would mean that, despite her unorthodox assertions about doctrine, she thinks of herself as militantly orthodox. Although her position has something in common with Lollardy, I would not posit her consciousness of that similarity.

tems. And when glosses lie by covering over unacceptable features in "naked texts," they resemble the self-serving, sexually tinged flattery Jankyn may be using on Alisoun.

The word itself embraces its own near opposite: to gloss is to disclose deep meaning, as Ambrose's glosses did for the young Augustine, or to prevent disclosure of deep meaning by presenting an attractive but deceptive surface, as Fortune's glosses do for her victims. Either Jankyn saw deeply into Alisoun, or he merely dazzled her with words.

## *Glossing Alisoun's Story*

These observations point to direct consequences for our glossing of Alisoun's story. If *On Christian Doctrine* authorizes and maintains an unquestioned logocentrism in medieval thought and social practice, Alisoun must be both wrong and wicked. But if other glossing systems compete with that logocentrism, or if glossing itself has come under suspicion, her story must be reassessed to admit other glosses of her Prologue, authorized by master texts other than patristic ones.

To read medieval texts according to Augustine's avowed design for stabilizing interpretive practice (rather than the modified view of it that I have developed here) may lead to D. W. Robertson's reading of Alisoun as a hopelessly "carnal and literal" exegete whose challenge to real *clerkes* is not to be read sympathetically. In Augustine's formulation the literalist is a slave and a type of Eve, causer of man's fall (it is handy that this misled exegete is also female). Alisoun is, therefore, "an elaborate iconographic figure designed to show the manifold implications of an attitude . . . the femininity she represents was in Chaucer's day a philosophical rather than a psychological concept."[13] Taking *On Christian Doctrine* as unproblematically logocentric, this approach claims that it is "manifesting a structure," the structure of Chaucer's fiction, by demonstrating the availability (indeed, the unavoidability) of a signifying code to both the originating author and his first readers. It calls other readings of this fiction misreadings on the grounds that "realistic," or "sentimental," or "psychological" inferences were not possible for Chaucer or his contemporaries. As a result we must read the Wife's utterances as providing a point-by-point contradiction of

13. D. W. Robertson, *A Preface to Chaucer* (Princeton: Princeton University Press, 1968), pp. 330–31.

what the author wants us to take as truth about life. To substantiate this reading, one could consult the great repository of types in the patristic glosses and note the differences between the teaching on the Scripture found there and Alisoun's "noble preching."

Robertson's argument has done medieval studies the inestimable service of locating and making known a rich cache of intertextual influences, deepening our sense of the philosophical seriousness of medieval writing and (far better than most of his opponents) conveying the assertiveness of the critic's task in mastering textual codes. Like Augustine's Tyconius before him, however, he promises too much certainty, too securely fixed and single a code. Other commentators before and since have provided other glosses, authorized by other master texts, which fix textual meaning differently.

Rather than Augustine and Jerome, Mary Carruthers, for example, selects medieval courtesy books and legal records as implicated in the fabric of meaning in the Wife's Prologue. By seeing Alisoun's argument as levered against the description of women's roles in contemporary courtesy manuals, Carruthers builds the portrait of "a wealthy west-country clothier managing to carve herself a bit of independence and social power by challenging older mores."[14]

It is not my purpose here to set these critical arguments against each other. It is to notice that both are glosses. Both proceed by selecting a particular set of details from the Wife's Prologue and linking those details together to tell a story that though blurred on the surface of the text, is brought into sharp focus by reference to a master text. Both allegorical stories include details that are not found on the textual surface—that Alisoun "is clearly not interested in 'engendrure,' " as Robertson claims, and that she "oversaw the whole process of cloth manufacture," as Carruthers argues. But that doubling of one text into another to yield clearer patterns of ideas is the point of allegorical interpretation.

Both readings make convincing points about Chaucer's rich text, but neither can stabilize it, "fully embody, with no residue, the internally dialogic potential" that the text itself is (Bakhtin, p. 326). No reading can proceed without first selecting markers for what is figure, what ground, and without devising a frame to link privileged details together.

14. Mary Carruthers, "The Wife of Bath and the Painting of Lions," *PMLA* 94 (1979), 209–22.

These are interpretive acts, and they cannot be retroactively located in the text itself—the text that "says what it means," as Talbot Donaldson said in replying to Robertson.[15] Reference to a Bakhtinian sense of a text's agitated social environment, then, opens it to various construals of its center and its appropriate contexts, textual and nontextual.

A Derridean critique would further "de-center" the text. The difference between Robertson's and Carruthers's doublings and the Derridean project of decentering texts is that the doubling is limited by supposed authorial intention where Derrida is just as attentive to the historical shifts that wrest a text's language away from its biographical author.[16] Again, the doubling readings are focused so that textual figures, tropes, and turns of phrase lead in a single direction, while Derrida is interested in showing conflicts and interferences among the various words and tropes of a text. He "deconstructs" by unfixing the text from its moorings in both authorial origins and thematic consistency.

These and other contemporary critical formulations should invite medieval studies to envision the linguistic and social abundance of its materials. Rather than argue over which gloss is the final word, we might begin to recognize the variousness of the languages that rich texts weave together and time allows to unravel. Historical research, released from the constraints of a fixed "medieval world view" to scrutinize instances, may come to reveal through studies of philology, intellectual life, the occupations, and for that matter the beasts and stones, the plenitude that such texts as the *Canterbury Tales* hold in play. Neither the implications of Alisoun's word *glose* nor our gloss of her text can be reduced and fixed once and for all, and even Augustine

15. Some critics who opposed Robertson, including E. Talbot Donaldson, apparently wanted to dissociate themselves from allegory altogether by reasserting "the right of a poem to say what it means and mean what it says, and not what anyone, before or after its composition, thinks it ought to say or mean." See Donaldson, "Patristic Exegesis: The Opposition," *Critical Approaches to Medieval Literature: English Institute Essays* (New York: Columbia University Press, 1960), p. 2. Taken literally, this view prohibits any commentary at all, for all commentary, as Northrop Frye points out, "is allegorical interpretation, an attaching of ideas to the structure of poetic imagery." See Frye, *Anatomy of Criticism* (Princeton: Princeton University Press, 1957), p. 89 and *passim.*

16. In *Of Grammatology,* Derrida describes his rather dismissive term "doubling" as an attempt to recreate the intended text of the original author "respectfully," a necessary step in intrepretation but one that "protects" rather than opens a reading and must therefore be surpassed (p. 158).

cannot be unproblematically enlisted as the intellectual force that closes the *debat*.

Alisoun of Bath may become, then, a figure for the garrulous, incorrigible, inexplicable text, always *wandrynge by the weye,* always escaping from any centralizing authority that attempts to take over her story. She wants to be glossed and gives out a wealth of clues to reading her enigma, but no one reading will master the rest. And the glossing she invites is itself readable as the work of high intellect and spiritual insight, or the play of material forces and sexual cajolery, or both. With the plentitude of Mother Earth herself (and Father Logos), she offers too much.

# Models of Literary Influence in the *Commedia*

RACHEL JACOFF

Great poems, especially great poems that are complete and for which no drafts survive, present the reader with special problems; the reader must invent the questions and imagine the choices that subtend the extant text. This is a formidable task when a text teases us, as does Dante's *Commedia*, with a compelling illusion of total coherence, completeness, and perfection. Nonetheless, a poem as capacious and as self-conscious as the *Commedia* makes us want to query its modes of self-understanding and self-definition. This self-definition takes place in several explicit forms: in addresses to the reader, in the terminology used for the poem, and in the fascinating dedicatory letter to the *Paradiso,* which most scholars now believe to be authentic. These explicit statements, even when not totally congruent, provide us with one kind of gloss on Dante's self-awareness and his ambitions. But what concerns me in this essay is the way Dante implicitly generates hermeneutical guidelines by means of the encounters between his poem and its models and influences. The most interesting recent work on Dante has called attention to the ways in which Dante's use of his sources is polemical.

This essay has benefited from generous and helpful responses received when earlier versions were read at Boston University, the University of Pennsylvania, Yale University, and Cornell University. I express particular gratitude to Barbara Johnson and Margaret Ferguson for their suggestions.

Dante does not simply enhance or ornament his poem by the use of literary allusion; rather, he works with his sources to reframe, transform, and comment on the texts and traditions that he inherited, shaping and defining his own remarkable poem in the process. The effect of this activity is progressive and cumulative as Dante deploys a variety of strategies to dramatize and thematize the very nature of what we now call intertextuality. In this essay I examine some of these strategies and their role in Dante's uniquely rich poetics of literary influence.

Although the work of individual Dante scholars often assumes the problematic complexity of Dante's relationship to his models,[1] this assumption is not yet widely shared. Generations of source hunters have tended to identify sources rather than query how Dante used them as a glance at any commentary on the *Commedia* shows. Furthermore, modern critics rarely include Dante in more general speculation on the subject, and recent illuminating discussions of intertextuality in premodern texts characteristically begin with Petrarch. Yet analyses of the Renaissance theory and practice of imitation, such as those by G. W. Pigman and Thomas Greene, often seem so pertinent to Dante that one wonders why he is cited so peripherally in them. Pigman, for example, in a very suggestive article maps out a terrain that extends from Petrarch to Milton.[2] Greene's recent book, *The Light at Troy*, does open with a brief discussion of Dante, but it begins in earnest with Petrarch and concludes with Ben Jonson. Both studies are important responses to the fact that, until quite recently, theoretical discussion of intertextuality virtually limited itself to nineteenth- and twentieth-century writers. Harold Bloom's *Anxiety of Influence* had posited "a great age before the Flood, an age when influence was generous."[3] Pigman, and Greene even more so, address pre-Romantic texts in terms of the questions we have learned to bring to those texts which Bloom characterizes as postdiluvian. Such work is a salutary recognition of the tensions and inner conflicts characteristic of such

1. In addition to work specifically cited in this essay, see Teodolinda Barolini, *Dante's Poets: Textuality and Truth in the "Commedia"* (Princeton: Princeton University Press., 1984); John Freccero, *Dante: The Poetics of Conversion* (Cambridge: Harvard University Press, 1986); and Robert Hollander, *Il Virgilio Dantesco* (Florence: Olschki, 1983).

2. G. W. Pigman III, "Versions of Imitation in the Renaissance," *Renaissance Quarterly* 33 (1980), 1–32.

3. Harold Bloom, *The Anxiety of Influence: A Theory of Poetry* (New York: Oxford University Press, 1973), p. 122.

texts, and in fact of all interesting texts. If there was an age before the Flood, it is not clear who might represent it.

That subtle and theoretically nuanced studies of pre-Romantic intertextuality treat Dante as marginal to their subject is nonetheless puzzling. What does the virtual avoidance of Dante tell us about the intertextual models being developed and privileged? Is Dante's poem insufficiently problematic, or is it problematic in terms that readers accustomed to Renaissance texts do not properly recognize? Both Pigman and Greene set up a series of categories to define characteristic imitative strategies. Greene articulates this practice in terms of two closely related categories, heuristic and dialectical imitation. By heuristic imitation, Greene means the imitation that takes place when a text thematizes its relationship to its constitutive subtext so that the relationship between the two texts becomes part of the second poem's subject. Heuristic imitation shades into what Greene calls dialectical imitation when the relationship between the two texts generates a two-way movement. For Greene, this latter is the privileged form of imitation, because the risk taking that it involves guarantees the humanist text's authenticity. The text, says Greene, "has to expose the vulnerability of the subtext while exposing itself to the subtext's potential aggression. By exposing itself in this way to the destructive criticism of its acknowledged or alleged predecessors, by entering into a confict whose solution is withheld, the humanist text assumes its full historicity and works to protect itself against its own pathos."[4] Greene's language here edges very close to the notion of imitation as agon. As Greene assumes this agonistic model to be the most authentic form of imitation, Dante is a marginal figure in the book's larger argument.

By exploring the resonances of what Greene elegantly terms "heuristic imitation," I hope to open the question of whether dialectical imitation, the privileged form for him, *is* necessarily the most interesting model after all. The language in which Greene articulates this model makes it quite clear that it is a model of strife. Dante, I argue, reverses the priorities that Greene holds as evaluative standards, showing us that heuristic imitation can include and call into question the model of strife itself. In the *Commedia* heuristic imitation reveals itself as a nourishing strategy and theme.

4. Thomas Greene, *The Light in Troy: Imitation and Discovery in Renaissance Poetry* (New Haven: Yale University Press, 1982), p. 45.

I examine a group of episodes in which Dante dramatizes his poem's relationship to its privileged subtext, the *Aeneid.* Dante's use of the *Aeneid* is often mediated by other texts, literary and theological, and Virgil is by no means the only literary influence who is presented thematically in the *Commedia.* Ovid, in particular, forms part of an extended meditation on imitation. In fact, it is in his imitation of Ovidian metamorphoses, in the canto of the thieves, that Dante explicitly acts out the notion of imitation as competition. Dante interrupts his text to announce the competition: "Taccia Lucano," Dante begins, "Let Lucan now be silent.... Concerning Cadmus and Arethusa let Ovid be silent, for if he, poetizing, converts ["converte poetando"] the one into a serpent and the other into a fountain, I envy him not" (*Inf. XXV*, 94, 97–99). Dante's boast that he is outdoing Ovid is, however, in context subject to retrospective reinterpretation. Dante converts it into a metaliterary moment both in the apology with which he ends the canto and in the prologue and presentation of Ulysses, himself an over-reacher, in the following canto, showing us that such a claim belongs to the rhetoric of pagan poetry and is inappropriate, hubristic, and dangerous for a Christian poet. Insofar as Dante allows himself an overt expression of rivalry with his models, he stages it as an episode in his development, a temptation to be exorcised.[5]

Despite the significance of Ovid and other classical and vernacular poets to Dante's self-definition, the *Aeneid* is clearly the central text in terms of which Dante confronts and elaborates his own options. The *Aeneid* and its author enter the *Commedia* in the very first canto as Virgil meets Dante in the "selva oscura." Virgil's introduction of himself gives us a clue to Dante's particular way of reading the *Aeneid.*

> Nacqui *sub Iulio,* ancor che fosse tardi,
> e vissi a Roma sotto 'l buono Augusto
> nel tempo de li dèi falsi e bugiardi.
> Poeta fui, e cantai di quel giusto
> figliuol d'Anchise che venne di Troia,
> poi che 'l superbo Ilïón fu combusto.
>
> I was born *sub Julio,* although late, and I lived at Rome under the good Augustus, in the time of the false and lying

5. Cf. Peter Hawkins, "Virtuosity and Virtue: Poetic Self-Regulation in the *Commedia,*" *Dante Studies* 98 (1980), 1–18.

> gods. I was a poet, and I sang of that just son of Anchises
> who came from Troy after proud Ilium was burned.[6]

Virgil's characterization of Aeneas as the just son of Anchises will be paralleled in Canto II by Dante's description of Aeneas as the father of Silvius, underlining the centrality of father-son relations in both the *Aeneid* and the *Commedia*. The *Aeneid* is brought into the *Commedia*'s moral orbit both with the adjective "giusto" and with the coordinates "superbo Ilion" and, later in Canto I, "umile Italia." These are literal echoes from the *Aeneid*, but they acquire a new moral valence in Dante's appropriation of them, bringing the journey of Aeneas into relation to Dante's own journey from sinful pride to humility. Virgil is given a mysterious prophecy in Canto I in which he predicts the coming of a figure Dante calls the Veltro. There is much debate about who or what this Veltro is, but the form of Virgil's prophecy is itself significant, for in it he links an apocalyptic future to his own poem's version of a semimythical past. The Veltro, he says, "shall be the salvation to that low-lying Italy ["umile Italia"] for which the Virgin Camilla and Euryalus, Turnus, and Nisus died of their wounds" (I, 106-8). The poet Giuseppe Ungaretti noted that this particular choice of characters from the *Aeneid,* and the order of their naming, is revealing: they are characters who fought and died on both sides in the war for possession of Italy which the last six books of the *Aeneid* depict, a war that must be seen in retrospect as a civil war.[7] Here Dante shows himself sensitive to Virgil's own awareness of the pathos and price of any such war, sensitive to Virgil's special compassion toward the young and the brave who are war's most poignant victims. By situating these deaths in relation to a displaced apocalyptic fulfillment, Dante draws the *Aeneid* into his own, larger vision of providential history.

Throughout the opening cantos of the *Inferno* there are extensive Virgilian borrowings. Some are mere details or phrases, but often Dante's transformation of a Virgilian allusion becomes a commentary on the original. The famous and much imitated simile in Book VI of the *Aeneid*—the flock of souls awaiting entrance to the underworld

6. All quotations of Dante are from *The Divine Comedy*, trans. with commentary by Charles S. Singleton, Bollingen Series LXXX, 3 vols. in 6 (Princeton: Princeton University Press, 1970–75).

7. In *Letture Dantesche,* ed. Giovanni Getto, vol. 1 (Florence: Sansoni, 1964), pp. 5–23, esp. pp. 22–23.

compared to autumnal leaves falling—is taken over by Dante, and its emphasis radically changed. Whereas Virgil uses the comparison to suggest the sheer numbers of souls ("Quam multa . . . ") and the naturalness of their fate (the souls are compared to migrating birds), Dante thinks of the leaves falling one by one ("ad una ad una") and elaborates the comparison to underline the role of individual volition rather than cyclical (or seasonal) destiny. Dante's use of the simile not only is a way of describing an event in his own text but becomes an implicit commentary on Virgil's poem and its *gestalt.* In this case Dante counts on the reader to recognize the allusion and to take the measure of his refashioning of it. Elsewhere Dante calls attention to the borrowing by dramatizing it as an encounter between alternative versions, his own and Virgil's, of a similar event, most strikingly in Cantos XIII and XX.

In Canto XIII, the canto of the suicides, Dante's major source is Aeneas's meeting with Polydorus in Book III of the *Aeneid.* Aeneas, en route from Troy to Italy, first lands in Thrace; when he attempts to tear a branch from the soil to serve as a cover for an altar, he finds that unintentionally he has disturbed the grave of Polydorus, a son of Priam who was murdered by the greedy king of Thrace. The scene is important for Dante's reading of the *Aeneid*, and the *Commedia* contains at least two other allusions to it. The memory of the scene affects the action of Dante's poem when Virgil prompts Dante to reenact it in the wood of the suicides. At the opening of Canto XIII, Virgil tells Dante, "Look well, therefore, and you shall see things that would make my words incredible." He then urges Dante to break off a branch of one of the thornbushes that surround them. When Dante does so, the voice of the severed twig issues a lament that echoes the lament of Polydorus to Aeneas with its invocation of *pietas.* Virgil apologizes both for Dante and for himself, explaining that if Dante had believed Virgil's verses he would not have broken off the branch; but as Virgil himself urged him to it, what is at issue is Virgil's belief in his own text. It is Virgil who characterizes the situation as "la cosa incredibile"; and it is Virgil who introduces the episode by telling Dante that he will see things that will call Virgil's words into question ("torrien fede al mio sermone"[XIII, 21]).

Two points suggested by this interchange have ambiguous overtones. First, as most commentators note, Dante's scene actually does differ significantly from its Virgilian model, so that Virgil's verses do not provide an exact equivalent for the situation that Virgil and Dante encounter in the wood of the suicides.[8] Virgil's Polydorus is buried beneath the myrtle branches that Aeneas rends, not embodied in them. Only in Dante's version of the episode is the tree identical to the bodily form of the soul within it. Second, Virgil seems to be testing the credibility of his own invention: this is one of the very few places in the *Commedia* when we are asked to think about the *Aeneid* as fiction and not as history. The word "credere" (to believe) recurs in several forms throughout the canto, and the problem of belief is at the heart of the moral, political, and theological issues raised in the episode.[9] But the problem of belief in fiction is also at stake, and Dante raises it to suggest the superiority of his poem to Virgil's even as he calls explicit attention to his dependence on Virgil: first, with respect to daring of conception (the invention of the man-tree), and second, with respect to its truth claims, which go further than, or are of a different order from, those made by even the *Aeneid.*

If the status of the *Aeneid* is called into question in Canto XIII, in Canto XX it is blatantly problematized. In this, the canto of the soothsayers or diviners, the cast is a group of figures from ancient literature and modern times. The focus is on four figures, each of whom is drawn from one of the great Roman epics: Amphiaraus from Statius's *Thebaid,* Tiresias from Ovid's *Metamorphoses,* Arruns from Lucan's *Pharsalia,* and Manto from Virgil's *Aeneid.* Augury is an important subject in these epics, and particularly in Statius and Lucan, where its practice both fascinates and repels. Although the classical epics themselves already contain a critique of augury, a critique that is a Stoic commonplace, Dante rightly sees augury as a characteristic feature of pagan literary representation.

Virgil is the speaker for most of this canto, and it is he who points out and describes the classical augurs one by one. Dante's versions of these figures clearly draw upon his sources but also suggest, through subtle changes, a demystification of them.[10] In each case the original descriptive rhetoric is slightly deflated and undercut. The most per-

8. The classic treatment of this canto is by Leo Spitzer, "Speech and Language in *Inferno* XIII," in *Dante: A Collection of Critical Essays,* ed. John Freccero (Englewood Cliffs, N.J.: Prentice-Hall, 1965), pp. 78–101.

9. See William J. Kennedy, "Irony, Allegoresis, and Allegory in Virgil, Ovid and Dante," *Arcadia* 7 (1972), 115–34, esp. 119–21.

10. My reading of this episode is deeply indebted to Robert Hollander's richly detailed "The Tragedy of Divination in *Inferno* XX," in his *Studies in Dante* (Ravenna: Longo, 1980), pp. 131–218.

plexing shift comes in the longest and most overtly corrective of these rereadings. In what seems a literary retraction, Virgil tells the story of Manto and the founding of Mantua, his own birthplace, in terms that expressly deny the version of the story he had told in Book X of the *Aeneid*. Virgil's insistence at the end of his lengthy account that no other previous version is acceptable is a retrospective aggression against his own text. Nor is this all. Before the canto concludes, Virgil mentions yet another character from the *Aeneid*, the augur Eurypylus, and he mentions him in connection with an event in which, in the *Aeneid*, he has no part. The fact that Virgil is presenting a story at variance with his own text is itself not as important as the fact that he does so while denying it, for it is exactly at this point that Virgil says to Dante, "Thus my high Tragedy sings of him in a certain passage—as you know well, who know the whole of it" ["così 'l canta / l'alta mia tragedìa in alcun loco: ben lo sai tu che la sai tutta quanta"] (XX.113-114). This conjunction alerts the reader to the fact that such a misreading cannot be accidental. Because Dante makes Virgil its narrator, Virgil himself seems both to correct (in the Manto story) and misquote his own poem. The whole canto thus functions as a critique of the truth-value of ancient literature, a demystification of its prophetic claims, and a challenge to its inviolability. In fact, Dante here legitimates radical violence against a prior text by having the text's own author perform it.[11] This is only one of a number of stances that Dante takes toward ancient literature, but it is potentially the most negative.

Such negativity has to be set against Dante's most positive dramatization of the prophetic and salvific potential of classical literature, the Statius-Virgil encounter in *Purgatorio* XXI–XXII. It is one of the most inventive and richly imagined episodes in the *Commedia*, and I can sketch only some of its implications here.[12] Statius, a first-century Latin poet, is given a three-part autobiography. The three subjects of

11. See Margaret Ferguson, *Trials of Desire: Renaissance Defenses of Poetry* (New Haven: Yale University Press, 1983), pp. 126–30. Ferguson shows the connection between this scene in Virgil and Dante and its later development by Ariosto and Tasso. Her analysis of the bleeding tree episode as a figure for intertextual violence is very suggestive for what is a mere hint in Dante.

12. This episode has attracted great attention in recent years. In addition to Barolini, *Dante's Poets*, and Hollander, *Il Virgilio Dantesco*, see Robert Ball, "Theological Semantics: Virgil's *Pietas* and Dante's *Pietà*," *Stanford Italian Review* 2 (Spring 1981) 59–80, and Giuseppe Mazzotta, "Literary History," in his *Dante, Poet of the Desert* (Princeton: Princeton University Press, 1979), pp. 192–226.

his autobiography—his poetic, moral, and spirtual stories—are unified by each of them being made to turn on Statius's reading of Virgil. In his capsule poetic autobiography, Statius describes the generative and seminal influence of the *Aeneid* on his own poetry in a striking combination of metaphors.

> Al mio ardor fuor seme le faville
> che mi scaldar, de la divina fiamma
> onde sono allumati più di mille;
> de l'Eneïda dico, la qual mamma
> fummi, e fummi nutrice, poetando;
> sanz' essa non fermai peso di dramma.

> The sparks which warmed me from the divine flame whereby more than a thousand have been kindled were the seeds of my poetic fire: I mean the *Aeneid* which was in poetry both mother and nurse to me—without it I had achieved little of worth. (XXI, 94–99)

Earlier in the *Inferno,* Dante had figured Virgil as a solicitous mother, but here Statius speaks of the *Aeneid* itself as a nourishing mother. It seems "in character" that Statius should say this about the *Aeneid* because Statius's own poem, unlike Virgil's, gives extraordinary prominence to the figure of the mother. (As even the editor of the Loeb edition notes, Statius is visibly partial to the mother-son relationship.) This speech, echoing the conclusion to the *Thebaid* itself, expresses the tender *pietas* that marks the whole scene of Statius's encounter with his beloved master/mother.

The second stage of Statius's autobiography deals with his moral conversion from the sin of prodigality, which he has been purging on the terrace where Virgil and Dante meet him. This conversion Statius attributes to a reading of a line in the *Aeneid,* a line from the Polydorus episode that we have already seen Dante using in *Inferno* XIII. Statius's reading is actually a misreading, because he takes a line in which Virgil decries the murderous power of avarice and hears in it an injunction on the virtue of moderation. Nonetheless, his misreading is valorized as the "true" reading, that is, the one by which Virgil's words allow Statius to hear exactly what he needs to hear in order to effect his moral change. Interpretation becomes a function of an extratextual imperative. Statius's life takes precedence over Virgil's text, although it is Virgil's text that "authorizes" Statius's conversion. The connections between this moment in the *Purgatorio* and the canto of the *Inferno* to which the same episode from the *Aeneid* is central suggest a retrospective gloss on all of Dante's interpretive reworkings of Virgil. The *Aeneid,* as Ulrich Leo, Robert Hollander, and others have argued, is instrumental in Dante's conversion, but the very sign of its importance and instrumentality is Dante's willingness to sacrifice, to violate if need be, the integrity of the generative text. The importance of the Polydorus episode for Dante lies in part, I believe, in its sacrificial context, in its bringing together the sacred and the sacrilegious. *Pietas* and violence are inseparable even in the most overt celebration of the *Aeneid*'s power. Dante dramatizes here the necessary transcendence and transgression of the model as the very form of poetic conversion ("converte poetando").

In his third autobiographical narrative, Statius explains how he was converted to Christianity by reading Virgil's *Fourth Ecloque.* Although there is no known source for the idea that Statius became Christian, legends do exist about other pagans being converted by the *Fourth Ecloque,* and the first Christian emperor, Constantine, according to Eusebius, quoted it in public as a proof text. Dante's invention of Statius's conversion validates the prophetic power of Virgil at the same time that it maximizes the pathos of Virgil's predicament. "Through you I was a poet, through you a Christian," Statius says; he can be saved by Virgil's text, but Virgil cannot. There is never any question that Virgil is the greater poet of the two, and yet that greatness cannot be weighed on the only scales that count. Most readers see Statius as an embodiment of Dante's own relationship to Virgil, but that relationship must be calibrated to include more than homage. For Virgil's fate is never fully intelligible within the *Commedia*'s elaborately precise articulation of the necessary correspondence between sin and guilt, the identity of crime and punishment which Dante calls *contrapasso.* The gap between Virgil's being and his fate makes him the only truly tragic figure in the *Commedia.* The more power Dante attributes to Virgil's poetry, the more profoundly we feel that gap, the more haunting it seems.

Dante's most explicit interrogation of the *Aeneid* comes in *Purgatory* VI, where he asks Virgil to interpret the present action of the *Commedia* in terms of what he had said in the *Aeneid.* Dante has just encountered a series of purgatorial penitents who each urge him, after he returns from his journey, to speak of them to their loved ones whose prayers will speed their purgation. Dante asks Virgil about such prayer, with a reminder of Virgil's denial of its efficacy in the *Aeneid:*

> io cominciai: "El par che tu mi nieghi,
> o luce mia, espresso in alcun testo
> che decreto del cielo orazion pieghi;
> e questa gente prega pur di questo:
> sarebbe dunque loro speme vana,
> o non m'è 'l detto tuo ben manifesto?

> It seems to me, O my light, that you deny expressly in a certain passage that prayer bends the decree of heaven; and these people pray but for this—shall then their hope be in vain, or are your words not rightly clear to me? (VI, 28–33)

The "certain passage" to which Dante refers in this disingenuous question is the speech of the Sybil in Book VI of the *Aeneid,* in which she responds to the prayers of the unburied helmsman of Aeneas, Palinurus, that he be allowed to cross the Styx with Aeneas. The Sybil insists on the impossibility of such prayer: "Leave any hope that prayer can turn aside the Gods' decrees." Dante's request that Virgil interpret the purgatorial situation in terms of the *Aeneid* actually inverts the real question. Dante, of course, has no doubt of the efficacy of prayer; his question leads not to a discussion of Purgatory but rather to a critique of the limits of Virgil's ethos. Virgil explains to Dante that prayer was without value in his poem because then prayer was "disjoined from God." For Dante, this gap between man and God is filled by the Incarnation. At the same time the Christ event itself constitutes the gap between Virgil's poem and Dante's, between tragedy and *Commedia.* Because this extratextual event is posited as the source of Dante's superiority, it shifts the grounds on which any purely literary comparison can be made. This is not to say that any Christian poem is better than any classical one, but rather that Dante insists on something other than his own genius as the true dividing line between his poem and Virgil's.

Dante underlines this division in innumerable ways, but nowhere more brilliantly and concisely than in the extraordinary scene of Beatrice's arrival and Virgil's farewell which takes place in Canto XXX at the top of the mountain of Purgatory. As several critics have noted, Virgil's departure is enacted in a sequence of allusions. John Freccero was the first to point out that the sequence is actually the equivalent of a fadeout, moving from direct quotation, to translation, to allusive echo.[13] Dante's appropriation and transformation of these Virgilian quotations generates his most powerful commentary on the distance between his poem and Virgil's. Beatrice's arrival in the poem is accompanied by an extraordinary garland of allusions, beginning with a line from the Song of Songs, "Veni sponsa, da Libano," and the Gospel herald, "Benedictus qui venis," biblical citations that contribute to the Christological typology of her presentation. Dante links, actually rhymes, the line from Matthew with a line from the *Aeneid:*

> Tutti dicean: "*Benedictus qui venis!*"
> e fior gittando e di sopra e dintorno,
> "*Manibus*, oh, *date lilia plenis!*"
>
> All were crying, "Blessed is he who comes," and scattering flowers up and around, "give lilies with full hands." (XXX, 19–21)

The line from the *Aeneid* comes from one of its most resonant scenes. "Give lilies with full hands" is Anchises' funereal gesture toward the young Marcellus at the anticlimactic climax of his presentation of Rome's future heroic history to Aeneas. Marcellus was to have been Augustus's heir, and his death shadows the celebration of Roman achievement chronicled in this section of the poem. In context, the death of Marcellus reminds us of all the youthful deaths that the *Aeneid* sorrowfully recounts, all those sons who die leaving their fathers to mourn for them. Precisely because, as we have seen, the fates cannot be swayed by prayer, Anchises' mourning gestures dramatize a confession of futility and sadness:

> O boy whom we lament, if only you
> could break the bonds of fate and be Marcellus.
> Give lilies with full hands; let me
> Scatter these purple flowers, and with these gifts,
> at least be generous to my descendant's spirit,
> Complete this service, though it be in vain (*inani*).[14]

13. In lectures and now in John Freccero, "Manfred's Wounds and the Poetics of the *Purgatorio*," in *Centre and Labyrinth: Essays in Honour of Northrop Frye*, ed. Eleanor Cook and Chaviva Hošek (Toronto: University of Toronto Press, 1983), pp. 79–81; rpt. in *Dante: The Poetics of Conversion*, pp. 195–208.

14. All quotations from the *Aeneid* are from the translation by Allen Mandelbaum (Berkeley: University of California Press, 1971).

Virgil consistently associates the word *inani*, which occurs at the end of this passage, with death, in particular the death of the young. One Virgil scholar suggests that it actually comes to mean "lifeless" or "not having the power to save from death" or "not having the power to restore life."[15] *Inanis* is also associated with the phrase "lacrimae rerum" in the sculpted depiction of the death of Hector, which Aeneas confronts on his arrival in Carthage. In that scene, as in the Marcellus passage, mortality undermines historical promise, vitiating the power of both commemoration and representation. Dante appropriates the phrase "Manibus date lilia plenis" within the specific context of the Resurrection (Purg. XXX, 13–15), so that the triumphal advent of Beatrice transforms the lilies of mourning into those of the Easter celebration. As Beatrice too died young, her role as a counter-Marcellus who fulfills her promise after death, or in spite of death, is clear. A hopeless farewell becomes a joyous welcome made possible in part by the virtue of hope.

The full power of this particular allusion depends on the *Commedia*'s containing several other Marcellus figures (among them Charles Martel, Manfred, and Henry VII), whose cumulative effect suggests that this episode was as emblematic for Dante as for Virgil. For both poets, the early death of the politically promising hero is tragic. But for Dante that tragedy gives way to a larger vision of hope which places it in a perspective that is anything but "inanis."[16]

After Dante sees Beatrice, he records the effect of her power on him in a second Virgilian allusion. Here Dante translates from Virgil's Latin into his Italian the line in which Dido expresses her passion and foreboding as she first feels love for Aeneas, a love that will ultimately destroy her. Dante converts the line into an assertion of the continuity and the ultimately redemptive power of eros. By means of this line he

15. M. Owen Lee, *Fathers and Sons in Virgil's "Aeneid": Tum genitor natum* (Albany: SUNY Press, 1979), esp. p. 166.

16. "Inanis" is a key word in 1 Cor. 15. 12–14, which supplies a perfect gloss on the Dantesque understanding of Virgilian limitations in a comparable context: "Si autem Christus praedicatur quod resurrexit a mortuis, quomodo quidam dicunt in vobis quoniam resurrectio mortuorum non est? Si autem resurrectio mortuorum non est, necque Christus resurrexit. Si autem Christus non resurrexit, *inanis* est ergo praedicatio nostra, *inanis* est fides vestra" [Now if Christ is preached as raised from the dead, how can some of you say that there is no resurrection of the dead? But if there is no resurrection of the dead, then Christ has not been raised; if Christ has not been raised, then our preaching is in vain and your faith is in vain.] Cf. the conclusion of 1 Cor. 15: "quod labor vester non est *inanis* in Domino" [knowing that in the Lord your labor is not in vain.]

connects Beatrice's appearance in Purgatory with his first childhood awareness of her, and he links the *Commedia* to his first work, the *Vita Nuova*, in which he first recorded his love for her.

> Tosto che ne la vista mi percosse
> l'alta virtù che già m'avea trafitto
> prima ch'io fuor di püerizia fosse,
> volsimi a la sinistra col respitto
> col quale il fantolin corre a la mamma
> quando ha paura e quando elli è afflitto
> per dicere a Virgilio: "Men che dramma
> di sangue m'è rimaso che non tremi:
> conosco i segni de l'antica fiamma."

> As soon as on my sight the lofty virtue smote that had already pierced me before I was out of my boyhood, I turned to the left with the confidence of a little child that runs to his mother when he is frightened or in distress, to say to Virgil, "Not a drop of blood is left in me that does not tremble: I know the tokens of the ancient flame." (XXX, 40–48)

The last line of this verse is a translation of the Virgilian "Adnosco veteris vestigia flammae, " reminding us both of Dido and of the difference between her love and Dante's. The passage contains the same rhyme on "mamma-dramma-fiamma" present in Statius's tribute to the seminal power of the *Aeneid*.[17] Dante links these two moments in the duplicated rhyme schemes, incorporating Statius's tribute to Virgil into Dante's farewell to him, thereby linking Virgil's persona and poem in the moment of maximal pathos.

The last Virgilian echo is an allusion to the climax of the Orpheus story in the fourth book of the *Georgics,* where Eurydice's final loss triggers a threefold repetition of her name. In Dante it is Virgil's name that is repeated three times as he is lost to Dante and Beatrice takes his place.

> Ma Virgilio n'avea lasciati scemi
> di sé, Virgilio dolcissimo patre,
> Virgilio a cui per mia salute die'mi.

> But Virgil had left us bereft of himself, Virgil, sweetest father, Virgil to whom I gave myself for my salvation. (XXX, 49–51)

17. See Robert Hollander, "Babytalk in Dante's *Commedia,*" in his *Studies in Dante,* p. 129.

Taken together, this extraordinary cluster of Virgilian allusions dramatizes a series of reversals. The new context of resurrection and recovery displaces the original context of loss and death. Virgilian acknowledgments of the power of death over history, eros, and poetry are converted into Dantesque celebrations of the capacity of the Christ event to inform all three spheres with hope and triumph.[18]

Another series of reversals here has not, I believe, been remarked upon. In each of the three Virgilian allusions Dante's appropriation entails a gender reversal. Gender reversal is already present in the Gospel herald, a prelude to the whole passage, because Dante uses the masculine adjective "Benedictus" for Beatrice. Likewise each of the three Virgilian allusions reverses the original's gender designation: a line used about Marcellus is used for Beatrice, a line used about Aeneas is used for Beatrice, and the lines speaking of Eurydice are used for Virgil. Gender reversals pervade Canto XXX. In addition to the Virgilian allusions, Virgil is compared to a mother, Beatrice to an admiral.

The admiral simile is yet another Virgilian allusion, one that specifically addresses problems raised by Virgil's passionately patriarchal poem. The simile describes Beatrice as "Quasi ammiraglio che in poppa e in prora / viene a veder la gente che ministra / per li altri legni, e a ben far l'incora" [Like an admiral who goes to stern and bow to see the men that are serving on the other ships and encourages them to do well . . . ] (ll. 58–60). *Poppa* is important in other nautical metaphors in Dante and connects this moment in the poem with the Ulysses canto, in which Ulysses' *poppa* was turned backward, and with the journey of the souls to Purgatory guided by an angel Dante describes as a celestial helmsman standing on the *poppa;* it is a also key word in Beatrice's last prophecy in *Paradiso* (XXVII, 146).

The Italian word "poppa" points back to its Latin source, a key word in a crucial phrase in the *Aeneid,* a phrase that is almost a leitmotif in three occurrences in the epic.[19] The phrase is "stans celsa in puppi," [standing on the lofty stern], and it is used once of each of the poem's

18. I discuss this sequence of Virgilian allusions at greater length in a forthcoming essay on *Purgatorio* XXX for the *Lectura Dantis Californiana.* Cf. the fine essay by Christopher Ryan, "Virgil's Wisdom in the *Divine Comedy,*" *Medievalia et Humanistica* 11 (1982), 1–38.

19. The importance of this phrase in the *Aeneid* is discussed by Michael C. J. Putnam, "The Third Book of the *Aeneid:* From Homer to Rome," in his *Essays on Latin Lyric, Elegy, and Epic* (Princeton: Princeton University Press, 1982), p. 276.

key figures in the line of male succession at the moment when he takes control of his people and his destiny: Anchises (III.527), Aeneas (X.261), and Augustus (VIII.680). By making Beatrice his admiral, Dante is announcing his very un-Virgilian sense of the positive possibilities of female guidance. Although the role of the female and the feminine in Dante is too large a subject for this context, Dante corrects Virgil in this area. The value system of the *Aeneid* is clearly, if not relentlessly, patriarchal. *Pietas,* its highest virtue, is never exemplified by or in relation to a female figure. The shift from Virgil's *pietas* to Dante's *pietà* is made possible, as Robert Ball has recently argued, by female mediation. "Dante transcends the repetitive cycle of fathers and sons by adhering to a principle of female mediation rigorously excluded from the historical chain of origins and desires in the *Aeneid,* but recuperated by Dante as both a literary and theological mode in the course of his journey."[20] Ball's argument is particularly suggestive for this canto and its constellation of gender reversals. The whole notion of gender is called into question by the kaleidoscopic reversals and equations that Dante makes here. Within a single episode we see Virgil compared to a solicitous mother and Beatrice to an admiral; and immediately afterward, Beatrice is compared to a stern mother as well. As all this takes place after Dante has established Beatrice as a *figura Christi,* the gender reversals suggest the radical ways in which Christ himself can be thought to have called the status of gender into question.[21]

The instances of intertextuality I have been considering are just one way of opening up the question of Dante's relationship to Virgil; only with continued and communal meditation will be able to explore the question fully.[22] What seems constant is Dante's repeated linking of his poem to Virgil's, his paradoxical creation of both a continuity and a distance between the two texts, a distance that makes his own poem the ultimate arbiter of the *Aeneid's* meaning and status. There is, of course, a name for such a relationship between texts: biblical typology,

20. Ball, "Theological Semantics," p. 79.

21. As in the Letter of Paul to the Galatians: "There is neither Jew nor Greek, there is neither slave nor free, there is neither male nor female; for you are all one in Christ Jesus" (Gal. 3.28).

22. Such "communal meditation" is planned in the forthcoming collection *The Poetry of Allusion: Virgil and Ovid in Dante's "Comedy,"* ed. Rachel Jacoff and Jeffrey Schnapp.

the system that governs the New Testament's relation to the book it regards as the Old Testament and governs patristic and medieval theories of that relationship. Typology is a model for the relationship between sacred texts, that is, texts presumed in the ultimate sense to have the same author, namely God or the Holy Spirit, the only author whom Dante calls "verace." It is this true Author, unfolding His meaning in time, who guarantees the unity presumed to exist between the two parts of His Book.

From St. Paul on, this principle of relationship between the two testaments assumed an axiomatic status in Christian culture. The Old Testament was read as incomplete without the New, as a series of prophecies and prefigurations whose true meaning was comprehensible only from the point of view of the New Testament. Structurally, the hierarchical assumptions of this system of relationships accomplished an *a priori* privileging of the latecoming text in an assertive denial of priority as a source of power in and of itself. Typology thus claims *a priori* what, as we have seen, literary imitation sets out to accomplish. Dante conflates the typological way of reading associated with sacred texts with the kind of heuristic imitation we find in secular texts to situate his own poem in a unique middle ground. He extends the privileged vantage point that the New Testament adopts toward the Old to his own poem's relation to prior texts, and he assumes the right to do so by claiming in the last analysis that his poem's master-text is not the *Aeneid* but rather the Bible itself. The typological perspective allows Dante to think of the distance between himself and the ancients as an advantage. Virgil, like his character Marcellus, and like classical culture itself, remains a figure of incompletion.

Scripture thus provides Dante with an *ultra*-textual referent, and it is with this in mind that I turn to my last example of the *Commedia's* commentary on its relationship to other texts, its most explicit alignment with Scripture. In Cantos XXIV–XXVI of *Paradiso,* Dante undergoes examination by the apostles Peter, James, and John on the virtues of faith, hope, and charity. In response to St. James's question about the sources of his hope, Dante gives as twin sources the psalms of David and the saint's own epistle.

> "Spene," diss'io, "è uno attender certo
> de la gloria futura, il qual produce
> grazia divina e precedente merto.

> Da molte stelle mi vien questa luce;
> ma quei la distillò nel mio cor pria
> che fu sommo cantor del sommo duce....
> Tu mi stillasti, con lo stillar suo,
> ne la pistola poi, sì ch'io son pieno,
> e in altrui vostra pioggia repluo.

> Hope, I said, is a sure expectation of future glory which divine grace produces, and preceding merit. From many stars this light comes to me, but he first instilled it into my heart who was the supreme singer of the Supreme Lord. ...You afterwards in your Epistle did instill it into me, together with his instilling, so that I am full, and I pour again your shower upon others. (XXV, 76–78)

The internal rhymes, repetitions, and doublings here enact a language of plenitude: "Io son pieno," says Dante. Each text is empowered by the fullness of its predecessor and ultimately grounded in the fullness of the logos. The metaphors of light and water describe a system of filtration with which Dante elsewhere describes the operation of the cosmos itself. In the Neoplatonic cosmology of the *Paradiso,* the planets and stars are the filters (transmitters and differentiators) of the unitary divine light. The distribution of literary influence is, in the model invoked in *Paradiso* XXV, comparable to astral influence. This model of benign transmission is the ideal paradigm, yet the *Commedia* would be much less rich and complex were it the only one deployed.

I close with a glance at one of the greatest texts of antiquity, a text that Dante could not have known but that nonetheless offers a commentary on his ways of understanding and dramatizing intertextuality. It is the treatise *On the Sublime* whose author we call Longinus. Longinus proposes three different metaphors to represent possible relations between texts. In the first he speaks of Plato wrestling with Homer, of the strife that leads to achievement and encourages it, a strife that he says, echoing Hesiod, is good for mortals. This is the rivalry Dante dramatizes in *Inferno* XXV where he "takes on" Ovid and Lucan. In the second the figure of the predecessor-as-rival gives way to that of the predecessor-as-guide, the one who lights the way for his successor, the very image Dante uses for Virgil when he has Statius speak of him as "one who goes by night and carries the light behind him:" (*Purg.* XXII, 67-68). In Longinus's third formulation the predecessor becomes the source of power and inspiration:

> For many men are carried away by the spirit of others as if inspired. . . . From the great natures of the men of old there are borne in upon the souls of those who emulate them, as if from sacred caves, what we may describe as effluences, so that even those who seem little likely to be possessed are thereby inspired and succumb to the spell of others' greatness.[23]

For Dante, the effluences come not from sacred caves but from sacred scripture, which Dante claims "instills" and confers a trace of its own power on his poem.

These three models—the prior text as rival, guide, and empowering source—suggestively recapitulate the major typologies of influence dramatized in the *Commedia*. Longinus, as Greene points out, leaves these conceptions unreconciled and unresolved, capable of mutual amplification rather than brought into the status of contradiction.[24] Dante's *Commedia* reveals, enacts, and dramatizes a comparable multiplicity of models, but it does so in a hierarchical structure. Although each cantica includes more than one model, there is, as we would expect from Dante, a hierarchical advance that makes each one the locus of a more generous vision of literary influence, culminating in the cosmic metaphors of *Paradiso*. As the *Commedia* reaches its completion, Dante speaks of it as his sacrifice rather than his achievement, and he places its proud perfection humbly in the lineage of the Logos.

23. *Longinus on the Sublime*, trans. W. Rhys Roberts (Cambridge: Cambridge University Press, 1907), p. 81.

24. Greene, *The Light in Troy*, pp. 78–81.

# "Mothers to Think Back Through": Who are They? The Ambiguous Example of Christine de Pizan

SHEILA DELANY

My title comes from Virginia Woolf, who claims in the sixth chapter of *A Room of One's Own* that "a woman writing thinks back through her mothers." The book attempts to revive the tradition of the writing woman and to explore some of the special problems of that tradition. Woolf's notion of "mothers to think back through" poses a problematic of its own which I address in this essay, using as my test case the late-medieval French courtly writer Christine de Pizan.

The problem of antecedents has begun to be explored by contemporary gender-oriented scholars stimulated as much by the work of Harold Bloom as by that of Virginia Woolf. In *The Anxiety of Influence* (1973) Bloom advances a more or less Freudian and Oedipal theory of poetic history as a history of influence in which the strong poet "corrects" or completes the work of precursors. The poet does so through "strong misprision": a misreading or misinterpretation that is actually a complex defense mechanism permitting the poet to absorb and transcend the influence of the powerful precursor. Gender-oriented scholars have both appropriated and criticized Bloom's theory. Sandra Gilbert and Susan Gubar write that their well-known study of nineteenth-century female writers, *The Madwoman in the Attic* (1979), "is based in the Bloomian premise that literary history consists of strong action and inevitable reaction" (p. xiii). Simultaneously they point out that the female poet does not experience anxiety of influence as her male counterpart would do, for she experiences something much more fundamental: "anxiety of authorship," the fear that she cannot become a precursor. "The creative I AM cannot be uttered if the 'I' knows not what it is" (p. 17).

The consensus among those who have used Bloom's thesis, whether they are pro or con,[1] appears to be that Bloom's theory itself requires a strong "creative misprision," a rewriting that will free it from the male-oriented Oedipal perspective and allow the notion of influence or models to operate in the context of female experience. Such a rewriting must restore the social dimension that seems marginal in Bloom's project but that, as Virginia Woolf stresses, has profoundly molded the woman artist's relation to her work. It must recognize as a primary component of female experience the fact of exclusion—exclusion, often, from production and consumption of the means of culture; more generally, exclusion from that range of experience which writers write about, including the experience of personal and institutional power.

One of the aims of contemporary gender-oriented scholarship has been to acquaint us with our antecedents and to provide role models—"mothers to think back through"—by rehabilitating women writers whose work has been neglected. Thus we have learned, to mention only a few examples from my own period of specialization, about Hrotswitha, the tenth-century German nun and playwright; about some two dozen *trobairitz* (women poets of courtly love) in twelfth- and thirteenth-century France; about the women humanist scholars of quattrocento Italy; about women poets of the Renaissance; and about

1. See, for instance, Annette Kolodny, "A Map for Rereading; or, Gender and the Interpretation of Literary Texts," *New Literary History* 11 (Spring 1980), 451–67; Joanne Feit Diehl, " 'Come Slowly-Eden': An Exploration of Women Poets and Their Muse," *Signs* 3 (Spring 1978), 572–87; S. Delany, "Rewriting Woman Good: Gender and the Anxiety of Influence in Two Late-Medieval Texts," in *Chaucer in the Eighties*, ed. Julian Wasserman (Syracuse: Syracuse University Press, 1986). Also on the question of the experience of the woman reader or writer, see Judith Fetterley, *The Resisting Reader: A Feminist Approach to American Fiction* (Bloomington: Indiana University Press, 1978); Margaret Homans, *Women Writers and Poetic Identity* (Princeton: Princeton University Press, 1980); Ellen Moers, *Literary Women* (Garden City, N.Y.: Doubleday, 1976); Suzanne Juhasz, *Naked and Fiery Forms: Modern American Poetry by Women: A New Tradition* (New York: Octagon, 1976); Mary Jacobus, ed., *Women Writing and Writing about Women* (London: Croom Helm, 1979).

the early fifteenth-century courtly writer Christine de Pizan.[2] This rehabilitation is a valuable effort, and not only for women. Everyone needs to know what women have done and what they have not done, and the reasons why; for as the utopian socialist Charles Fourier long ago declared, the condition of women in any society is an index to the advancement and limitations of that society as a whole.

Paradoxically, however, the very effort to reconstitute a full understanding of women's participation in cultural history can result in a skewed perception of individual contributions and of history at large. This need not happen, but it can happen and has happened when we do not firmly anchor the figure in question in her own historical milieu. If we desire the full equality and genuine liberation of women, then we desire the transformation of social life; we cannot afford an inaccurate view of past or present, for that would condemn us to ineffectuality. If we do not wish to maintain a falsified history, then we have to assess every rehabilitated woman writer in relation to her social context. Without a rounded and balanced analysis of this kind, the search for "mothers to think back through" becomes simply a scholarly version of that "sisterhood" which the revived women's movement in our era has confronted as one of its basic theoretical and political questions. In this essay I challenge the idea that the act of writing by itself suffices to qualify an early woman writer as a feminist, a radical, a revolutionary, or a model for us. We have, in short, to *select* the mothers we wish to think back through.

Christine de Pizan has a place-setting in that powerful and controversial monument to "sisterhood," Judy Chicago's installation *The Dinner Party*. One criterion for inclusion in *The Dinner Party* was ability to "present a role model for the future," and this criterion gave

2. Ann L. Haight, ed., *Hroswitha of Gandersheim: Her Life, Times and Works* (New York: Hroswitha Club, 1965); Meg Bogin, *The Woman Troubadours* (New York: Paddington, 1976); Patricia LaBalme, ed., *Beyond Their Sex: Learned Women of the European Past* (New York: New York University Press, 1980); Margaret King and Albert Rabil, eds., *Her Immaculate Hand . . . The Women Humanists of Quattrocento Italy* (Binghamton: Center for Medieval and Early Renaissance Studies, 1983); Albert Rabil, *Laura Cereta, Quattrocento Humanist* (Binghamton: Center for Medieval and Early Renaissance Studies, 1981); Ann Jones, "Assimilation with a Difference: Renaissance women Poets and Literary Influence," *Yale French Studies* no. 62 (1981), 135–153; E. Jeffrey Richards, trans., *The Book of the City of Ladies: Christine de Pizan* (New York: Persea, 1982).

the artist a moment of doubt. "As I worked on research for *The Dinner Party*," she writes, "and then on the piece itself, a nagging voice kept reminding me that the women whose plates I was painting, whose runners we were embroidering, whose names we were firing onto the porcelain floor, were primarily women of the ruling classes."[3] But Judy Chicago shies away from the difficult implications of this nagging voice with the truism that "history has been written from the point of view of those who have been in power. It is not an objective record of the human race." Are we then to reject the notion of ruling class or to reject all historical data recorded by men? Chicago's evasion implies a total skepticism that would render any historical understanding impossible, including that of *The Dinner Party*, which reveals a strongly biased (and inaccurate) conception of history. The nagging voice that Chicago dismissed is the one to which I pay attention, arguing that we need not clasp every woman writer to our collective bosom merely because—as Virginia Woolf remarked of the eighteenth-century novelist Eliza Haywood—"she is dead, she is old, she wrote books, and nobody has yet written a book about her."[4]

Christine de Pizan requires a hard historical look because of the large claims that have been made for her. Jeffrey Richards, for example, translator of Christine's *Livre de la Cité des Dames*, adopts a tone nearly hagiographical, in which the vocabulary of "mothers to think back through" is very pronounced. We are told of "the experimental and innovative nature of her prose" (p. xxi), "her enormous range" (p. xxii), "her participation in the intellectual currents of her age" (p. xxvi). Christine is "revolutionary . . . profoundly feminist," completely dedicated "to the betterment of women's lives and to the alleviation of their suffering" (p. xxviii). This appreciation, which seems to me wrong on every count, is one of the most extreme, and particularly odd because the view of Christine as protofeminist is not a new one.[5]

3. This and the following quotation are from Judy Chicago, *The Dinner Party: A Symbol of Our Heritage* (New York: Doubleday, 1979), p. 56.

4. "A Scribbling Dame," in *Virginia Woolf: Women and Writing*, ed. Michele Barrett (New York: Harcourt Brace Jovanovich, 1979).

5. Earlier versions of Richards's position were put forward by Rose Rigaud, *Les idées féministes de Christine de Pisan* (1911; rpt. Geneva: Slatkine, 1973), who writes of "cette femme 'moderne,' féministe convainçue . . . 'précurseur' " (p. 25) and of "la théoricienne du féminisme moderne" (p. 142); also by Léon Abensour, *La femme et le féminisme avant la Révolution* (Paris: Leroux, 1923), who claims that Christine "élabore un corps de doctrine féministe . . . avec la même méthode que les modernes défenseurs

The notion emerged and was debated a century ago, in the heyday of the international feminist movement; it was laid to rest as early as 1912 by Matilde Laigle in her study of Christine's *Le Livre des Trois Vertus.* Later I suggest some reasons for the latter-day revival of this "querelle de Christine."

My purpose in presenting a cautionary dossier on Christine is to show that she was not, even by the standards of her own day, a reformer or protofeminist; that she is at best a contradictory figure, admirable in some respects, deplorable in others. I approach Christine as a reader and a writer who has been moved by Christine's account of her own "anxiety of influence" at the beginning of *Cité des Dames,* where she confronts head-on the literary tradition of medieval clerical misogyny. I believe I have understood her subversive propagandistic effort to

---

des droits de la femme" (p. v). Though Lulu M. Richardson begins her book on *The Forerunners of Feminism in French Literature of the Renaissance* (Baltimore: Johns Hopkins University Press, 1929) with a chapter on Christine, she nonetheless concludes that there is nothing in Christine's work that "could give any one any grounds for calling Christine a radical feminist" (p. 33); and even Rigaud is circumspect enough to place Christine "à la droite du mouvement actuel" (p. 143).

More recently, Angela Lucas sees Christine as "dedicated to championing women's interests in her society," *Women in the Middle Ages* (New York: St. Martin's, 1983), p. 169; Joan Kelly characterizes Christine as a feminist who "defined what was to become the modern feminist sensibility," in "Early Feminist Theory and the *Quérelle des Femmes,* 1400–1789," *Signs* 8 (Autumn 1982), 4–28. Jean Rabant describes her as "la première féministe connue," *Histoire des féminismes français* (Paris: Stock, 1978), p. 19; and two militants of the French women's movement have taken the names of two women whom they obviously consider precursors and role models: Annie de Pisan and Anne Tristan, *Histoires du M.L.F.* (Paris: Calmann-Lévy, 1977). The irony is that neither Christine nor Flora Tristan was a feminist if by feminist we mean someone who draws the sex line before the class (or race) line. Christine was loyal first and foremost to the French aristocracy, Flora Tristan to the international proletariat.

Recent scholars who have seen Christine as conservative or even reactionary include F. Douglas Kelly, "Reflections on the Role of Christine de Pisan as a Feminist Writer," *sub-stance* no. 2 (Winter 1972), 63–71; Joseph L. Baird and John R. Kane, *La Quérelle de la Rose: Letters and Documents* (Chapel Hill: University of North Carolina Press, 1978), p. 18; Judith M. Davis, "Christine de Pisan and Chauvinist Diplomacy," *Female Studies* VI (Old Westbury, N.Y.: Feminist, 1972), 116–22. In 1975 Charity C. Willard warned against using Christine for ideas that she did not really express, observing that Christine's role in the *Roman* quarrel does not bear out the recent view of her as forerunner of modern feminists: "A Fifteenth-Century View of Women's Role in Medieval Society: Christine de Pizan's *Livre des Trois Vertus,*" in *The Role of Women in the Middle Ages,* ed. Rosemary T. Morewedge (Albany: SUNY Press, 1975). This reverses an earlier opinion, for in the introduction to her edition of the *Livre de la Paix* (The Hague: Mouton, 1958), Professor Willard had urged us to see Christine as "precursor . . . of the whole feminist movement" (p. 14).

"rewrite woman good" in that text.[6] I have been charmed by some of her lyrics, impressed by her determination to educate herself and above all by her will to write. Yet I have also been terminally bored by the tedious, mind-numbing, bureaucratic prose of *Cité des Dames,* imitated from the style of royal notaries and civil servants.[7] I have been angered by Christine's self-righteousness, her prudery, and the intensely self-serving narrowness of her views. I have been repulsed by the backwardness of her social attitudes, attitudes already obsolescent in the early fifteenth century when she lived and wrote. If in this essay I emphasize the negative axis of my response to Christine de Pizan, it is to bring into the foreground the kind of historical interrogation that is necessary in selecting the literary mothers we wish to think back through.

We know a good deal about Christine's life, much of it from her own pen.[8] She was Italian by birth, the daughter of a prominent physician-astrologer who took up residence at the French court under Charles V. Christine was born about 1365, educated at home by her father, happily married to one Etienne de Castel (a notary in the royal service), widowed at twenty-five with three children and a mother to support. With small inheritance and only a little land, Christine eventually turned to writing as her profession, maneuvering skillfully among the murderous rivalries that plagued the French ruling houses. She was a prolific author with a substantial reputation among the French and English aristocrats whose patronage was her livelihood. The *oeuvre* on which her reputation rests was mainly produced over some fifteen years.

6. See "Rewriting Woman Good." The two texts are Christine's *Cité des Dames* and Chaucer's *Legend of Good Women.* In *Writing Woman: Women Writers and Women in Literature* (New York: Schocken, 1983), I offer a sympathetic view of Christine in the last chapter, "A City, A Room: The Scene of Writing in Christine de Pisan and Virginia Woolf."

7. See Maureen Curnow, "*The Livre de la Cité des Dames of Christine de Pisan: A Critical Edition*" (diss. Vanderbilt University, 1975), vol. 1, chap. 5. For a different perspective on Christine's style, see E. J. Richards, "Christine de Pizan and the Question of Feminist Rhetoric," *Teaching Language through Literature* 22 (1983), 15–24.

8. There is autobiographical material in *Cité des Dames;* in the *Mutacion de Fortune,* ed. Suzanne Solente (Paris: Picard, 1959–66), 4 vols. in Société des Anciens Textes Français (SATF); and in *Lavision Christine,* ed. Sister Mary L. Towner (New York: AMS, 1969). The two most recent of several full biographies are by Enid McLeod, *The Order of the Rose* (Totowa, N.J.: Rowman & Littlefield, 1976), and Charity C. Willard *Christine de Pizan: Her Life and Works* (New York: Persea, 1984).

Later, for more than a decade (1418–29), Christine withdrew to a convent at Poissy, outside Paris, and evidently wrote only a single work, a religious contemplation of the Passion. She was one of many courtiers who followed the dauphin into "exile" upon the Burgundian invasion of Paris in 1418. Her last work, a patriotic poem honoring Charles VII and Joan of Arc, was produced in 1429.[9] We do not know Christine's response when Charles betrayed La Pucelle the following year, nor exactly when Christine died, except that she was dead by 1432. Until 1600 or so her reputation flourished, with translations of her works into several languages.[10]

Those who are not familiar with the period of transition from feudalism to capitalism—Christine's period—are often surprised by its radical aspects, for it was a self-consciously modern age that had begun in theory and in practice to attack traditional ideas and institutions. What was the social context in which Christine lived and wrote? What would "radicalism" actually mean in early fifteenth-century Europe?[11]

To begin with, the Catholic church was in crisis. Clerical abuses and high living had generated a tradition of anticlerical sentiment on both scholastic and popular levels. (At the latter level one would include, for instance, German polemical poetry, French *fabliaux* and the *Roman de Renart,* and several of Chaucer's *Canterbury Tales.*) Simultaneously there flourished, from the eleventh century on, a network of popular heresies that, despite the variety of their origins and programs, challenged the church by practicing pacifism or apostolic poverty, denying the sacramental nature of marriage, and advocating the right of laymen to administer the sacraments, the right of women to preach, or salvation through women. The church was sufficiently worried about the appeal of such heresies that it founded not only the Inquisition to combat

9. Christine's "Ditié de Jehanne d'Arc" has been edited by Angus J. Kennedy and Kenneth Varty in *Nottingham Mediaeval Studies,* 18 and 19 (1974, 1975).

10. On the later fortunes of Christine, see Gianni Mombello, "Per un'edizione critica del' 'Epistre Othea' di Christine de Pizan," *Studi Francesi,* 8 and 9 (1964, 1965), 29–55 and 53–76.

11. There is a vast bibliography on the topics summarized in these paragraphs. Two convenient surveys of the period, with ample bibliographical references, are Barbara Tuchman, *A Distant Mirror: The Calamitous Fourteenth Century* (New York: Knopf, 1978), and William C. Jordan, Bruce McNab, and Teofilo Ruiz, eds., *Order and Innovation in the Middle Ages* (Princeton: Princeton University Press, 1976). See also G. de Lagarde, *La naissance de l'esprit laïque au déclin du moyen âge* (Paris: Béatrice, 1934–46), 6 vols., and A. C. Crombie, *Medieval and Early Modern Science* (New York: Doubleday, 1959), vol. 2.

them but also the orders of preaching friars. Moreover, a low-level but widespread skepticism about the efficacy of prayer and priestly ministration was probably inevitable: the Crusade movement failed, the Black Death invaded Europe in 1348, and the Great Schism in the church from 1378 to 1417 produced the unedifying spectacle of rival popes excommunicating one another. Reinforcing these centrifugal tendencies was the consolidation of national monarchies and, in Italy, of city-states or communes governed by elected councils of the high bourgeoisie. Monarchs and republicans had their theoreticians—the corpus of lawyers, scholars, and theologians, such as Marsilius of Padua, Pierre DuBois, John Quidort, and William of Ockham—whose task was to rationalize the dismantling, or at least the limiting, of ecclesiastical power in the temporal sphere. The English Protestant Reformation was still more than a century in the future when Christine de Pizan died, but already in the thirteenth century the nobles of France had formed a society for the disendowment of the church.

On the intellectual scene, philosophers of the *via moderna*—the revolutionary new "nominalistic" logic—were well established at the universities of Europe and nowhere more firmly or more notoriously than at the University of Paris. They challenged the certainty of orthodox doctrine on such basic questions as creation *ex nihilo* and transubstantiation. The goodness of God and even His existence were interrogated as logical propositions and found wanting. In science the diurnal rotation of the earth was already proposed by Nicolas Oresme, economic adviser to Charles V and a colleague of Christine de Pizan's father. Yet while Tommaso da Pizzano stuck with astrology, the work of Oresme in physics and astronomy anticipated that of Copernicus and Galileo.

Socially, feudalism was dying, stifled by the efflorescence of international commerce and the political and economic demands of the urban bourgeoisie. The order of the day was social mobility both vertical and horizontal: that is, changes in social rank and travel. Symptomatic of these changes were major revolts in every European country and involving every social class: peasants, artisans, bourgeois, university intellectuals, even aristocrats. I list a few of the best-known of these insurrections to give the flavor of the period, but each is only the tip of an iceberg, preceded and followed by decades of struggle that often erupted into strikes and lockouts, sit-ins and occupations, armed confrontation and guerrilla warfare.

There was the great antifeudal revolt of English peasants and artisans in 1381, which nearly took London. There was a workers' government in Florence for six weeks during 1378 when textile workers—the Ciompi—demanded reform of labor legislation and the right to participate in municipal government. There was the people's militia in Flanders led by the wealthy merchants Jacob van Artevelde and his son Philip, who twice during the fourteenth century ousted the count of Flanders. There was the guildsmen's overthrow of the city government of Freiburg in Germany in 1388.

In France—mother of revolutions—the normal tensions of the transition period were exacerbated by war with England and by a ruling elite whose self-indulgence turned every holiday into a national financial disaster. The country was in a constant turmoil that during the lifetime of Christine de Pizan coalesced into several nationwide insurrections. The Jacquerie, the great national peasant revolt of 1358, linked up with dissatisfied bourgeois in many cities who were already organizing general strikes against royal fiscal policy. The Maillotin insurrection of 1382 brought to a head months of tax riots by bourgeois and artisans in major cities, taking its name from the police mallets seized by the rebels. During 1383 and 1384 guerrilla warfare was carried on throughout the south by bands of dispossessed peasants and urban poor, the so-called Tuchins.

Christine herself witnessed and wrote about one of the most important of these insurrections, the 1413 Cabochian revolution, centered in Paris.[12] Here, a multiclass coalition (today we would call it a popular front) developed around a program of fiscal reform. The bloc was led by Jean Sans Peur, duke of Burgundy and Christine's long-time patron, who saw the reform movement as a convenient anti-Orléanist weapon. His main bloc partner was the pro-Burgundian University of Paris, official thinktank of the day. The muscle of the coalition was the working population of Paris—artisans, apprentices, servants, shopkeepers, guildsmen—headed by the wealthy guild-corporations of skinners and butchers, whose leader, Simon Caboche, gave his name to the rising. The rebels placed under house arrest princely advisers and courtly hangers-on, including fifteen of the queen's ladies-in-waiting. They forced the king to "dis-appoint" (*désappointer*) officials and re-

12. The standard study is by Alfred Coville, *Les cabochiens et l'ordonnance de 1413* (Paris, 1888; rpt. Geneva: Slatkine, 1974).

place them with the rebels' university allies; they made the king establish a committee of inquiry into abuses and proclaim a series of reform ordinances. The rebels achieved, in other words, a short-lived period of dual power. But it is typical of cross-class blocs that the threat of force, while effective, alienates the ruling-class partners, and so the nobles and the university dumped their embarrassing allies along with the reforms already won. A new coalition was formed, its slogan of "Peace at all costs" appealing to the high or "respectable" bourgeoisie who had no particular desire for fiscal reform. (It was this new party that won the sympathy of Christine de Pizan.) The reform ordinances were revoked, the corporations of butchers and skinners destroyed, and the country returned to the *status quo ante* just as the rebels had warned: civil war and economic disaster.

Such was the tenor of the Parisian life that Christine observed. Even at court, though, there was a long tradition of criticizing government and royalty, continued by—among others—Christine's fellow poets and courtiers Eustache Deschamps and Alain Chartier. Deschamps sympathized with the poor whose labor produced the country's wealth:

> This grain, this corn, what is it but the blood and bones of the poor folk who have plowed the land? Wherefore their spirit crieth on God for vengeance. Woe to the lords, the councillors and all who steer us thus, and woe to all who are of their party, for no man careth now but to fill his bags.

Chartier went so far as to give voice to the peasant directly.[13] To be a courtier, clearly, one did not have to suspend all critical faculties.

The last aspect of medieval society I refer to is the role of the urban middle-class woman, which changed, like other aspects I have mentioned, to reflect the radical social changes of the epoch.[14] From the

13. In "Le debat du heraut, du vassault et du villain," the *vilein* interrupts the other two to present the views of the peasantry on the state of society; J. C. Laidlaw, ed., *The Poetical Works of Alain Chartier* (Cambridge: Cambridge University Press, 1974). Deschamps is cited by Tuchman, *A Distant Mirror*, pp. 396–97. Kenneth Varty makes the point about criticism of government in his edition of Christine's *Ballades, Rondeaux and Virelais* (Leicester: Leicester University Press, 1965), p. 164.

14. For information in this paragraph, see Frances and Joseph Gies, *Women in the Middle Ages* (New York: Crowell, 1978); A. Abram, "Women Traders in Medieval London," *Economic Journal* 26 (1916), 276–85; Alice S. Green, *Town Life in the Fifteenth Century*, 2 vols. (Boston 1894; rpt. New York: Blom, 1971); Sylvia Thrupp, *The Merchant Class of Medieval London* (Chicago: University of Chicago Press, 1948);

eleventh century, expanding mercantile and manufacturing capital had called more and more women into the labor force and given them numerous legal and social rights (to be lost during the Renaissance). In Christine's day the bourgeois woman owned, inherited, and bequeathed property independent of her husband; she sued and was sued in court; she lobbied Parliament; in some cities she held minor public office, in others voted in municipal elections. She apprenticed, worked in, owned, and operated virtually any trade or profession, from apothecary to shoemaker, brothel-keeper to weaver. The huge food and textile industries were often staffed and controlled by women, who also joined the guilds of their craft. Though women were not admitted to university, they could receive education at home or at church or public schools. Some Italian women scholars gave public orations or lectures at university. The ideal of the educated woman penetrated even the literary romances of the day: some of them present a heroine skilled in languages, literature, and science.

In the late Middle Ages, in sum, dissent from received norms was neither impossible nor unusual. Radical ideas and practices were current in this pluralistic and seethingly modern society—but not in the work of Christine de Pizan.

She was, of course, a courtier and a foreigner. In an age of international marriages, alliances, and cultural exchange, many Italians lived and worked in France. Few can have been so intensely loyal to their employers as Christine, who—the Rosemary Woods of her day—praises her corrupt and fratricidal patrons as the most benign and humane nobility in the world.[15] When Christine, "plus royaliste que le roi," asserts it is literally a sin to criticize king or nobles—"Je dy que c'est pechie a qui le fait"[16]—she is very much in the rearguard of social thought of the period. Christine seems to think little of parlia-

---

Georges Renard, *Guilds in the Middle Ages* (1918; rpt. New York: Kelley, 1968); Barbara Kanner, ed., *The Women of England from Anglo-Saxon Times to the Present: Interpretive Bibliographical Essays* (Hamden, Conn.: Archon, 1979). On the Italian women scholars see LaBalme, *Beyond Their Sex,* and King and Rabil, *Her Immaculate Hand.* In *The Court of Richard II* (London: Murray, 1968), Gervase Mathew lists at least a half-dozen well-educated romance heroines (p. 193).

15. *Le Livre du Corps de Policie,* ed. Robert H. Lucas (Geneva: Droz, 1967), III, vii. Further citations to this work will appear in my main text, as will references to *Le Livre de la Paix,* ed. Charity Cannon Willard (The Hague: Mouton, 1958).

16. In Varty, *Ballades,* no. 118, or in the *Oeuvres Poétiques,* ed. Maurice Roy (Paris: Didot, 1886), 1:263, as no. XLIX.

ments, councils, cabinets, or any of the institutional means whereby a ruler might consult the ruled. Republican government with rotating administration, which already existed in Bologna and elsewhere, she rejects. The principle of electoralism frightens her deeply: why, if a ruler can be elected, he can also be deposed (*Policie,* III, ii)! For the Parisian reformers and their project Christine shows nothing but hatred and contempt. The *Livre de la Paix* is filled with her execrations against "le vile et chetive gent, le fol gouvernment de menu et bestial peuple" (*Paix,* II, i) who flout the will of God in their dissatisfaction with the nobility (*Paix,* III, ix and x). Even an Italian despot is better than such people, who should keep silent "de ce de quoy ne leur apertient a parler" (*Policie,* I, iii). Her sketch of a political meeting—"celle diabolique assemblee" (*Paix,* III, xi)—is nothing short of vicious. For Christine, social justice and harmony consist in each rank fulfilling its divinely appointed duties according to its divinely determined nature (*Paix,* III, x and xi). By the fifteenth century this model was sadly outmoded, completely out of touch with late-medieval social life and political theory. The image that comes to mind is of King Canute trying to beat back the tide with a broom; so Christine tries to beat back the tide of social change, of protest and nascent democracy, with her little broom of pious anecdotes and exhortations gathered from the Bible and other ancient authorities. In a time when even courtiers and clerics wanted change, Christine continues in her quiet neo-Platonic hierarchies and her feudal nostalgia.

It is not inconsistent with a static, neo-Platonic world view that Christine should consider rural laborers the most necessary social group of all and advise us to be grateful for their services. She merely repeats the truisms of classical and Christian rhetoric: Adam and Noah tilled the soil, so did some famous Romans, therefore we ought not to have contempt for those who till the soil. Besides, a life of poverty is the most morally perfect of all (*Policie,* III, x). Christine herself did not, of course, aspire to this particular form of perfection but strove mightily to avoid it. In fact her brief, edifying reflections on rural life consist of a set of literary *topoi* echoing the pastoralism then in vogue with the French nobility.[17] Perhaps Christine was among the retinue of Queen

17. As for the urban poor, her treatment is equally literary. Brian Woledge calls attention to passages in the *Mutacion* in which Christine writes vividly of the suffering of city dwellers who have been reduced to poverty by misfortune: "Le thème de la pauvreté dans la *Mutacion de Fortune* de Christine de Pisan," in *Fin du Moyen Age et*

Isabel when the latter retreated, as she often did, to her farm-estate, Hostel des Bergeries, the gift of her fond husband Charles VI, "pour esbattement et plaisance."

What about Christine as champion of women? Surely this is the arena in which, for feminists, her credentials as protofeminist are decisive. The *Cité des Dames* is usually cited as the strongest evidence of Christine's dedication to the cause of women. Here Christine offers models of female courage, intelligence, and prudence to show that women are indeed capable of these virtues and to bolster women in a positive self-image undermined by clerical misogyny. The aim is laudable, but it is surely minimal given the already prominent role of women in medieval social life. Moreover, in several ways the text subverts its own "subversion." We are told of ancient warriors, queens, goddesses, and scholars, and of a few present-day noblewomen said to be of surpassing virtue. But for all the book's valorization of female strength and ingenuity, we hear of no modern working woman, whether rich or poor. The sole exception is a painter, Anastasia, who illuminated some of Christine's manuscripts (*CD,* I, chap. xli). France was full of strong, clever, industrious, and ambitious women, but one would never guess it from *Cité des Dames*. The reason, I suspect, is that these women were of a class that Christine had little affection for—they were, after all, the realm's trouble-makers, and the considerable virtues of the bourgeois or artisan woman were lost on our arch-courtier. In the same text Christine's *porte-parole*, Dame Rayson, justifies the exclusion of women from public office on the grounds that it is not their God-given place (I, xi). Though many women were their husbands' partners, both domestically and commercially, Christine fears the implicit egalitarianism of such an arrangement, advising the married woman to submit humbly to whatever comes her way (III, xix).

In *Le Livre des Trois Vertus,* Christine ignores the independent woman of her day, presenting her only in relation to a husband's "professional conscience." It is the wife's duty to ensure her husband's honesty, especially if the husband should be a rural laborer:

---

*Renaissance: Mélanges . . . offerts à Robert Guiette* (Antwerp: Nederlandsche Boekhandel, 1961). On medieval poverty and attitudes toward it, see C. Lis and H. Soly, *Poverty and Capitalism in Pre-Industrial Europe* (London: Harvester, 1979); M. Mollat, *Les pauvres au moyen âge* (Paris: Hachette, 1978); David Aers, "*Piers Plowman* and Problems in the Perception of Poverty: A Culture in Transition," *Leeds Studies in English,* n.s., 14 (1983), 5–25.

> If your husbands work land for others, they should do it well and loyally, as if for themselves, and at harvest they should pay their master in wheat... and not mix rye with the grain.... They shouldn't hide the best sheep with the neighbors to pay the master the worst ones... or make him believe the sheep have died by showing him the hides of other animals, or pay the worst fleeces or give short count of his goods or fowl. (Laigle, p. 300, my trans.)

Thus Christine sees woman as domestically "the angel in the house," socially an agent of control on behalf of the ruling elite.

Christine is sometimes mentioned as an early crusader for the education of women. The notion is far from the truth. In reality Christine argues merely the standard Catholic truism that women are *capable* of learning. Despite her own thirst for knowledge, though, she does not recommend education for women generally, her point being that most women do not require an education to fulfill their social obligations. They need neither Latin nor scholarly texts such as Christine herself knew: vernacular romances and saints' lives will do for most girls, and only as much arithmetic as will enable them to keep household accounts (Laigle, pp. 173-86). One need not wonder what Christine's countrywoman, the learned Laura Cereta, would have thought of such a limited program. We know what her countryman Giovanni Boccaccio thought, for he denounced the narrow domestic aspirations of women—who "have in common the ability to do those things which make men famous." We know, too, how highly the fourteenth-century French theologian Pierre DuBois valued the capacities of women, for he proposed to the pope a scheme for sending a large corps of educated women into the Muslim East, to regain by propaganda and fraternization what the Crusades had lost.[18] By contrast with such ideas of her contemporaries, Christine's proposals seem timid at best.

18. Boccaccio, *De Claris Mulieribus*, trans. by Guido A. Guarino as *Concerning Famous Women* (New Brunswick: Rutgers University Press, 1963), p. 188 (Chap. 84, Cornificia); see also p. 220 (Chap 95, Proba). This text was a primary source for Christine's *Cité des Dames*. Pierre's scheme is mentioned by Shulamith Shahar, *The Fourth Estate: A History of Women in the Middle Ages* (London: Methuen, 1983), p. 155. A similar program was in fact established by the Bolsheviks after the Russian Revolution of 1917 in order to bring literacy and other social benefits to Muslim areas; see Gregory J. Massell, *The Surrogate Proletariat* (Princeton: Princeton University Press, 1974). Christine's failure to recommend advanced learning to her contemporaries is addressed by Susan Groag Bell, "Christine de Pizan (1364–1430): Humanism and the Problem of a Studious Woman," *Feminist Studies* (Spring/Summer 1976), 173–184. Bell seems to agree with Christine's view that "it is woman's work to keep the fabric

The last aspect of Christine's career I consider here is her part in the well-known debate on the *Roman de la Rose,* one of the most popular, influential, and durable works of the entire Middle Ages.[19] It is not difficult to see why the *Roman* has often been interpreted as a subversive text. The poem denounces numerous social ills, among them clerical hypocrisy and the perversion of justice by wealth. It propounds a rationalistic—though by no means unorthodox—Christianity threatening to conservative churchmen such as Jean Gerson, chancellor of the University of Paris and Christine's ally in the debate. It offers a fictional representation of fornication—that is, sex without benefit of the marriage sacrament—which implicitly removes sexuality from the ecclesiastical control to which it had been subjected in the ecclesiastical reforms of the eleventh and twelfth centuries: a campaign that also established clerical celibacy, persecuted homosexuality, and intensified clerical misogyny.[20]

If we can speak of a Phyllis Schlafly of the Middle Ages, surely that title belongs to Christine. Her main complaint against the *Roman* is that its author talks dirty. In a discussion of the nature of justice, Jean de Meun has Dame Raison recount the story of Saturn's fall. Raison's narration includes a reference to "les secrez membres"—specifically the "coilles" (testicles)—of Saturn, whose castration by his son Jupiter ended the Golden Age. Raison argues (as did many defenders of the *Roman*) that because all creation is good, such naming is permissible. Christine refutes this justification of obscene language: as the beauty of creation is a paradisal condition, to name the genitals is to deny the

of society intact," and the three reasons she offers for Christine's limited educational policy do not convince me: that Christine had in mind the necessity of repopulation during a period of war; that she realized most women had insufficient time to study anyway; that as a writer—an isolated woman doing "man's work"—Christine "outgrew her female friends and became estranged from the essential female network of her society." These strike me more as excuses than as reasons. See also Astrik L. Gabriel, "The Educational Ideas of Christine de Pisan," *Journal of the History of Ideas* 16 (1955) 3—21.

19. See Eric Hicks, *Le débat sur le Roman de la Rose* (Paris: Champion, 1977); Baird and Kane, *La Quérelle;* and Pierre-Yves Badel, *Le Roman de la Rose au XIVe Siècle* (Geneva: Droz, 1980).

20. See Georges Duby, *Le chevalier, la femme et le prêtre: Le mariage dans la France féodale* (Paris: Hachette, 1981). I am not suggesting that Jean de Meun advocated fornication—indeed, I tend to agree with John V. Fleming's interpretation of the work in *Le Roman de la Rose: A Study in Allegory and Iconography* (Princeton: Princeton University Press, 1969), though Fleming ignores the social context of "sexual politics" which Duby illuminates and which surely affected response to the *Roman.*

polluting effects of original sin, and hence it is an act not only socially offensive but also virtually heretical. Nor may we excuse an author because a fictional character spoke: Christine insists that an author take full responsibility for every word written. Luckily Christine did not explicitly apply this criterion to her contemporaries: Geoffrey Chaucer, for one, would scarcely have passed muster with his apologias for plain speaking (*Canterbury Tales,* General Prologue 725–46 and Fragment A 3167-86). French popular literature must have been agony for Christine: such words as "con," "foutre," "merde," "vit," and "pet" were quite common in *fabliaux,* riddles, jokes, and popular songs, even finding their way occasionally into the *chansons de geste* and other courtly literature.[21] It was not, by and large, a prudish age.

After castigating the book's use of obscenity, Christine objects to the *Roman*'s potential influence. As human nature is already inclined to evil, the *Roman* will encourage abominable behavior and dissolute living through its portrayal of unmarried love. It is a dangerous book, and all the more so for being well written. Finally, the author or his characters (for Christine, the same thing) slander women by portraying in certain episodes their love of gossip and their ability to deceive a jealous husband. (Curiously, Christine ignores numerous examples of virtuous women in the text.)

Christine's solution to the *problème de la Rose* is simple: burn the book. She proposes it not only in her letters but in a *balade,* where she self-righteously compares herself to Aristotle and Socrates, who had also been attacked for telling the truth. "Le Roman," she writes, "plaisant aux curieux, / de la Rose—que l'en devroit ardoir!" Interestingly, Jean Gerson, the most influential of the several parties to the debate, seems virtually obsessed with fire: the imagery of fire recurs constantly in his letters, in proverbs and metaphors as well as in actual recommendations. Gerson demands the flames not only for the *Roman* and for the letters of those who defend it but also for the works of Ovid, for popular songs, poems, or paintings that incite to lubricity, for homosexuals or those who practice any other "vice against nature"

21. See the collection of riddles and jokes in Bruno Roy, ed., *L'érotisme au moyen âge* (Montreal: Aurore, 1977); Charles Muscatine, "Courtly Literature and Vulgar Language," in *Court and Poet,* ed. Glyn S. Burgess (Liverpool: Cairns, 1981); Betsy Bowden, "The Art of Courtly Copulation," *Medievalia et Humanistica* n.s., 9 (1979), 67-85; Philippe Menard, *Le rire et le sourire dans la littérature courtoise*... (Geneva: Droz, 1969).

(which for Gerson included sodomy, oral copulation, and abortion). "Justice les arde!" "Au feu! bonnes gens, au feu!" he writes, in the exalted hysteria of Crusade rhetoric. Gerson's recommendations would have decimated the ranks of the church and society at large, as well as a good deal of medieval literature and art.[22] Fortunately neither the ecclesiastical nor the civil powers were as committed as Gerson to the salubrious ministrations of the flames.

Censorship was a genuine issue in Christine's day, and burning—of books and of people—was its most extreme expression, not common but possible. Need we recall that many of the heretics burned before and during Christine's lifetime were women, that most of the witches who would later go to the stake were women, and that Christine's heroine Joan of Arc met her death by fire? Political censorship was not unknown at the French court. In 1389 Christine's colleague Philippe de Mézières proposed a ban at court on all poets except those using moral or religious themes, and in 1395 Charles VI forbade all poets and balladeers to mention the pope or the schism. Burning had been rare in France since the extermination of the Cathars in 1330, but at the time of the *Roman* debate Jean Gerson was engaged in polemical struggle against a sect of which a group had been burned in Paris in 1372 for heresy. As Pierre-Yves Badel has shown, there was for Gerson a close association between the errors of the *Roman* and those of the heretics, particularly on the subject of sex.[23] Christine does not go so far as to demand the burning of individuals, not even Jews: she merely denounces them, endorsing Fortune's continual punishment of them, though such uncompromising hostility was neither the "official" position nor held by all educated laymen and clerics.[24] Yet Christine's advocacy of book-burning has a logic of its own that should give us

22. On homosexuality and the evolution of ecclesiastical attitudes toward it, see John Boswell, *Christianity, Social Tolerance, and Homosexuality* (Chicago: University of Chicago Press, 1980); for methods of and attitudes toward contraception, John T. Noonan, *Contraception . . .* (Cambridge: Harvard University Press, 1965).

23. Badel, *Le Roman de la Rose,* pp. 447–61.

24. *Mutacion,* 8413–42. For this reference I am indebted to the unpublished dissertation of Nadia Margolis, "*The Poetics of History: An Analysis of Christine de Pizan's Livre de la Mutacion de Fortune*" (Stanford University, 1977). Though Margolis claims Christine "was no more anti-semitic than any other Christian living in France or Italy at that time" (p. 205), see to the contrary Richard Schoeck, "Chaucer's Prioress: Mercy and Tender Heart," in *The Bridge; A Yearbook of Judaeo-Christian Studies,* 2, ed. John M. Oesterreicher (New York: Pantheon, 1956), and reprinted in *Chaucer Criticism,* 2 (Notre Dame: University of Notre Dame Press, 1960), 245–58.

pause: Gerson's intervention in this seemingly innocuous literary debate was motivated by no chivalrous gallantry but by the most conservative of political interests. And although I do not doubt Christine's sincerity any more than I do Gerson's, I do not forget that she first publicized what began as a private literary discussion and thereby effectively enhanced her career at court.

Christine's role in the *Roman* debate shows her once again less the friend of woman than of the powers that be, at their most oppressive: a position no more inevitable in her time than in ours. If Christine stood in advance of her day, it was in anticipating the prudish moralism of nineteenth- and twentieth-century literary censorship. If Christine was correct on the *Roman de la Rose,* then so were the censors of James Joyce, Henry Miller, and D. H. Lawrence. If Christine was correct, then we should not read Djuna Barnes or Anaïs Nin either. In fact it was Christine's opponents, the defenders of the *Roman*—male, clerical, arrogant, and patronizing though they were—who made the arguments that today permit us to read some of the most interesting writers, male and female, of our own time.

This completes my short dossier on Christine de Pizan, and I return now to the late twentieth century and to gender-oriented criticism. The kind of overestimation that I have tried in this chapter to correct is not limited to Christine. I note it, for instance, in some scholarship on the American feminist Charlotte Perkins Gilman, who shows interesting parallels with Christine and whom I have elsewhere characterized as "representative of a day that was drawing to a close rather than as harbinger of a day that was dawning."[25] Phyllis Rose, a biographer of Virginia Woolf, has warned against imbalanced appreciation of women writers. "Recent feminist biography," she notes, "has been challenging in exciting ways our accepted notions of major and minor. But just because an artist has been underappreciated does not mean her work is major.... This partisanship, this absence of perspective produces some outrageous statements."[26] Nor is the phenomenon limited to literary studies. In reviewing two books about activist women, the sociologist Berenice Fisher writes that "it is especially important that we do not incorporate role models uncritically. We need to examine

25. "Two American Feminist Utopias," in *Writing Woman.*
26. *New York Times Book Review,* June 26, 1983.

carefully our portrayal of women as models, to ask ourselves what message these images convey." Fisher goes on to call for "the radical social analysis that shows the objective constraints under which individual women have achieved."[27]

I believe that the data assembled here are conclusive with respect to Christine's conservatism. What doubtless remains open for some, though, is interpretation. Was Christine's view of things inevitable or predictable precisely because of "objective restraints?" Bluntly, was she forced into ultraconservatism by complete dependence on royal patrons, a dependence created by lack of opportunities for women? If so, ought we not to sympathize rather than to judge? The first is primarily a historical question, the second moral. To treat them fully would require another long paper, but I shall address what seem to me the major problems with this approach.

Historically, the position is less tenable for Christine's epoch than for those preceding and following it. The tenth century, or the sixteenth, might offer more convincing evidence, but the high and late Middle Ages did in fact open significant opportunities to women. Moreover, ultraconservatism is only one possible response to constraint; many medieval women found others. Thus women participated in the rebellions of the time, joined heretical sects, banded together in collectives to do good works (the Beguines), ran businesses, petitioned Parliament for legislative change in their industries, and regularly disobeyed the church's teachings on contraception, abortion, and sexuality.

Nor was Christine herself without resources. She might have remarried. She might have chosen to live at a convent (as in fact she would do later in life), there to continue her scholarship and social life, as was normal for well-placed convent boarders. She might have retired to the Château de Mémorant, a property given her father by King Charles V and which Christine eventually sold to Philippe de Mézières. She might have gone into business as a bookseller, a notary, or a copyist, or in some other branch of the burgeoning book industry. She might have accepted invitations from Henry IV to take up residence at the English court, where her son was companion to the young prince, or from the duke of Milan to grace his court. These invitations and refusals were made in 1400 and 1401—"even before she had begun to produce

27. "The Models Among Us: Social Authority and Political Activism," *Feminist Studies* 7 (Spring 1981), 100–112.

her major works," as Charity Willard points out.[28] In France she was supported by many members of the royal family, male and female. All this suggests that the search for patronage was considerably less urgent a matter for Christine than it must have been for many another courtly writer.

Despite the opportunities available to urban women in general, and to Christine in particular, even an exceptional woman had neither complete freedom nor complete equality with men. Nor do we today, and there can be no doubt that the special oppression of women deforms consciousness. Nonetheless, to adduce special oppression, then or now, in mitigation of reactionary social attitudes strikes me as condescending, naive, and ultimately irresponsible.

Condescending, because it implies that we should exempt women from moral or political polemic because of their gender. About Christine it implies that her stated opinions were insincere. Indeed, in its effort to exculpate Christine from the unfashionable charge of conservatism, the defense from sheer economic necessity (besides being inaccurate) paradoxically reduces her to a completely unprincipled and hypocritical opportunist. I prefer to think that she understood the choices available to her and chose as she believed. To think so preserves at least her dignity.

Naive, because the position implies that an individual can hypothetically be removed from her social environment and inserted into an ideal, ahistorical existence, one in which special oppression no longer deforms her consciousness and in which therefore her "true," "authentic" opinions can be known or guessed. In literary terms this is a version of the old sincerity fallacy. For better or worse, though, all we have is the text, and all we have is individuals in their social context.

Irresponsible, because although any opinion surely has both personal and social determinants, these do not, in my view, justify the denial or abdication of choice. Here I mean both Christine's choice and ours. To take an extreme instance: in our day the woman fascist or the woman racist can be understood; the special oppression of women is doubtless relevant to her position; but then what? or even so what? If we do not accept a passive-deterministic attitude toward life, then we ought not to gloss over reactionary views, though they be voiced by a woman and in the name of womanhood.

28. Willard, *Life and Works*, p. 165.

What I find interesting about the revival of Christine's reputation as proto-feminist is that it seems to reflect a much more conservative feminism than was typical of the women's movement two decades ago: a backlash, if you will, observable in academic life, among the organized left, in the labor movement, in national electoral politics. It is a telling sign of the times that Jeffrey Richards can adduce, as Christine's fellow so-called revolutionary, the humble pacifist Martin Luther King, whose slogan "If there is blood in the streets, let it be ours" was rightly denounced twenty years ago by activists of both races and varying political persuasions. But if King is your idea of a revolutionary, then the leap to Christine de Pizan is not hard to make. If the censorship of pornography strikes you as progressive social action—as it does some feminists today—then to see Christine as progressive will not be hard. If you cannot imagine any alternative to the institution of the family as it now exists, then you may well endorse Christine's admonitions to women. And if you believe that the special oppression of women—even the exceptional woman—foredooms women to conservatism, then Christine's conservatism will appear perfectly "natural."

But I suggest another model in keeping with the metaphor of "mothers to think back through" with which I began. We learn from our mothers in various ways, not exclusively by imitation.[29] We also learn by struggling against them, by coming to terms with our ambivalence about them, by making the effort to understand historically their success and their failure.

29. My thanks for this perception to Sandra Gilbert, who heard an earlier version of this paper.

# PART III

# *The Reader*

# Affective Criticism, the Pilgrimage of Reading, and Medieval English Literature

PETER W. TRAVIS

It is more than a slight understatement to assert that scholars of medieval English literature have not been centrally engaged in contemporary critical theoretical debate. In the titles of the most recent medieval English literary studies, for instance, one rarely finds a term or metaphor suggesting indebtedness to any structuralist or poststructuralist critical theory. Similarly, the notes of these studies rarely yield even a passing recognition of such critics as Barthes, Jameson, Lacan, Kristeva, de Man, Derrida, Poulet, Hartman, and Gadamer. Yet such theoretical conservatism is to be found less uniformly in the scholarship of other medieval literatures. One need mention only the French medievalist Paul Zumthor, the German medievalist Hans Robert Jauss, and the Italian medievalist Umberto Eco to recognize that English medieval scholarship is anomalous in not having produced a critic who contributes significantly both to the study of medieval texts themselves and to the evolution of contemporary critical discourse. The reasons behind the apparent xenophobia of medieval English literary criticism are many, and several respectable arguments in defense of this parochialism could be advanced. In fact, medievalists should all be experiencing a peculiar kind of *déjà vu* as they observe the ongoing modern critical debate brought on by the perceived divorce of words from their referents: the classical *res-verba* covenant of a logocentric aesthetic, tried and tested by various medieval poets, is now dissolving into an uncentered vision where the man-made logos has no apparent stable or stabilizing significance. Yet the very fact that medievalists can recognize the redeployment of various medieval linguistic problems and the replication of certain medieval philosophic issues suggests that modern theoretical discourse not only derives from, but is partially applicable to, medieval literary aesthetics.

My concern in this essay is to argue the natural application to medieval literature of what, in general terms, I will call affective criticism—criticism that emphasizes the prominent role of the reader or audience in determining the meaning of a literary or dramatic work of art. Reader-response criticism, as employed by Stanley Fish, Wolfgang Iser, Norman Holland, and others, pays scrupulous attention to the reactions of an individual reader as he or she gradually proceeds through a text in time. Whereas earlier twentieth-century scholarship had accorded either to the author or to the text itself the power of determining meaning, reader-response criticism focuses upon the role of the reader as the ultimate authority in determining a text's significance. This reader tends to be ahistorical or modern and may be either "real" (as in Holland's psychological studies) or "ideal" (as in Fish's projections of his own reading experiences as exemplary if not universal). At the other wing of affective criticism is *Rezeptionsästhetik,* which likewise assumes that artistic meaning is determined by the way a text is received by its audience. But unlike reader-response criticism, *Rezeptionsästhetik* emphasizes the historicity and alterity of literary works from the past. Despite a work's historical otherness, however, Hans Robert Jauss, the leading proponent of *Rezeptionsästhetik,* believes that the role of a general audience contemporary with a medieval work can be adequately reimagined.[1]

Both forms of affective criticism are, I believe, explicitly inscribed in the strategies of various kinds of medieval literature. Reader-response criticism naturally suits the more bookish and self-reflexive literary forms, and *Rezeptionsästhetik* more appropriately obtains to oral and dramatic forms addressed to a large public audience. Rather than undertake a sustained application of affective criticism to one work, in

1. A full, annotated bibliography of reader-response and *Rezeptionsästhetik* critical works is included in Jane P. Tompkins, ed., *Reader-Response Criticism: From Formalism to Post-Structuralism* (Baltimore: Johns Hopkins University Press, 1980), pp. 233–72.

this essay I intend to accomplish three things: first, to demonstrate ways that certain medieval literary works foreground the role of their viewers and readers as cocreators of artistic meaning; second, to suggest ways that these works resist or undercut a straightforward application of various kinds of affective criticism; and third, to outline one way that reader-response criticism, with its ahistorical and individualistic commitments, can be integrated with a *Rezeptionsästhetik* emphasizing the historical contextualizations of a more general, and generic, interpretive experience.

One need turn only to Chaucer to find that the power of the reader to create a text's meaning is not a modern discovery. In Book III of *Troilus* the narrator actually beseeches the reader to rewrite his story:

> For myne wordes, heere and every part,
> I speke hem alle under correcioun
> Of yow that felyng han in loves art,
> And putte it al in youre discrecioun
> To encresse or maken dymynucioun
> Of my langage, and that I yow biseche.[2]

As he explicitly encourages his readers to modify and displace his authorial words, feelings, and narration with their own, Chaucer is indirectly asking them—through his narrative persona—whether in fact such a rewriting of his tale is not precisely the interpretive process in which they have been already and always engaged. Chaucer's understanding of his readers' creative contributions to the *sentence* of his own narrative is a perception that modern reader-response critics share. There is no such thing, they argue, as a purely autonomous text containing a stable authorial intention whose significance the reader passively receives in a distilled extrapolation called "meaning." "Rather than intention and its formal realization producing interpretation," Stanley Fish has written, "interpretation creates intention and its formal realization by creating the conditions in which it becomes possible to pick them out."[3] Throughout his career Chaucer was unusually sensitive to and concerned about the power of established interpretive schemes to define the form of his poetry and its perceived *entente*.

2. *Troilus and Criseyde* III, 1331–36, in *The Works of Geoffrey Chaucer*, ed. F. N. Robinson, 2d ed. (Boston: Houghton Mifflin, 1957), p. 435.

3. Stanley Fish, *Is There a Text in This Class? The Authority of Interpretive Communities* (Cambridge: Harvard University Press, 1980), p. 163.

Because of this sensitivity, and because of the malleability of his own verbal medium, Chaucer often foregrounds in his own poetry a heightened awareness of the subtle chemistry of the reading process, as text and reader interpenetrate in a mutual act of interpretation and transformation.

Not only does Chaucer directly call attention to his readers' habit of collectively rewriting his own narrations, but elsewhere in *Troilus* he dramatizes the fact that each one of his readers is involved in a private interpretation deeply colored by past personal experience. Using the "thou" form rather than the "yow," Chaucer in the Proem to Book II singles out individuals in his audience:

> Ek scarsly ben ther in this place thre
> That have in love seid lik, and don, in al;
> For to *thi* purpos this may liken *the,*
> And *the* right nought, yet al is seid or schal.[4]

Addressing one listener who may respond to his narrative with pleasure and then another who may respond with an equal amount of displeasure, Chaucer articulates the same artistic dilemma that Lou Myers portrays in his celebrated "reader-response" cartoon: a woman reads a book while two men read over her shoulders—one laughing hysterically, one weeping voluminously, while she reads soberly on.[5] Chaucer recognizes that—like the book in the cartoon—his text is likely to generate as many different readings as there are listeners in his audience. The reason for this, he implies, is that each of his auditors has lived and loved differently. "Scarsly ben ther in this place thre / That have in love seid lik, and don, in al"; scarcely, therefore, are there three who will respond identically to the same love narrative. The main reason Chaucer so highlights the plurality of his text's interpretations, it could be argued, is that he wishes to confront his audience with the nature of their readings. Yet Chaucer's clear understanding that the *entente* of one's poetry is defined ultimately by the creative (mis)prisions of one's audience is a perception not only fundamental to reader-response theory but fundamental also to the strategies of narration so distinctive of Chaucer's own poetic style.

4. *Troilus and Criseyde* II, 43–46, my emphasis.
5. Reprinted on the cover of Tompkins, *Reader-Response Criticism.*

Such strategies as Chaucer's many uses of irony and ambiguity, his various manipulations of generic form and narrative personae, all grant to the reader an unusual freedom as a creative participant in the process of making poetic meaning. These strategies Chaucer has also designed, and integrated, in such a way as to accord to his reader a considerable amount of responsibility in choosing how to "rede aright." To guide the reader in the direction of right reading, Chaucer in each of his longer works intimates the outlines of a "mock audience"—a caricature reader whose interpretive habits any "ideal" reader would wish to escape from by developing a more refined and self-critical set of interpretive norms. To delineate fully the role of Chaucer's reader ("mock," "real," and "ideal") would be an ambitious undertaking, requiring not only a reader characterization evoked from each poem's mode of address but also an outline of the reader's progress from the text's beginning to its end. If successful, however, such a critical enterprise would in my opinion manage to approximate the intended effect of Chaucer's poetry more closely than any other form of critical analysis currently in use.

One reason Chaucer's poetry is so patently open to reader-response criticism is that it is highly conscious of itself as linguistic artifice and of its readers' role as coconspirators in the art of making fiction. Chaucer's poetry, in other words, is for its era unusually self-reflexive. For this very reason, I now turn away from Chaucer to consider the applicability of affective criticism to the kinds of literature that men and women of the Middle Ages were accustomed to experience. This literature is often "naive" and "propagandistic": it addresses its audience not as readers but always as auditors; it thinks of itself not as "art" but rather as a performance designed to effect in its listeners a positive and therapeutic effect. As is confirmed by such diverse evidence as the poetry handbooks of the medieval universities and the poetics-in-practice of the Franciscan lyrics, the liberal art to which medieval literature was most closely aligned was rhetoric: like rhetoric, poetry is a series of affective and suasive tropes directed at an audience whose thoughts and emotions are meant to be evoked, charged, and transformed. Because of its primary concern with social efficacy, then, medieval literature generally speaking fits into that category which R. G. Collingwood has called "magical art": "a representation where the emotion evoked is an emotion valued on account of its function, and fed by the generative or focusing magical activity into the practical life that needs it."[6]

Collingwood, however, disregards the audience as itself an active part of that generative activity: the identity of the audience and the nature of its participation both valorize the "magic" of the art-event. Or, in slightly different terms, each work of medieval literature was a speech-act whose full significance can now be recaptured only by reconstructing the original audience and its involvement in the experience of the literary event. There are, I believe, essentially three ways of reconstructing that audience and its role. The first brings together all the available historical information to try to read the work from the perspective of its target listeners: *The Wanderer,* for instance, is one poem if it was addressed to a recently Christianized eighth-century *comitatus* group and another if it was written for a tenth-century order of monks; *The Owl and the Nightingale* could be more confidently interpreted if we knew that it was a poem written exclusively for university scholars; the fifteenth-century play *Wisdom* shifts emphasis if one believes it was composed for a London street audience, or for a wealthy manor house, or for the monks of Bury St. Edmunds on the occasion of the visit of the king of England.

Whereas this historical contextualization has been a staple of medieval scholarship for years, the second way of reconstructing the role of a medieval audience is of quite recent vintage. This is the application of anthropological methods, paradigms, and terms to the "ritual" of an audience's attending a narrative or watching a play. Only medieval drama, to my knowledge, has been examined in this light, and then only occasionally. The best such study remains C. Clifford Flanigan's examination of early Latin liturgical drama, a performance that Flanigan insists must be seen as ritual rather than drama precisely because it was so perceived by the religious congregation for whom it was originally enacted.[7] But clearly other kinds of medieval literature could be studied from a sympathetic anthropological perspective, especially from one that focused upon the audience's participation, active and imaginative, in the shared reification of the truths represented by the artistic event.

6. R. G. Collingwood, *The Principles of Art* (Oxford: Clarendon Press, 1938), p. 68.

7. C. Clifford Flanigan, "The Roman Rite and the Origins of the Liturgical Drama," *University of Toronto Quarterly* 43 (1974), 263–84.

The third approach, even though it is the most "literary," has not yet been adopted by scholars of medieval English literature. Formulated on the Continent and developed in Germany by Iser and Jauss, *Rezeptionsästhetik* contends that a work of literature is a historical event that speaks to us now only if we are able to rediscover the imperfections of the audience to which that work was originally addressed. It is to Jauss's theory, and especially to his early notion of the audience's horizon-shift (a notion he has more recently revised), that I now turn.

Jauss's thesis of horizonal change can be boiled down to a point of almost embarrassing simplicity. A change in an audience's horizon of expectation is effected when a literary masterwork succeeds in moving its audience from a presupposed to a more sophisticated aesthetic vision. In *Toward an Aesthetic of Reception,* Jauss defines two kinds of art, the first of which, "culinary art," is designed to gratify an audience's expectations with no shift in horizon. Culinary art, writes Jauss, is

> characterized by an aesthetics of reception as not demanding horizonal change, but rather as precisely fulfilling the expectations prescribed by a ruling standard of taste, in that it satisfies the desire for the reproduction of the familiarly beautiful; confirms familiar sentiments; sanctions wishful notions; makes unusual experiences enjoyable as 'sensations'; or even raises moral problems, but only to 'solve' them in an edifying manner as predecided questions.[8]

The second form of art, the masterpiece, Jauss has difficulty defining, but he implies that in most ways it is the antithesis of culinary art, even though in generations after its original reception it may be perceived, like culinary art, as confirming familiar sentiments and solving predecided questions. The masterpiece at its time of creation enjoyed neither the classical form nor those eternal truths later generations are wont to find there. Rather, Jauss argues, it subverted its original audience, undermined their expectations, and worked to effect in them a transformation to a more critical perspective. To recapture the original effect of these masterworks, modern critics must "read against the grain" to recover the very reading sensibility that the work of literature itself succeeded, over time, in transcending.

With one problem of Jauss's thesis I am quite sympathetic: its def-

8. Hans Robert Jauss, *Toward an Aesthetic of Reception,* trans. Timothy Bahti (Minneapolis: University of Minnesota Press, 1982), p. 25.

initions of the two audience-horizons must remain general and open-ended because such phenomena can be specified in detail only as they are actualized in individual works. To test Jauss's thesis, then, I consider briefly two instances of medieval religious drama that focus intently upon their audiences. The first is the twelfth-century Fleury *Visitatio,* an Eastertide liturgical drama sung in Latin celebrating the visit of the Marys to the sepulchre. This short play is a carefully constructed sequence of scenes: the three Marys seeking Christ are met at the tomb by an angel who tells them Christ is resurrected; then the Magdalene, unpersuaded, laments alone, to be convinced finally by Christ's calling her name as he appears before her in the guise of a gardener; the play concludes with Christ appearing triumphantly before his viewers, wearing his sacerdotal vestments. Throughout the play, as the stage directions clearly indicate, the lay congregation *(populum)* are directly addressed as viewers whose faith is necessary to confirm the truth of these sacred events. Having just heard the angel's words, the three Marys immediately turn to the audience *(conversae ad populum)* to share their experience: "We came mourning to the tomb of the Lord; we have seen an angel of God sitting and saying that he has risen from death." Mary Magdalene, having just been persuaded that Christ is risen in the flesh, likewise turns to the *populum:* "Congratulate me, all you who love the Lord, for . . . I saw my Lord, alleluia." And at the play's end the viewers are granted the occasion to become one with the drama as they, Christ, the Marys, and the choir all sing the *Te Deum* in unison.[9]

The Fleury *Visitatio* clearly traces within its own formal boundaries a major shift in horizon, moving from doubt to belief and from *tristia* to *gaudium.* But I suspect that Jauss (perhaps reluctantly) would categorize the play as a form of culinary art because it is not designed to subvert its audience and transform a prior "standard of taste." Rather, the play is a "reproduction of the familiarly beautiful": a reenactment of a most sacred event celebrated in a liturgical context that had changed only imperceptibly over the years. If Jauss's thesis does pertain to the Fleury play, then it must be divested of its modernist assumption that any art-form that confirms the prior beliefs of its viewers is culinary. The *Visitatio* does in fact help effect a horizon-

9. I use the edition by David Bevington in *Medieval Drama* (Boston: Houghton Mifflin, 1975), pp. 39–44.

shift in its audience, but this shift is the deepening of a traditional faith that is ever in danger of regressing into facile trust. For as the play is performed, Christ is truly dead: he was crucified on Good Friday, and all in the congregation are in mourning, hoping that the impossible may happen again and that, incredibly, he will rise from the tomb and appear in the flesh before his faithful. Where Jauss's approach is limited (and this limitation he came to appreciate in his subsequent critical writings) is in its assumption that literary history is a sequence of one-time advances, each effected by a work whose relationship to its audience is subtly adversarial. The relationship of the audience to the Fleury *Visitatio* is indeed of primary importance, for without their belief and their participation the performance would be merely a "play." But that relationship is one of shared values and interdependent trust, the foundation of which is a faith in beliefs that need never change.

My second instance of the role of the medieval dramatic audience is found, with slight variations, in three of the four extant fifteenth-century English Corpus Christi cycles. This is Christ's address from the cross, a fierce and poignant lyric that focuses unswervingly upon the viewers as themselves responsible for nailing Christ on the cross and causing his present suffering. The opening two stanzas of the Wakefield address from the cross indicate the power of Christ's words:

I pray you pepyll that passe me by,
That lede youre lyfe so lykandly,
heyfe vp youre hartys on hight!
Behold if euer ye sagh body
Buffet & bett thus blody,
Or yit thus dulfully dight;
In warld was neuer no wight
That suffred half so sare.
My mayn, my mode, my myght,
Is noght bot sorow to sight,
And comforth none, bot care.

My folk, what haue I done to the,
That thou all thus shall tormente me?
Thy syn by I full sore.
What haue I greuyd the? answere me,
That thou thus nalys me to a tre,
And all for thyn erroure;
where shall thou seke socoure?
This mys how shall thou amende?

when that thou thy saveoure
Dryfes to this dyshonoure,
And nalys thrugh feete and hende![10]

Whereas the Fleury *Visitatio* depends heavily upon its viewers as cocelebrants and active witnesses verifying the sacred truth of the dramatized events, the Wakefield *Crucifixion* assails its audience as miscreants whose brutal indifference is responsible for their Savior's emotional torment, physical suffering, and imminent death. Because the people in the Wakefield audience are made fully aware of what they are doing, the play's merciless strategies define them as even less forgivable than Christ's original, unwitting tormentors. By so brilliantly integrating the fiction of drama with its affectivist function, the play forces the viewers into a position of near-paralysis: they cannot but allow the crucifixion drama to happen, even while that allowance is dramatically interpreted as proof of their murderous guilt. Situated at the center of one of the most powerful pageants in the cycle, this address to the viewers summons forth a welter of colliding emotions, a complex mixture of pity, piety, grief, horror, guilt, and awe.

We do not necessarily have to "read against the grain" to recapture the Wakefield audience's original horizon of expectation, nor of course should we accept this audience profile as the Wakefield dramatist's fully accurate depiction of his viewers' spiritual condition. Rather, this kind of address is found in a variety of late medieval art forms and constitutes the dark side of what art historians have called the aesthetics of "affective piety": the viewer's guilt is probed by treating the viewer as a doubting Thomas, or a pagan, or an Old Testament Jew living in the age of grace. Wakefield's mock-audience profile is a savage caricature, which like all caricature may bear a disturbing amount of verisimilitude. The expected reaction of the viewers, the role the viewers are intended to play in the remaining drama, is to shift as far as possible away from this profile of spiritual indifference by responding as fully defined Christians to the many remaining events that fill out the cycle's drama of human history. Further, the viewers are expected to translate this dramatic experience into Christian actions performed in their daily lives, such as the works of corporal mercy which Christ articulates in the cycle's concluding play of the Last Judgment. Jauss's general model

10. *The Towneley Plays,* ed. George England and Alfred W. Pollard, Early English Text Society, 71 (London, 1897), pp. 265–66.

thus applies, with certain modifications; for the Wakefield cycle, despite its epic proportions, is indeed not designed as a classical, self-contained, formally complete work of art. Rather, a Jaussian study of an English Corpus Christi cycle would show how the play's various strategies of audience manipulation and participation succeed, ideally, in effecting a major shift in horizon, not only during the play but after, as the viewers define a special kind of artistic closure by grounding that new vision in their lives. As with the Fleury *Visitatio*, however, this newly realized horizon is not a radical break from past modes of interpretation; rather, it is a paradigm of the Christian life that thousands of believers had sought yet rarely achieved throughout the Middle Ages.

The antiformalism of reader-response criticism is very much in harmony with the aesthetic theories implicit in much late medieval literature, for both assume that a work of art's ultimate meaning is defined by the nature of the responses of the individuals who constitute its audience. Of course, deconstructive critics also insist that literature is open-ended and that meaning is never ultimately determined by the constraints of the text. For deconstructionists, however, the meaning of a literary text tends to recede indefinitely into a linguistic abyss. In sharp contrast to the deconstructionists' desire to prove that literature has no ultimate or stable meaning, reader-response critics tend to insist on the heuristic, even the therapeutic, value of the process of interpreting a literary work—even if that process involves a succession of corrective reinterpretations. For example, Jauss's horizon-shift is clearly a model of literature's power to effect a positive human advance. Wolfgang Iser, Jauss's compatriot, holds that the reading process "build[s] a better self through the interpretive enterprise." For Walker Gibson reading literature critically is an act that "refine[s] one's moral sensors"; for Michael Riffaterre it brings one "ever closer to the truth"; and for Stanley Fish it develops a "sharpened awareness of the mental processes the language engages us in."[11] Compared to claims made by some medieval and Renaissance apologists of poetry, these neohumanistic defenses of the value of reading literature are modest and cautious. Nevertheless, they belong to the same tradition as their forebears and stand as twentieth-century aesthetic positions still defending the significant interdependence of audience and text as subjects and objects of a useful (albeit not salvific) communicative enterprise.

11. All quotations taken from Tompkins, *Reader-Response Criticism,* pp. xv-xvi.

That affectivist critics so often discuss only the Ideal Reader (usually a transparent extension of themselves) is one complaint leveled against their methodology. Another valid complaint is that they often tend to look at works of literature through either one end or the other of a telescope. Jauss, for example, will define the horizon-shift of a great masterpiece in a few paragraphs, while Fish is capable of taking up several pages scrutinizing the experience of reading a single sentence. For long and complicated works of medieval literature, it would be advantageous to develop a middle ground of affectivist interpretation: set half-way between the very general and the extremely specific, this proposed interpretive method would focus upon the "real reader," who is of course a hypothetical construct shilly-shallying in that large area between the mock reader and the ideal. This real reader makes only sporadic progress in understanding the work, being easily diverted, often sentimental, given to *longueurs* of boredom punctuated by spurts of passionate interest. To trace this reader's progress requires a critic's close reading both from the reader's perspective and from the perspective of an author aware of the real reader's uncanny ability to miss the main point. For a critic to move from this close appreciation to a middle-ground critical perspective, it may often prove fruitful to consider the variety of available literary genres through whose conventions a specific work may be read. In his study of *Piers Plowman*, for instance, Morton Bloomfield suggested that six major literary and religious genres informed the construction of the poem.[12] A reader-response analysis of *Piers* might trace the real reader's pilgrimage through the poem by reading its historical narrative from a perspective dominated by one generic vision. If the critic were a member of the liberal wing of modern reader-response criticism, this reading would be proffered as one of many equally valid interpretations of a polygeneric and pluralistic text. If the critic were less liberal, however, this partial perspective would be seen as one horizon of expectation that the poem appeals to but seeks gradually to transform into a more sophisticated generic vision. The real reader's progress then becomes a halting pilgrimage that manages in a middling way to comprehend the integration of less familiar genres but never succeeds in understanding adequately the horizon toward which the work is pointing.

12. Morton W. Bloomfield, *Piers Plowman as a Fourteenth-Century Apocalypse* (New Brunswick: Rutgers University Press, 1962), p. 10.

The image of the pilgrimage, a standard medieval metaphor of man's life, can, I think, be usefully employed as a paradigm of the reader's progress through many medieval literary works. The pilgrimage model I am specifically referring to is a generic hybrid itself, a conflation of the fall of man and the return of the prodigal son. This popular narrative form was given early expression in *Parabola I* (attributed to Bernard of Clairvaux) and is amplified in various later medieval poems, such as Lydgate's *Reason and Sensuality* and *The Pilgrimage of the Life of Man*. In broad outline, the pilgrim-Everyman figure falls from grace, supplants his reason with his worldly passions, and wanders into a strange land of inverted identities (the "land of unlikeness") where he is tempted by various human vices, assumes outlandish clothes as part of a transformed self, and finally approaches satiation and despair. At the eleventh hour a semidivine figure helps restore his reason and guides him to a virtuous castle within which he may seek grace and forgiveness. In his excellent recent study of this Bernardine trope, Edgar Schell traces its various implementations in five medieval and Renaissance plays, beginning with *The Castle of Perseverance* and concluding with the trope's tragic undoing in the figure of King Lear.[13]

This pilgrimage model can be shifted from literary protagonist to literary reader so as to serve as a general pattern of the progress of the individual through the reading experience. When the narrative fiction is at the very least a distant simulacrum of salvation-history (and many longer medieval works are), this reading model is even more appropriate. Beginning with images of the fall, closing with restoration and judgment, such narratives vary most dramatically in their middles: some adhere closely to the world-history archetype, others take the Christian life as their model, others wander into a world of bivalent imagery, false gardens, allegorical figures, twisted tropes. As Bernardine pilgrim the reader is drawn into this middle world of verbal and visual space and must read these images (sacred or profane) as both likenesses and unlikenesses, as appealing guises masking his own features and projecting his own errant progress toward judgment.

One of the most dramatic moments in the land of unlikeness is the penultimate one when Everyman sits—sated and dumb and careless—wondering what else life holds in store. Then, suddenly, the voice of

13. Edgar Schell, *Strangers and Pilgrims: From "The Castle of Preservance" to "King Lear"* (Chicago: University of Chicago Press, 1983).

spiritual authority speaks. In the English morality plays the audience shares the power of this moment from their own vantage as viewers, for typically they are by now glutted with the distracting but ultimately wearisome carryings-on of the figures of vice. The voice of truth breaking into their play-world is nevertheless a dramatic shock—chilling, comforting, harrowing. In medieval works whose interior mimetic design does not conform neatly to the Bernardine pilgrimage, this arresting moment is yet central to the audience's experience. Consider two different cases. In the English Corpus Christi cycles, this penultimate moment intervenes between history past (concluding with Pentecost) and history future (the Last Judgment). Up through Pentecost the viewers had been observing the experiences of historical individuals who for all their immediacy were somewhat removed by their pastness and their otherness. Then, suddenly, timeless and generic human figures embracing the audience and all humankind are summoned to final judgment. At that judgment, Christ explains to the saved and damned souls that he, in whose image they were made, was himself to be found "disguised" in many human figures of history. Retrospectively, then, and guiltily, the audience must reinterpret the play as having contained human images reflective both of themselves and of their relationship to their Savior. For all its historical verisimilitude, then, the play was a kind of "land of unlikeness" containing disguised images of the viewers' own states of ill and well-being.[14]

Consider also the *Canterbury Tales* and specifically the head-link to the Manciple's Tale, when the Cook falls off his horse dead drunk. Like the vice figures in the morality plays, whose cure for sensual indulgence is more sensual indulgence, Harry Bailley forces the Cook to drink even more wine to freshen him up; weirdly, the Cook is able to right himself, although he is still too drunk to speak. What follows this, perhaps the most distasteful scene on the Canterbury way, is the Manciple's Tale, which is not a clear-voiced summons to repentance but a gross burlesque of wisdom literature uttered by one of the most cynical of the Canterbury pilgrims. Yet all the tale's topics are appropriate: the power of words, vicious conduct, the effect of truth-telling, physical metamorphosis, poetry, rage, self-delusion. If one constructs

14. The Chester cycle takes this exploration of images one dramatic step further in the stage-figure of Antichrist. See my *Dramatic Design in the Chester Cycle* (Chicago: University of Chicago Press, 1982), pp. 223–54.

a reading pilgrimage through the *Canterbury Tales* to this point and views the tales—their various genres, voices, and guises—as a poetic land of unlikeness in which the reader has failed to discover his similitude, the fierceness of feeling behind the Manciple's Tale may seem urgently appropriate. A grotesque travesty of the Bernardine moment when Wisdom calls her errant darling to reason, the Manciple's Tale may for the reader-pilgrim possibly succeed—for all its unlikeness—where a sermonic address would have failed.

If my real readers should respond to this short defense of affectivist criticism with a mumbled "We knew most of this stuff already," I have made my point, for the initial horizon-shift I am proposing in the critical study of medieval literature is extremely modest, perhaps little more than the emboldened use in scholarship of certain pedagogical strategies already used in the classroom. Because of the lasting influence of New Criticism and the mid-century distrust of subjectivity it embraced, scholars of medieval English literature still are often unwilling to speculate about anything they believe is not patently in the text. Yet, ironically, American reader-response criticism developed directly out of New Criticism, taking New Criticism's fascination with irony and ambiguity one logical step further to examine the affective and temporal decoding and recoding of those linguistic and literary devices. With its object of study a literature that habitually addresses its readers and viewers, medieval scholarship should be ready to embrace many of the methods of reader-response criticism; but because the historical alterity of those readers and viewers constitutes a major hermeneutical issue, medieval scholarship should be prepared to refine some of the methods of *Rezeptionsästhetik* criticism even while blending them with the stategies of affectivist scholarship. In time, perhaps, the grafting of these two critical methods will lead medievalists toward exploring some of the headier forms of poststructuralist theory. And in time, perhaps, such an exploration would generate a distinctive school of literary criticism, a school native to the field of medieval English literary studies and particularly responsive to its medieval and modern needs.

# Hermeneutics of Reading in the *Corbacho*

MARINA SCORDILIS BROWNLEE

If a critical methodology is to be useful in the decoding of literature, it must account for the disparity of interpretations—diachronic as well as synchronic—which any text inevitably undergoes. Why do two eras (not to mention two contemporaneous readers, or even one reader rereading the same work) yield such divergent results?

One of the most promising recent critical formulations to focus on this interpretive relativism is literary hermeneutics. Like its etymon Hermes, mediator between the gods and men, hermeneutics involves both reception and transmission mediating between a text viewed as self-referential system and as participant in an extratextual system—another mind, another era, an alien discourse.

In considering both the evolution of hermeneutics and the particular relevance of this critical discipline for the study of medieval literature, Eugene Vance makes an important distinction between medieval and modern hermeneutics: "When modern critics, whether structural or hermeneutical, speak of 'narrative' they seem to take for granted, first, that they are referring to an object of science that exists as some kind of universal in human culture and, secondly, that the object of their science is perfectly distinct from the cognitive instruments brought to bear upon them by the perceiving subject . . . [Yet] the performance of narrative in the Middle Ages was *not* understood as being distinct from what we might call a 'structural' or 'hermeneutical' performance."[1] Narration and interpretation were perceived as one and the same act. Hence Augustine could devote the last four books of his autobiographical *Confessions* to an exegesis of Genesis in a way totally integral to the medieval way of thinking and reading, although modern readers frequently (and anachronistically) view this exegetical material as extraneous to the autobiography, or at least as optional.

The virtue of hermeneutic criticism, more broadly speaking, is that it incorporates valuable structuralist principles of analysis while at the same time reinstating the primacy of referentiality, which the structuralist model neglects. Reader-oriented criticism acknowledges the inescapable fact that literature and its reception are culturally determined, that there is no such thing as an autonomous text.

In this context, Wolfgang Iser and others have devoted considerable attention to the "logic of reading": its conditions, processes, and effects.[2] This research has resulted in a new awareness of reading as temporally determined yet as both linear and circular in nature. While reading from the first to the last page of a book is an undeniably linear procedure, it is not merely cumulative but also cyclical: the reader is constantly reading retrospectively as well as prospectively. Connections, assumptions, and speculations are progressively being revised and adjusted to conform to the additional accretions of information yielded by further reading. Beyond this synchronic type of temporal mediation of the reading process by the individual reader is a diachronic, historico-cultural factor in textual interpretation. The informed reader of any era draws on a storehouse of tacit knowledge of communication in general, and literary conventions in particular. If we read a current advertisement for a "user-friendly" computer, we do not anticipate that the computer possesses a human affect. Similarly, when Cervantes wrote "In a certain village of La Mancha, which I do not wish to name, there lived not long ago a gentleman," he does not refuse to identify the village for fear of compromising its inhabitants. Rather, his omission stems from a desire to defy the relentless neo-Aristotelian insistence on precision of detail in the act of narration.

1. Eugene Vance, "*Pas de Trois:* Narrative, Hermeneutics, and Structure in Medieval Poetics," in *Interpretation of Narrative,* ed. Mario J. Valdés and Owen J. Miller (Toronto: University of Toronto Press, 1981), p. 119.

2. Wolfgang Iser, *The Act of Reading* (Baltimore: Johns Hopkins University Press, 1978), and "Narrative Strategies as a Means of Communication," in Valdés and Miller, *Interpretation of Narrative,* pp. 100–17.

Such ability to decipher various codes illustrates what is meant by "literary competence." It involves knowledge of particular kinds of discourse as well as certain literary categories, and its features may vary radically from one historical epoch to another. All authors assume some form of literary competence on the part of their readers. The language used by a given writer implies one range of possible audiences rather than another. A particular implied reader is thus necessarily encoded in any individual text. Yet granted that we acknowledge such uniformity of readership (the informed readers' shared familiarity with the "givens"—the linguistic, generic, and social parameters of what they are reading), why, then, do texts persistently generate such a multiplicity, indeed disparity, of meanings? In part this interpretive divergence stems from the obvious fact that diachronically different audiences vary tremendously, each one identifying certain conventions of literature as dominant and others as recessive. Romanticism grafted textual interpretation upon the biography of the author, New Criticism anchored itself in the autonomy of the text, just as reader-response theory privileges an epistemology of the reader.

This perennial, ultimately irreducible margin of interpretive relativism on both the diachronic and the synchronic planes results from the omnipresence of textual "gaps" or "indeterminacies," facets of the text which are dependent upon the individual reader's interpretation. It is in recognition of this indeterminate dimension of the text that Tzvetan Todorov distinguishes between "signified" and "symbolized" facts: "Signified facts are *understood:* all we need is knowledge of the language in which the text is written. Symbolized facts are *interpreted;* and interpretations vary from one subject to another."

Todorov illustrates this difference by positing four stages in the reading process:

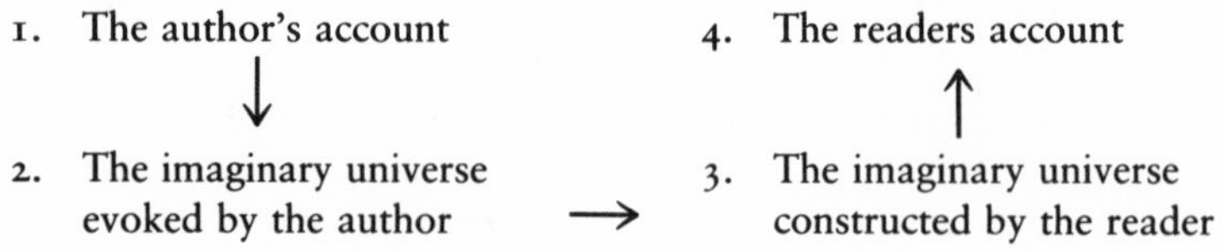

| | | |
|---|---|---|
| 1. The author's account | | 4. The readers account |
| ↓ | | ↑ |
| 2. The imaginary universe evoked by the author | → | 3. The imaginary universe constructed by the reader |

Accordingly, "the relationship between 2 and 3 . . . is one of symbolization (whereas the relationship between stages 1 and 2, or 3 and 4, is one of signification)."[3]

3. Tzvetan Todorov, "Reading as Construction," in *The Reader in the Text,* ed. Susan R. Suleiman (Princeton: Princeton University Press, 1980), p. 73.

I propose here to examine this critical interpretive space between the imaginary universe posited by the author and the reader's reconstruction of it. My chosen context is the fifteenth-century Spanish *Corbacho*, written by Alfonso Martínez de Toledo, Archpriest of Talavera.

Talavera—notorious as the arch-misogynist of medieval Spain because of this book—based his text of 1438 on Book III of the *De amore* of Andreas Capellanus. Three related factors lead to this conclusion. Both texts are treatises that overtly juxtapose the two fundamental (and seemingly irreconcilable) medieval authorial stances toward woman: her idealization, as articulated in the idiom of courtly love; and her condemnation, based on biblical and patristic discourse. These radically opposed perspectives on the love of women form the two poles in the dialectically structured texts of both the Archpriest and Capellanus concerning love, its nature and its effects. In addition, the *Corbacho* bears the subtitle "Reprobación del loco amor," which mirrors the title of the *De amore's* third book, "De reprobatione amoris."[4] Finally, as Per Nykrog observes, the *Corbacho* contains numerous textual reminiscences of Book III of the *De amore* "up to the point where he starts out on the Ten Commandments and the Seven Sins, [the Archpriest] must have written with Andreas' book under his eyes; on every other page there is a borrowing and these hidden quotations appear in the same order as they appeared in *De amore*."[5]

Despite the acknowledged filiation of the *Corbacho* to the *De amore*, however, the precise extent to which Capellanus's misogynistic third book informs the Spanish text continues to provoke considerable controversy. Some see the influence of Capellanus more or less throughout,[6] others see it only in the first half of the *Corbacho*,[7] while still others see it exclusively in Part I.[8] In short, no consensus exists. The matter

4. In point of fact, it is quite possible that Talavera did not label his work "Reprobación del loco amor." The Spanish subtitle has been included in all printed editions, although the only surviving contemporary copy (by Antonio de Contreras—a defective copy of 1466) does not contain the subtitle.

5. Per Nykrog, "Playing Games with Fiction: *Les Quinze Joyes de Mariage, Il Corbaccio, El Arcipreste de Talavera*," in *The Craft of Fiction: Essays in Medieval Poetics*, ed. Leigh A. Arrathoon (Rochester, Mich.: Solaris, 1984), p. 445.

6. Erich von Richthofen, "Alfonso Martínez de Toledo und sein 'Arcipreste de Talavera,' ein kastilisches Prosawerk des 15 Jahrhunderts," *Zeitschrift für romanische Philologie* 61 (1941), 417-537.

7. David O. Wise, "Reflections of Andreas Capellanus's 'De Reprobatione Amoris' in Juan Ruiz, Alfonso Martínez, and Fernando de Rojas," *Hispania* 63 (1980), 507.

8. E. Michael Gerli, " 'Ars Predicandi' and the Structure of 'Arcipreste de Talavera,' Part I," *Hispania* 58 (1975), 438.

is complicated by the absence of consensus as to the structural division of the *Corbacho*. Many perceive the structure as being defined by four (very unequal) parts that are identified by the narrator, in addition to an independent Prologue and Epilogue.[9] Recently and to my mind convincingly, however, it has been noticed that the work in fact falls into three structural units of equal length: the first part consisting of the Prologue and Book I; the second, Books II and III; the third, Book IV and the Epilogue.[10]

The *Corbacho*'s Epilogue is also controversial. Indeed, it is not infrequently omitted entirely from modern editions of the work. It has been interpreted as apocryphal,[11] as a belated *capatatio benevolentiae* designed to mollify outraged female readers,[12] or, at the very least, because it refutes the Archpriest's misogynistic discourse by affirming the genuine pleasures to be had from the company of women, as a calculated publicity gimmick.[13] The very last words of the Archpriest's *refutatio* (and of the text as a whole) read: "¡ guay del cuytado que siempre solo duerme . . . e en su casa rueca nunca entra todo el año! Este es el peor daño" [Woe to the unfortunate man who sleeps alone . . . and in whose house a distaff does not enter all year long! This is the worst of all evils.][14]

Despite this clear recanting of his didactic perspective, the Archpriest (like Capellanus) is read as the author of a seriously exemplary didactic treatise. Yet it is impossible, I submit, to do so. For in moving backward

9. Joaquín González Muela, ed., *Arcipreste de Talavera o Corbacho* (Madrid: Castalia, 1970), pp. 12–14. All Spanish quotations are from this edition.

10. Colbert I. Nepaulsingh, "Talavera's Imagery and the Structure of the *Corbacho*," *Revista Canadiense de Estudios Hispánicos* 4 (1980), 335.

11. Alfonso Martínez de Toledo, *Arcipreste de Talavera: Corvacho, o Reprobación del amor mundano*, ed. Martín de Riquer (Barcelona: Selecciones Biblófilas, 1949), p. 13.

12. Von Richthoven, "Alfonso Martínez de Toledo," pp. 464–65.

13. Mario Penna is inclined to believe that the Epilogue to the *Corbacho* was very likely written by Talavera, although "che . . . possa essere apocrif[o]non e, certamente, impossible . . . la burlesca epistola finale poteva servire molto bene per vendere il libro e quindi nulla di inverosimile che il primo stampatore, o chi l'avrà coadiuvato nell' impresa, se sia inventata"[the possibility that (it) is apocryphal should not be ruled out . . . the parodic final letter could have served to sell the book and therefore, it is not hard to imagine that the first printer or his assistant would have invented it]. Penna, ed., *Arcipreste de Talavera* (Turin: Rosenberg & Sellier, 1951), p. xlviii.

14. Translations from the Epilogue are mine. All others are from *Little Sermons on Sin: The Archpriest of Talavera*, trans. Lesley B. Simpson (Berkeley: University of California Press, 1959).

and forward through the text, as the reading process necessitates, we find the authority of the clerical misogynistic stance irreparably damaged. I propose to reexamine both the extent and the function of the relationship between the *Carbacho* and the *De amore.* The Spanish text employs not simply Book III but the entire *De amore* as structural and hermeneutic model in a programmatically and architectonically conceived design—with regard both to tripartite division and to a contradictory set of exemplary discourses. In point of fact, this is a carefully structured *double inversion,* for the Spanish text reverses each of the *De amore's* three parts. We see the Archpriest employing Capellanus as a privileged model to undermine his own ostensibly misogynistic discourse—to subvert misogyny, valorizing in its place love between the sexes. Moreover, this valorization effected by the Archpriest is designed as an indicator not simply of existential preference but of epistemological truth—the potential as well as the limitations of the reading process itself.

In the texts themselves we observe several hermeneutic assumptions that the Archpriest and Capellanus have in common. First, it is important to note that each author speaks of his text as *system.* Capellanus mentions his systematic treatment early in Book I (chap. VI: *Qualiter amor acquiratur et quot modis*):

> Nunc igitur sequenti restat loco videre quibus modis amor sit acquirendus. Et quorundam fertur narrare doctrina quinque modos esse quibus amor acquiritur, scilicet formae venustate, morum probitate, copiosa sermonis facundia, divitiarum abundantia et facili rei petitae concessione. Sed nostra quidem credit opinio tantum tribus prioribus modis amorem acquiri, duos autem ultimos modos omnino credimus ab aula propulsandos amoris, sicut mea tibi suo loco *doctrina* monstrabit.

> Next it remains for us to examine in what ways love is to be gained. Some are said to teach that there are five means of winning love—namely, a handsome appearance, honesty of character, fluent and eloquent speech, abundant riches, and a readiness to grant what the other seeks. But my own view is that love is gained solely by the first three of these, whereas the last two ought in my opinion to be utterly expelled from the court of Love, as my *instruction* will in its due place demonstrate. (41-43)[15]

15. *Andreas Capellanus on Love,* ed. and trans. P. G. Walsh (London: Duckworth, 1982). All Latin and English citations are to this edition.

Similarly, the Archpriest writes that "desordenado amor es causa de cometer los siete pecados mortales, e uno non fallece que por los amantes non sea cometydo, segund verás aquí por el *proceso*" (101) [Love is the cause of our committing the seven deadly sins, for there is not a single one which is not committed by lovers, as you will see (by my *system*) (77)].

Each author thus offers a systematic treatment of the nature of human love and its relation to divine love. And although Capellanus begins by putting more stock in human than in divine love while the Archpriest starts from the other extreme, both undergo a reversal, ending up at opposite ends of the spectrum, subverting their initial premises.

Both likewise appeal to explicitly inexperienced readers. Capellanus's interlocutor, Walter, we are told in the Prologue, is unschooled in the ways of love. In like fashion the Archpriest informs us that he writes "para algunos que non han follado el mundo, nin han bevido de sus amargos bevrages, nin han gustado de sus viandas amargas, que para los que saben e an visto, sentydo, e hoydo non lo escrivo nin digo, que su saber les abasta para se defender de las cosas contrarias" (41) [For those who have not yet trod the ways of the world, or drained its bitter cup, or tasted its sour dishes. I do not write or speak for those who have done so, for their knowledge will suffice to protect them from evil-doing (11)].

For both authors, the inscribed reader is thus to be instructed, edified. By the time the reading of the text in question is finished, the reader will have internalized the proper mode of comportment and the proper values. Each text presents itself as exemplary; likewise, each one explicitly guarantees its pedagogical efficacy by its reliance on the power of reading. Yet, as we shall see, the ethical and behavioral codes advocated and articulated until virtually the end of each text are finally inverted and, therefore, subverted. In addition, these reversals are, of course, hermeneutic as well as structural—for the initially articulated principles of each text are unambiguously deflated. What Capellanus and the Archpriest seek to illustrate by such exploitation of narrative parataxis is, I maintain, the irreducible distance between *signans* and *signatum*—that is, the fact that a reader will not necessarily be persuaded by what he or she reads, that interpretation like beauty and evil is in the eye of the beholder. In their respective treatises both authors dramatize the questionable efficacy of such persuasive rhetoric.

The author who speaks from his own experience in an attempt to inform and convert others to his ethical system through the act of reading immediately brings to mind Augustine and his *Confessions,* which exerted an enormous influence in a variety of literary as well as extraliterary contexts throughout the Middle Ages.[16] Augustine figures in the *Corbacho* on three separate occasions; indeed, no Latin *auctor* is cited more frequently in the Spanish treatise. The citations from Augustine serve to refute his theory of reading, however, to undermine the status of exemplary discourse per se. Talavera recalls Augustine's belief in and appeal to man's rational faculty (specifically his memory), whose ultimate efficacy was demonstrated in Book VIII of the *Confessions* with the author's own conversion and with the metaleptic act of handing the Bible to the next reader, Augustine's friend Alypius.

The generative function of reading in the *Confessions,* as in Scripture, is dramatically illustrated at the moment of Augustine's conversion. Having just understood the relevance of a key biblical passage to his life—having for this reason undergone conversion—Augustine immediately passes the Bible to Alypius:

> Tum interiecto aut digito aut nescio quo alio signo codicem clausi et tranquillo i am uultu indicaui Alypio. At ille quid in se ageretur—quod ego nesciebam—sic indicauit. Petit uidere quid legissem: ostendi, et attendit etiam ultra quam ego legeram. Et ignorabam quid sequeretur. Sequebatur uero: *Infirmum autem in fide recipite.* Quod ille ad se rettulit mihique aperuit. Sed tali admonitione firmatus est placitoque ac proposito bono et congruentissimo suis moribus, quibus a me in melius iam olim ualde longeque distabat, sine ulla turbulenta cunctatione coniunctus est.[17]
>
> Closing the book, then, and putting my finger or something else for a mark I began—now with a tranquil countenance—to tell it all to Alypius. And he in turn disclosed to me what had been going on in himself,

16. Marcia Colish, speaking of Augustine's tremendous influence on medieval thought in general, calls him "the most profound and prolific of the Latin fathers of the Church; in the Middle Ages he became an authoritative source second only to the Bible." Colish, *The Mirror of Language: A Study in the Medieval Theory of Knowledge* (Lincoln: University of Nebraska Press, 1983), p. 7. In this context, see also the encyclopedic study by Pierre Courcelle, *"Les Confessions" de Saint Augustin dans la tradition littéraire* (Paris: Etudes Augustiniennes, 1963).

17. Saint Augustine, *Confessionum Libri XIII,* ed. Lucas Verheijen, Corpus Christianorum, Series Latina XXVII (Turnholt: Brepols, 1981). All citations are to this edition.

> of which I knew nothing. He asked to see what I had read. I showed him, and he looked on even further than I had read. I had not known what followed. But indeed it was this, "Him that is weak in faith, receive." This he applied to himself, and told me so. By these words of warning he was strengthened, and by exercising his good resolution and purpose—all very much in keeping with his character, in which, in these respects, he was always far different from and better than I—he joined me in full commitment without any restless hesitation.[18]

As John Freccero explains, "this moment points to his newly acquired vocation, for he . . . passes the Bible to Alypius, thereby suggesting that his own text is to be applied metaleptically to the reader himself as part of the unfolding of God's Word in time."[19]

The Archpriest, however, discerns a paradox in this Augustinian model. On the one hand, Augustine repeatedly states that a given reader's comprehension of a text is a function of that reader's own moral condition, hence that any text will necessarily be subject to many different interpretations. On the other, we have the Augustinian premise that the writing of the *Confessions* can work to achieve not only Augustine's salvation but that of his "universal reader" as well. The *Confessions* is presented simultaneously as a record of Augustine's personal conversion and as a paradigm for his readers, as a model or mechanism for conversion which is designed to be emulated. However, since by Augustine's own admission no universal reader exists, his text cannot logically function as a conversionary impetus for those readers who are not already thus inclined or predisposed. Although this logical discrepancy—which involves the resolution of textual gaps in a prescribed way—is not problematic for Augustine, for Talavera it is. He will replace Augustine's "mystical hermeneutics" with "logical hermeneutics."[20]

This problematization of the reading process is foregrounded by the *Corbacho*'s three explicit references to Augustine's text. In the first, Talavera takes issue with the bishop of Hippo on the above-mentioned

18. Saint Augustine, *"Confessions" and "Enchiridion,"* trans. Albert C. Outler (Philadelphia: Westminster Press, 1955). All translations are from this edition.

19. John Freccero, "The Fig Tree and the Laurel," *Diacritics* 5 (1975), 37.

20. The fourteenth-century Spanish *Libro de buen amor,* to which Talavera alludes, provides another striking example of the programmatic recasting of the Augustinian paradox. See in this connection Marina Scordilis Brownlee, *The Status of the Reading Subject in the "Libro de buen amor"* (Chapel Hill: University of North Carolina Press, 1985).

logical inconsistency. Man—Talavera asserts—if he so chooses, will not be deceived by woman, he can choose not to become involved, he is a priori aware of the deceitful behavior of the daughters of Eve. Man, therefore, does not need to learn (to be instructed) to reject such lustful inclinations, which is the underlying narrative strategy of the *Confessions*. Augustine is recalled in this connection as follows:

> sy guardarse quisiese onbre, non le engañaría muger—e aunque en esto pone dubda Sant Agostín—; mas el onbre fíase de la muger, e fiándose quiérele a las veses conplaser e dexase della engañar e vencer por la contentar. E esto es más herrar por voluntad desordenada que por falta de saber ser engañado. Destos enxenplos las mugeres tomarán plaser e se glorificarán del mal, porque las pasadas mugeres a los más sabios engañaron. (77-78)

> [Men] are not deceived because of their learning, for, if a man so desired, no woman could deceive him, although St. Augustine, to be sure, has some doubt about this. But a man trusts a woman, and, trusting her, wishes to please her and allows himself to be deceived by her—which is to err from disordered willfulness rather than from ignorance. Women take pleasure in such yarns and boasts of the tricks that the women of old played on the wisest men. (51-52)

As an illustration of this belief, the Archpriest offers the legendary example of Virgil left hanging in a basket, the helpless victim of a disgruntled female. Aristotle suffers a similarly ignominious fate [I, xvii]. Clearly education—learning—is not the issue, given the universally recognized wisdom of these two *auctores*. For Augustine, however, the fundamental premise of the *Confessions* is that education can enable us to reject our lustful inclinations. Talavera's attitude undermines the basic pedagogical strategy not only of the *Confessions* but of his own work as well, as set down in the Prologue—that is, to teach the ignorant.

Augustine is cited for a second time in yet another ostensible appeal to man's rational faculty. Here too, however, the Archpriest is minimizing the heuristic function of reading as presented in the *Confessions:*

> quien en esto pensase e fiziese cuenta en este mundo como que vee aquellas penas e las padesce, e ya en esta vida ge las dan, ¿faría tanto mal como de cada día faze? Dubda Sant Agostín en ello. Por ende, non alegue ninguno: "non lo sope, nin lo sentí, nin fuy avisado, nin me lo

> dixeron"; que sería gruesa ygnorança non saber lo que es notorio a todos. (118)
>
> If a man would only think upon this, ponder it, mourn over it, know it, remember it, have it engraved upon his heart, and keep vigil over it, evil-doing would not be possible for him. If he would bear in mind the pains he suffers in this world, would he do the evil that he does each day? St. Augustine doubts it. Let no one plead, therefore, saying: "I didn't know; I didn't hear; I wasn't warned; I wasn't told about it," because it would be gross ignorance not to know what is notorious to all the world. (96)

We see Talavera here further diminishing the validity of Augustine's exegetic method, the cognitive function of reading, while at the same time continuing to underscore his own belief in man's fundamentally irrational nature.

The third Augustinian reference corroborates Talavera's textual self-presentation as incapable of combating ignorance through "education":

> como nuestro Señor dize en el su santo Evangelio: "Señor, muchas cosas a los sabyos e prudentes de tus secrectos escondiste, las cuales a los pobrezillos revelaste, e esto porque asy plaze a Ty."
>
> E demás, por conclusión, dixeron algunos grandes letrados, santos de Dios escogidos, en especial Sant Agustín: "Veemos unos violentos onbres que el mundo los aborresce e los tyene en estima de non nada por synples, pobres, e de poca ciencia e auctorydad, que roban e arrebatan los altos cielos por fuerça e con grand furia e violencia; que non ay detenimiento en ellos. E nosotros, con todo nuestro saber e ciencia, somo[s] çabullydos en los ynfiernos."
>
> Asy que non lo pongo en conparación esto por ser tal, nin uno de los violentos, porque me pesa; byen uno de los que poco saben e la merced de Dios esperan. (177-78)
>
> As Our Lord says in His Holy Gospel: "Lord, many secret things didst Thou conceal from the wise and the prudent which Thou didst reveal unto the humble, as was Thy Will." In conclusion, many great men of letters, the saints and God's chosen, were of the same opinion, especially St. Augustine, who said: "We see in the world certain men of violence who are hated by mankind and held in small esteem by the simple, the poor, the ignorant, and the weak, who rob and ravish heaven itself with force, fury, and violence, and there is no moderation in them. And we, with all our wisdom and learning, are cast into the abyss!"
>
> I do not make this comparison because I am one of the wise or one

> of the violent, for I know well enough that I am merely one of the ignorant who hope for God's compassion. (162-63)

This undoing of the initial claim that he writes to teach his readers in a well-ordered fashion why they should eschew the love of women is clearly the work of a devious narrator. The Archpriest presents himself here not as a wise man wishing to impart his learning but as simply a man, an Everyman figure.

Additional indeterminacies in the text of the *Corbacho* show it to be the work of an unreliable narrator. As one important indicator, the only two vernacular *auctores* cited by Talavera are Juan Ruiz (whose *Libro de buen amor* he refers to as a didactic treatise, a *tractado*), and Boccaccio (as author of the *Decameron* and *Corbaccio*).[21] The works of both Juan Ruiz and Boccaccio are, as has been amply demonstrated elsewhere, playful manipulations of exemplary discourse. They offer the reader conflicting signals that cast serious doubt on their expressed didactic intent, when considered collectively, prospectively as well as retrospectively in the unfolding act of reading. Talavera carefully employs citation to privilege his hermeneutic affinity with Juan Ruiz and Boccaccio in this context. A medieval generic "tradition" of pseudo-didacticism is suggested, in which—for Talavera—Andreas Capellanus is the single most important structural model.

The preceding argument suggests that the tripartite *Corbacho* inverts the three books of the *De amore*. The overall pattern of this three-part inversion is clearly symmetrical.

Part I of both texts treats:

*The nature of human love* (THEORY)

| | |
|---|---|
| For Capellanus it is very desirable. | For Talavera it is a scourge. |

Part II of both texts treats:

*The possibility and advisability of sustaining such love* (PRACTICE)

| | |
|---|---|
| For Capellanus it is possible | For Talavera it is impossible. |

Part III of both texts treats:

21. Talavera recalls Boccaccio as a written authority on "los arreos de las mujeres, de sus tachas, e cómo las encubren" (134–35)[of the ways women deck themselves out, and of their blemishes and how they conceal them (115)], which von Richthoven attributes to the *De casibus virorum illustrium*. Yet it is more likely, given the subject matter, that Talavera has in mind the *Decameron* and *Corbaccio*.

*A rejection of the type of love advocated by the preceding two sections* (REVERSAL)[22]

| For Capellanus: Flee carnal love. | For Talavera: Woe to the man who lacks the company of a woman. |
|---|---|

In addition to this paratactic, fundamentally contradictory narrative structure, we find, not simply in the third part but also in the first two parts of *both* works, further blatant contradictions.

The *De amore*'s Book I, Chapter VI, for example, puts forth no fewer than four mutually contradictory definitions of "nobility." The first asserts:

> Nam quum omnes homines uno sumus ab initio stipite derivati unamque secundum naturam originem traximus omnes, non forma, non corporis cultus, non etiam opulentia rerum, sed sola fuit morum probitas quae primitus nobilitate distinxit homines ac generis induxit differentiam. (44)

> Honesty of character alone truly enriches a man with nobility, and makes him thrive with glowing beauty. Since all of us are descended originally from one stock and have all taken the same origin in nature's way, it was not beauty or bodily adornment or even material wealth but only honesty of character which originally brought distinction of nobility and introduced difference of class. (45)

The second definition states: "Sed plures quidem sunt qui ab ipsis primis nobilibus sementivam trahentes originem in aliam partem degenerando declinant: 'Et si convertas, non est propositio falsa'" (44) [There are indeed many whose seed is sprung from those first nobles but who have gone downhill and declined to the opposite condition; on the other hand, "Reverse the statement; it will be true." (45)]

This assertion is followed immediately by a third distinction, a discussion of social class and its various gradations of nobility: "Ad hoc imprimis istam tibi trado doctrinam, quod mulierum alia est plebeia, alia nobilis, alia nobilior. Item masculus alius est plebeius, alius est

22. For two interesting discussions of Capellanus's structure, see Irving Singer, "Andreas Capellanus: A Reading of the *Tractatus*," *Modern Language Notes* 88 (1973), 1288–1315, and Wesley Trimpi, *Muses of One Mind* (Princeton: Princeton University Press, 1983), the chapter entitled "Capellanus and Boccaccio: From *Questione* to *Novella*."

nobilis, alius nobilior, alius nobilissimus" (44) [The instruction which I now give you is especially important in this connection. Women belong either to the common stock or to the nobility or higher nobility. So too with men—they are either common, or noble, or of the higher nobility, or of the highest nobility. (45)]

This discussion ends with the introduction of a fourth—and wholly different—concept of nobility: "Praeterea unum in masculis plus quam in feminis ordinem reperimus, quia quidam masculus nobilissimus invenitur, ut puta clericus" (46) [In addition, we find one rank more in men than in women, because there is one type of man of the highest nobility, for example the cleric. (47)]

Indeed, the *De amore* abounds in such contrary pronouncements on the most fundamental of issues. Douglas Kelly focuses on several of these problematic nexuses, chief among them Capellanus's initial offering of exempla for didactic purposes (as set out in the Prologue) and his subsequent refusal to do so—in this case having to do with the courting of nuns (I, VIII). This refusal is revealing, for, as Kelly explains, it illustrates the narrator's calculatingly inconsistent, unsystematic discourse: "First [Capellanus] admits to knowing, from personal experience, how to court nuns, and thus the dangers of such a love. Second, the refusal to give any instructions runs counter to [Capellanus's] practice in the *De amore,* where he condemns various kinds of love and lovers, but at the same time is not adverse to giv[ing] pertinent information on courting, should the lover be unable to restrain himself."[23]

Here we see Capellanus questioning the very foundation of his instructional method, namely *descriptio,* a written example for his readers of that which is to be avoided.

The Archpriest voices precisely the same epistemological doubt (in I, XXIV). Referring to the existence of ten different types of jealousy in the world, he refuses to describe them for fear of disseminating evil to his readers: "omito e dexo de dezir[las] por non ser prolixo e avisador de mal fazer" (93) [I shall not describe (them), lest I be prolix and a teacher of evil (68)].[24]

23. Douglas Kelly, "Courtly Love in Perspective: The Hierarchy of Love in Andreas Capellanus," *Traditio* 24 (1968), 125.

24. Further skepticism of this sort regarding the effects of reading is voiced by the narrator, for example, in I, XIX: "loco será byen el que lo sopyere leer o lo entendyere, sy de algo dotrina non tomare de lo que aqui dyré, syquiera en parte, aunque en todo

This structure, shared by Capellanus and Talavera—simultaneously advocating and denigrating the validity of explanatory description—is paratactic, not hypotactic, in nature. It is dualistic not gradualistic, and programmatically so.[25] Moreover, this kind of structure irreversibly undercuts the ostensibly didactic narrator's credibility (his exemplary status for the reader). Because the reader must make the ultimate decision as to which discourse is to be privileged, the *reader* thus becomes the figure of authority.

Let us look more closely at the *Corbacho*. To take one of numerous examples, in Book I, Chapter IV we find Talavera asserting of men who pursue fleshly temptations that "el que a tal delectación se da en grand quantydad, pierde el comer" (74) [He who indulges in such pleasures loses his appetite in great part (48)]. However, in Chapter XXXIV he totally contradicts this statement, affirming that "el quinto pecado mortal es gula. Deste non se puede escusar el que ama o es amado de muchos excesivos comeres e beveres en yantares, cenas, e plaseres con sus coamantes, comiendo e beviendo ultra mesura" (106) [The fifth deadly sin is gluttony. He who loves women, or is loved by them, cannot avoid eating and drinking to excess with his mistress, at breakfasts and suppers and dinner parties (82)].

In a similarly problematic vein, Talavera invokes the ninth Commandment ("Thou shalt honor thy neighbor's wife as thine own") at the beginning of I, XXVIII, having argued in the fifth chapter the virtues of loving the wife of a friend or relative (González Muela 54-55; Simpson 27). On the nature of virtue, the Archpriest avers in I, VIII, that a man is either completely virtuous or completely evil, since these qualities are mutually exclusive (59; 32), while shortly thereafter, in I, XV, we are informed that continence is such a great (that is, convenient) virtue because it serves as a "cloak"—to hide a multitude of sins (73; 47).

This procedure of exposition by contradiction reaches its climax, in a sense, when we observe Talavera after lengthy criticism of women (whom he categorizes as a plague to be avoided at all costs) extolling

---

non" (87) [He will be mad who, able to read and understand what I say here, learns not some lesson from it, at least in some degree, even though not entirely (61)].

25. For a discussion of gradualism see Arthur Lovejoy, *The Great Chain of Being* (Cambridge: Harvard University Press, 1936), pp. 73–74, and Henning Brinkmann, "Zur geistesgeschichtlichen Stellung des deutschen Minnesangs," *Deutsche Vierteljahrsschrift* 3 (1925), 615–41.

the many varieties and complexities of men. Yet this discussion of male attributes becomes increasingly negative, culminating in a pointed aside to his female readers in which he exclaims: " ¡O de la loca desaventurada que tyene firmeza con todo onbre!" (189) [Woe to the mad and wretched woman who is faithful to any man! (178)]. Thus the wholesale vilification of women in favor of men is reversed, as Talavera unambiguously sides with the ladies.[26]

Contributing further to the unexemplary effect of such obviously self-contradictory diction, is the casting of the narrator in an unmistakably comical light: at places in his text he claims that he will say no more, not wishing to be liable to the charge of prolixity, a female trait. It is precisely at these junctures in the text that he rambles on.[27] Similarly significant is the fact that his proofs of a given precept become shorter and shorter as do the proofs of Capellanus as the work progresses.[28]

Beyond the *Corbacho's* ironic self-presentation as misogynistic tract to which its contradictory discourses and uncontrollable prolixity bear witness, further proof of Talavera's unreliability is provided by the narrator's remarks on the genre of his text. He boldly affirms that "non es esto corónica nin ystoria de cavalleria, en las cuales a las veses ponen c por b" (119) [This is not a chronicle or romance of chivalry, in which at times white is made black (96)]. The pairing of the two genres here is significant because neither traditionally nor by definition do they form a pair, being regarded instead as opposites: the chronicle presents itself as "truth," an accurate account in which white is presented as white and black as black, whereas the romance is an obvious fiction and presents itself as such. By allying chronicle and romance, Talavera is once more drawing our attention to his devious narrator—he *is* in fact making white black.[29]

Finally, the Archpriest provides an important, explicit substantiation of the *Corbacho*'s unexemplary self-presentation when he identifies his book as being "unbaptised," an admission that he makes in the prefatory description preceding his Prologue: "Syn bautismo, sea por

26. This reversal is further underscored, as Nykrog, "Playing Games," p. 443, observes, in that "the final 'date' given to the 'letter' is couched in astrological terms (Jupiter in the sign of Venus!)."

27. E.g., pp. 73, 110, 113–14.

28. Gerli situates this phenomenon in the tradition of sermonic strategy (" 'Ars Predicandi,' " p. 437) in the context of Part I.

29. For a different interpretation of this passage, see Nepaulsingh, "Talavera's Imagery," p. 331.

nonbre llamado "Arcipreste de Talavera" (39) [Without benefit of baptism let this book be called the "Archpriest of Talavera" (9)]. The *Archpriest of Talavera*—not technically the *Corbacho*—is the work's true title.[30] The identification of this unbaptised text as consubstantial with its wayward narrator figure, the Archpriest, moreover, accords perfectly with the unbaptised ("fallen") discourse he employs to expose the overly ambitious degree of control over reader-response which, in his estimation, any exemplary text presupposes.

All of these various structural and discursive features, along with their resultant gaps, serve—individually and collectively—to undermine for the reader the *Corbacho*'s status as exemplum, because they definitively deflate the authority of the enuciating subject. Talavera's explicit, hypotactic manipulation of the Augustinian subtext reinforces what the implicit, paratactic manipulation of the Capellanean subtext reveals—namely, the inadequacy of exemplary discourse. For the underlying premise of any exemplary text is that the hermeneutic act can be regulated, that the reader can be transformed from bad to good by the act of reading itself. And it is the fundamental limitation of this premise which Talavera's book illustrates.

We have thus come full circle, for the *Corbacho* thematizes the fact that textual indeterminacies cannot be resolved, prescribed, or predicted by didactic discourse. The problematic issues of modern reading theory with which we began are, in fact, inscribed into the dynamic structure of this late medieval Spanish text. And it is thus entirely fitting to end this essay by citing Talavera's assertion that his book will invariably be subject to radically differing interpretations:

> seré de algunos reprehendido por non saber ellos mi entición . . . porque algunas cosas pongo en práctica dirán que mas es avisar en mal que

30. "La obra . . . debe llamarse *Arcipreste de Talavera,* por voluntad de su autor, pero ha pasado a la historia con el nombre de *Corbacho,* y el subtítulo de 'Reprobación del loco amor,' a partir del incunable de Sevilla de 1498. La obra de Boccaccio, el *Corbaccio,* era conocida en España por la traducción catalana que antes de 1397 hizo el mercader Narcís Franch, pero nuestro arcipreste no piensa en ella tanto como en otros libros de Boccaccio" [The work . . . should be called *Arcipreste de Talavera,* as stipulated by its author, yet it has come down through history with the title of *Corbacho* and with the subtitle "Reprobation of Foolish Love" beginning with the incunabulum published in Seville in 1498. The work by Boccaccio entitled *Corbaccio* was known in Spain before 1397 through the Catalan translation by the merchant Narcis Franch. But our Archpriest does not have it in mind so much as he does other works by Boccaccio] (González Muela, *Archipreste de Talavera,* p. 10).

corregir en byen. Diga cada qual su voluntad . . . las que saben que ge lo entienden, de algo dello se dexarán.

Pero non piense alguno o alguna que de mí presuma que otro non aya escripto más mill vezes destas cosas que yo he dichas e diré, como so el sol non sea oy cosa nueva. (164-65)

I shall be scolded by some [readers] for setting down these things, for they will say that I teach wickedness instead of correcting it; but they are ignorant of my purpose . . . [But] if they are wise and understanding, [they] will abate their evil-doing in some degree. And let no man or woman think I pretend that what I write here has not been written a thousand times already by others, because there is nothing new under the sun. (148)

# Oral-Formulaic Rhetoric: An Approach to Image and Message in Medieval Poetry

ALAIN RENOIR

The theory of oral-formulaic composition first came into being as the result of efforts to answer the ancient question concerning the means whereby the Homeric poems had acquired the general form in which we know them today. Although a somewhat analogous hypothesis had already been suggested over three decades earlier for Old English verse, we must trace the emergence of the theory to 1928 and Milman Parry's famous studies of the *Iliad* and the *Odyssey*.[1] Over the years Parry, and later Albert Lord, went on to the comparative analysis of Homeric Greek and current oral-traditional South Slavic poetry, and in a seminal essay Francis Peabody Magoun availed himself of the theories and empirical findings of Parry and Lord to argue that the bulk of Old English narrative poetry must have been composed orally.[2] Yet it was not until 1960 and the publication of Lord's prodigiously influential *The Singer of Tales* that large numbers of linguists, anthropologists, and literary scholars began applying the theory and various modifi-

1. Milman Parry, *L'épithète traditionelle dans Homère: Essai sur un problème de style homérique* and *Les formules et la métrique d'Homère* (both Paris: Belles Lettres, 1928), in English in *The Making of Homeric Verse: The Collected Papers of Milman Parry*, ed. Adam Parry (Oxford: Clarendon Press, 1971).
2. Francis P. Magoun, Jr., "Oral-Formulaic Character of Anglo-Saxon Narrative Poetry," *Speculum* 28 (1953), 446–67.

cations thereof to all kinds of ancient, medieval, and modern texts composed in practically every language normally taught at a university.[3]

In a simplified form the theory argues that, within certain language groups, properly trained traditional oral poets come equipped with a set of flexible paradigms which are drawn from a pool common to the group's poetic tradition and function at three different but complementary levels of composition to make it possible to produce, on the spot or after a period of reflection and without access to writing materials, poems of considerable length with a controlled structure: (1) metrical, as well as grammatical paradigms which make it possible to shape practically any one-sentence utterance or part thereof into a proper metrical unit usually called a formula or verse-formula; (2) themes which act as paradigms for all kinds of mimetic situations and make it possible to select appropriate verse-formulas and organize them into coherent narrative units often called type-scenes; and (3) larger traditional topics which guide the selection of narrative units and make it readily possible to organize them into an entire narrative often called poem or song, whose duration may be adjusted to the expectations and reactions of a live audience.

To illustrate the system with a familiar text: (1) nearly every metrical unit of the *Odyssey* is demonstrably constructed on a formulaic paradigm, so that the expression "Odysseus of many devices" ("polýmetis 'Odysseýs") occurs over and over again throughout the poem (e.g., 5.214, 7.240, 12.1) and is likewise found in the *Iliad* (e.g., 3.200), where the flexibility of the system allows the poet to shift the word order to suit the requirements of the meter (e.g., 3.268: "'Odyseýs polýmetis"). (2) The scene at the end of the thirteenth book, where Athena transforms Odysseus into an old beggar, conforms to the paradigm of an oral-formulaic theme whereby a returning hero is expected somehow to avoid immediate recognition upon reaching his destination. The paradigm is likewise found under a variety of shapes in traditional South Slavic oral epics. (3) The entire *Odyssey* conforms to the paradigm of a traditional oral-formulaic topic which is also embodied in the same South Slavic epics and is known as the return song.[4]

3. Albert B. Lord, *The Singer of Tales* (Cambridge, Mass., 1960; rpt. New York: Atheneum, 1965).

4. The primary texts quoted in this essay are, in order of citation, Homer, *Odyssey*

The foregoing remarks should suffice to indicate that what I call the theory of oral-formulaic composition can be either straight empirical information or pure theory, depending on the context. It is empirical information when scholars deal with actual observations concerning the performances of live oral singers, but it is theory when they draw upon these observations to surmise how ancient anonymous poems must have been composed. When we deal with works composed under circumstances unknown, the situation is complicated by the fact that oral poets trained in the art of written composition have been known to write—that is to say, to compose in writing—poems in the style of oral-formulaic rhetoric. The result is that, whereas nearly everyone accepts the general validity of the principles of oral-formulaic composition outlined above, we have no consensus when it comes to determining whether a particular anonymous formulaic poem of the past was actually composed orally or in writing.

A vast amount of medieval poetry extant today is in the oral-formulaic style, but the fact that much of it is anonymous and provides no reliable clues about the circumstances of its composition seems at first sight to warrant our relegating the oral-formulaic approach to the status of an interesting but extremely frustrating exercise in futility. Luckily for its practitioners, however, the oral-formulaic approach of-

---

and *Iliad,* ed. and trans. A. T. Murray, Loeb Classical Library (Cambridge: Harvard University Press, 1925 and 1919 respectively); *La Chanson des Quatre Fils Aymon,* ed. Ferdinand Castets (Montpellier: Coulet, 1909); *Das Hildebrandslied,* in Wilhelm Braune, *Althochdeutsches Lesebuch,* rev. Karl Helm, 11th ed. (Halle: Max Niemeyer, 1949); *Beowulf* and other Old-English poems, in *The Anglo-Saxon Poetic Records: A Collective Edition,* 6 vols., ed. George P. Krapp and Elliott V. K. Dobbie (New York: Columbia University Press, 1931–1942); Robert Burns, "A Red, Red Rose," in *The Norton Anthology of Poetry,* ed. Alexander W. Allison et al., rev. ed. (New York: Norton, 1975); *Gunnlaugs Saga Ormstungu,* ed. P. G. Foote and trans. R. Quirk (London: Nelson, 1957); Johann Wolfgang Goethe, *Faust,* ed. Franz C. Andres (Basel: Schwabe, 1949); Christopher Marlowe, *Doctor Faustus,* ed. Irving Ribner (New York: Odyssey, 1966); Jean Giraudoux, *La Guerre de Troie n'aura pas lieu,* ed. Henri J. G. Godin (London: University of London Press, 1963); Matthew of Vendome, Poem 56 ("Description d'Hélène") in his *Ars Versificatoria,* in *Les arts poétiques du XII*[e] *et du XIII*[e] *siècles,* ed. Edmond Faral (Paris: Honoré Champion, 1958); *Das Nibelungenlied,* ed. Karl Bartsch, rev. Helmut de Boor, 12th ed. (Leipzig: F. A. Brockhaus, 1949); *Sir Gawain and the Green Knight,* ed. Israel Gollancz (London: Oxford University Press, 1940); John Lydgate, *The Life of Saint Alban and Saint Amphibal,* ed. J. E. van der Westhuizen (Leiden: E. J. Brill, 1974); John Gower, *Vox Clamantis,* in *The Complete Works of John Gower,* ed. G. C. Macauley, 4 vols. (Oxford: Clarendon Press, 1902); Marie de France, *Le Lai de Lanval,* ed. Jean Rychner (Paris: Minard, 1958).

fers much that does not depend on the actual circumstances of composition. It can make—and is making—impressive contributions in areas where it buttresses other approaches as well as in areas where the other approaches have proved partly or totally ineffective. Speaking strictly from the point of view of literary studies (in contrast to linguistic or anthropological investigation), I believe that the areas in which the approach can yield the quickest and most rewarding returns are those in which the actual mode of composition (either written or oral) is of lesser importance but the rhetorical tradition (either written or oral) is of major importance. After all, the art of writing and its literary byproducts did not replace oral traditions overnight whenever medieval monks inaugurated a new scriptorium in a district. Quite on the contrary, it seems that oral and written traditions found means of cohabiting for a period of time, and there is evidence that this was the case within the very walls of the monastery. This assumption necessarily leads one to suppose that poets could have been composing oral-formulaic poetry in writing for the benefit of an audience familiar enough with the relevant tradition of oral-formulaic rhetoric to interpret the resultant texts accordingly, and there is convincing circumstantial evidence to bolster the supposition.

Just as this argument assumes that, for the purpose of this essay, there can be such a thing as written oral-formulaic poetry, so it further assumes that written literature can be orally composed. After all, many a poet has felt inspiration when pen and paper were unavailable and has nevertheless turned out a poem whose structure and texture satisfy all the requirements of written rhetoric. The language of such poetry usually reflects the author's conscious effort to find the right words and organize them into statements capable of dealing as exclusively and effectively as possible with the specific situation at hand. In brief, it tends to reveal a striving toward originality rather than an effort to make the particular situation fit into a traditional pattern expressed through the manipulation of age-old themes and formulas drawn from a common pool; and accordingly it may not be considered part of oral-formulaic composition, regardless of the circumstances under which actual composition took place.

In contrast, oral-formulaic rhetoric reveals no concern for originality, which strictly oral-formulaic poets would almost certainly shun if they understood the concept, and it makes the particular situation fit traditional patterns. The principle stands illustrated in the fact that, as noted, both the adventures of Odysseus and those of certain South Slavic warriors are made to fit the same traditional narrative topic of the return song and that the observation holds true on the level of the theme as well. Although most extant verse-formulas are probably more recent than narrative topics and themes, the antiquity of the system may be tentatively inferred from the fact that, in addition to formulaic similarities between Greek and South Slavic texts, versions of another narrative topic have been identified in German, Irish, and Iranian, while versions of another theme have been identified in Greek, English, and German, and the process has been repeated with other themes and languages. Especially in respect to the theme, the recurrence of these oral-formulaic elements in a variety of Indo-European languages is much too frequent to be attributed to sheer accident; so we must recognize the possibility that the origins of the system may go back several millennia to a time when the Indo-Europeans had not yet subdivided into Satem and Centum groups. However this may be, the system is surely ancient enough to have originated with preliterate societies and thus to warrant the use of the compound adjective *oral-formulaic* to differentiate it from systems of written rhetoric which have developed formulas of their own.

The facts and surmises discussed thus far suggest several contributions which the oral-formulaic approach can make to the study of either oral or written medieval poetry composed within the tradition of oral-formulaic rhetoric. Perhaps the most immediately obvious of these is the realization that verse-formulas are by their very nature a form of repetition, whether the repetition be predominantly word for word—as we have seen is the case with Homeric Greek and as is also the case with the medieval French epic—or modified by variations on a concept, as in Old English poetry. This fact makes it difficult to blame all repetitions on authorial ineptitude, and it should prompt us to worry less about the density of repetitious elements than about their nature and affective function within the context of a society familiar with the rhetorical tradition of the poem. If we consider, for instance, that the style of the *Chanson de Roland* has long been the object of superlative encomia while one would have to reach far and wide to find one word of praise for the style of the *Chanson des Quatre Fils Aymon,* it is worth noting that both epics make frequently repeated use of nearly similar formulas to introduce direct discourse. The difference lies in the use to which these formulas are put: whereas the former epic uses them so skillfully that they function as integral parts of the narrative, the latter inserts them with such mechanical clumsiness that their cumulative effect is both obtrusive and ridiculous, as in the case of the direct-address formula " 'X,' said Y": " 'Baron,' dist Charlemaigne" (1. 28), " 'Barons,' dist l'archevesque" (1. 18,348), " 'Sires,' dist li dus Naymes" (1. 101), " 'Sire,' dist Enguerrans" (1. 162), and so forth at a rate often exceeding one instance in twenty lines.

I must reiterate that what really matters here is the skill with which formulas are used rather than the mere frequency of repetition. The *Hildebrandslied,* for instance, repeatedly uses the formula "X spoke, Y's son" to introduce direct discourse, thus identifying the speaker's background as well as the speaker himself. When considered out of context, the fact that the same speaker may be identified more than once in this manner reminds us of the intrusive repetitions in the *Quatre Fils Aymon,* especially when two instances of the identification occur only a few lines apart (e.g., $14^{a\text{-}b}$ and $36^{a\text{-}b}$: "Hadubrant gimahalta, Hiltibrantes sunu"). Even for the most casual student of early Germanic verse there should be no question about the oral-formulaic nature of the utterance, because we find several instances of precisely the same formula, as well as variations thereof, in *Beowulf* (e.g., $957^{a-b}$ and $2425^{a\text{-}b}$: "Beowulf maþelode, bearn Ecgþeowes") and other well-known works of the period. Within the context of the whole German poem, the repetition is so skillfully manipulated that it works to impress the audience with the nature of the blood relationship which is the basis of a story in which a father must kill his only son as a result of the latter's refusal to recognize him. Thus we are made to share the father's tragedy.

If, in addition, we keep in mind that in traditional societies the general outline of a traditional oral-narrative topic must by definition be familiar to at least part of the intended audience, we need no formal analysis to feel the impact of the layers of tragic irony revealed when the brash young man who has just now been introduced as the son of the experienced warrior whom he will insist upon fighting to the death opens his very first statement in the very next line by proclaiming that he is that same warrior's son—"dat sagettun mi usere liuti/... dat Hiltibrant hætti min fater" ($15^{a}$–$17^{a}$) [our people have told me that my father was named Hildebrand]—and proudly goes on to boast of that warrior's heroic accomplishments for the next twelve lines ($18^a$–$29^b$). Here we note that the irony results *not* from the juxtaposition of individual words but from the juxtaposition of formulaic elements, for the practice of naming one's father when called upon to identify oneself is as formulaic as the convention which causes the prospective speaker's father to be mentioned by name. In this respect, students of *Beowulf* will recall that the same thing occurs when young Beowulf identifies himself to the Danish coast guard ($262^a$–$64^b$: "wæs min fæder . . . / . . . Ecgþeow haten") and goes on to boast about his own father ($264^a$–$66^b$). One is tempted to say that from an affective point of view, the skill with which formulaic elements are handled in the *Hildebrandslied* deserves some credit for the recognition which the poem has earned as "the crown of our Germanic poetry."[5]

Just as the oral-formulaic approach teaches us to examine the function and quality of formulas instead of dismissing them as clumsy repetitions, so it teaches us to think hard before dismissing seemingly illogical episodes which may prove to be thematic elements required by the narrative topic. By the standards of written rhetoric to which most of us are accustomed, something awkwardly unnecessary is taking place when a returning warrior who has spent twenty arduous years away from home and has presumably grown quite unrecognizable in the process must nevertheless be disguised lest his return be detected by people who were mostly unborn or very young when he left. In contrast, the chances are that the original audience of the *Odyssey* would have been seriously disappointed if this episode had been left out. Likewise the oral-formulaic approach teaches us not to bring charges of plagiarism to bear every time we find a similar episode in a later oral-formulaic work, because the chances are that the author merely dipped into the common pool for the theme which the narrative topic required at this point. Thus freed from the need to censure the work for plagiarism and faulty logic, we may turn our attention to the more rewarding business of studying the artistry with which the episode is or is not handled.

In addition to helping us think twice before recoiling in horror at the sight of repetitions, apparent faults of logic, and would-be instances of plagiarism which may prove to be parts of a sophisticated system of rhetoric and to have a positive affective impact once their functions

5. Georg Baesecke, ed., *Das Hildebrandslied* (Halle: Max Niemeyer, 1945), p. 7.

are understood, the oral-formulaic approach has been of great help in dealing with a variety of largely factual problems in medieval texts. I believe, however, that the most important contributions it can make to the study of literature are in the area of interpretation, as the remainder of this essay attempts to illustrate.

Even though the critical trends of the second half of the twentieth century have taught a large part of the literary establishment to look askance upon text and context, many of us still need both a text and a context before we can interpret responsibly a given literary utterance—or any kind of utterance, for that matter. A glance at the opening lines of Robert Burns's *A Red, Red Rose* will illustrate those aspects of the proposition which are relevant to the present discussion:

> O my luve's like a red, red rose,
> That's newly sprung in June.

To interpret this statement and to communicate our interpretation to others, we must first agree that the text establishes a relationship between the speaker's love and a rose. That much should be easy enough, but it is by no means so, because the word *luve* may refer either to the speaker's emotion or to the object of that emotion, and we have no means of determining which meaning is correct unless we hear or see it within the context of the whole poem. Moreover, solving this problem to our satisfaction would still leave us with a gap in communication because, to turn illustration into caricature, the word "rose" is unlikely to mean the same thing to an Eskimo hunter near the Arctic Circle as it does to a flower gardener in Florida. Even within the context of Western Europe and America, the years between the publication of the poem and our own time have witnessed the metamorphosis of roses from delicate and relatively small flowers into the obese products of genetic engineering which we purchase on Mother's Day, so that it seems that the intended impact of the image has been irretrievably lost to the general public.

These surmises imply a modicum of agreement with the view advanced by some psychologists of literature to the effect that, "clearly, meaning is not simply 'there' in the text; rather it is something that we construct within the limits of the text," either consciously or unconsciously.[6] Yet these scholars also assume that such interpretive re-

6. Norman N. Holland, *The Dynamics of Literary Response* (1968; New York: Norton, 1975), p. 25.

creations as may take place in our minds are primarily representative of assumptions and expectations common to our culture. Anthropologists and folklorists, who concern themselves with this kind of problem have reached similar conclusions in respect to entire cultures, within which certain literary techniques reflect the degree to which individual members of a given community share the same background and concomitant expectations. In so-called high-context cultures (communities in which everyone is assumed to share the same background and concomitant expectations), for example, the relationship between image and message in literature tends to remain unexpressed, presumably on the assumption that the audience will make the connection automatically; in so-called low-context cultures (communities in which few people are assumed to share the same background and concomitant expectations), the relationship between image and message tends to be stated explicitly, presumably on the assumption that not every member of the audience will make the connection automatically.

To apply this principle rigidly, we would have only to return to the opening simile of Burns's poem and point out that the speaker uses the preposition *like* to express the relationship between his love and a rose instead of merely juxtaposing the two elements of the comparison and letting the reader infer the relationship. We would then argue the possibility that the cultural context within which the poem was composed did not include an automatic connection between love and roses, so that Burns must have felt the need to make the connection explicit. In contrast, the following Old Icelandic poem from the *Gunnlaugs Saga Ormstungu* offers us no specific verbal assistance to establish the precise relationship between image and message:

> Roðit var sverð, en sverða
> sverð-Rǫgnir mik gerði;
> váru reynd í rǫndum
> randgǫlkn fyr ver handan;
> blóðug hykk í blóði
> bloðgðǫgl of skǫr stóðu,
> sárfíkinn hlaut sára
> sárgammr enn á þramma.

> My sword was reddened, but the sword-god sworded me also; / shield-fiends were tested on shields over the ocean; / I think that blood-stained blood-goslings stood in blood around my head; / once more it was the lot of the wound-eager wound-vulture to wade the river of wounds.

Comparison between *A Red, Red Rose* and this Icelandic poem may be arbitrary, but it reminds us that medieval Iceland was culturally much more homogeneous—that is to say, high-context—than the public for which any eighteenth-century poem printed for general distribution in the United Kingdom or Western Europe must almost necessarily have been. In other words, the Icelandic poet did not have to explain his imagery because he used images that everyone in his society understood and expected.

Of course, a society can be low-context in some respects and high-context in others. This principle is what enables scientists from widely different parts of the world to understand and enjoy the same scientific jokes even though they may not even speak the same human language. When applied to literature, it goes a long way toward explaining why readers from vastly different cultures can, under certain circumstances, recognize and enjoy allusions to a common literary background.

It is no secret that until fairly recently the French seemed to cultivate dirty toilets and show an inordinate fondness for snails fried in garlic butter, while Americans were wont to rate civilizations according to the cleanliness of toilet bowls and look upon extremely bland gelatine desserts as the greatest accomplishment of gastronomy. We may accordingly assume that a community filled in equal parts with French and American people would have produced a low-context culture. Yet neither the French nor the Americans needed graduate degrees in literature to appreciate at a glance what Goethe is doing when he has a character apostrophize Helen of Troy as an awesomely aristocratic woman ("o herrliche Frau") in *Faust II* (1.6516) and to have great fun if they should happen to compare the implied description to the "face that launched a thousand ships / And burnt the topless towers of Ilium" in Marlowe's *Doctor Faustus* (5.1.99–100) or to the oversexed and charmingly simple-minded Helen who sees the world through a book of colored pictures ("un album de chromos") in Jean Giraudoux's *La Guerre de Troie n'aura pas lieu* (1.9.62). Nor need we call upon the services of the Department of Psychology to guess what even greater fun those who *did* take graduate degrees in literature must have had when they first came upon Geoffrey of Vinsauf's famous *Description of Helen*, which devotes thirty lines to assuring us that the lady's snow-white teeth are straight (line 28, "pares in statione") and that the remainder of her anatomy follows the commendable example of her dentition. The point is that nearly all reasonably intelligent graduates from reputable academic high schools would have had enough classical learning to know that Homer's brief but magnificent portrait of Helen, in the third book of the *Iliad,* avoids all specific details beyond noting that she comes equipped with white arms (3.121 "`Elénēi leykōlénoi") and a substantial bank account (3.70, 72, 91, "ktēma"). In brief, regardless of the toilets their respective cultural contexts had trained them to choose, they had been given a classical training which enabled them to interpret in very similar ways a great many literary statements composed over the past two-and-a-half millennia in Greek, Latin, English, French, German, and other languages by authors whose immediate cultural contexts had very little in common. They may have been members of a low-context world, but when it came to literature they operated in a high-context international group.

These observations are relevant to the present argument because, as suggested earlier, certain oral-formulaic elements transcend time, geography, and language boundaries within the Indo-European family; so their affective impact upon otherwise disparate audiences must have been similar to that of classical learning from the eighteenth century to the beginning of the twentieth. The audiences and oral poets whom Lord interviewed in the mountains of Yugoslavia had probably never heard of Homer and had certainly not received a classical education; yet they were thoroughly attuned to an oral-formulaic tradition which they shared to an astounding degree with Homeric poetry. This aspect of the tradition is particularly useful when we deal with works whose authorship, date, geographic origin, and even circumstances and original language of composition—that is to say, their high-context environment—are partly and sometimes totally unknown to us, as is not seldom the case with medieval poetry in the vernacular.

Much to my chagrin, for instance, I have not the least idea of who composed the *Hildebrandslied,* or for whom, or why, or where; the only thing I know about the date is that the poem must have been composed before the first quarter of the ninth century, when the only extant manuscript seems to have been written, and I can do no better than guess at the language of the original of the manuscript copy. The result is that I am deprived of almost any historical context, either high or low, from whose point of view I could approach interpretation and determine whether mentions of snails or toilets, if there were any in the poem, ought to be construed as laudatory or pejorative. In contrast, interpreters approaching their task from the point of view of the oral-formulaic tradition will be off to a rather more promising start.

As already noted, the formulaic nature of certain key lines in the poem is obvious if we have had some previous contact with Germanic verse. In addition, because the opening line—"Ik gihorta ðat seggen" [I heard it said]—happens to be the most common opening statement in the extant corpus of early Germanic oral-formulaic poetry, properly trained interpreters are alerted from the outset to look out for additional oral-formulaic elements which may have an affective impact. The most cursory glance at one of these elements will illustrate the principle and its application.

Immediately before and after the middle of the poem, our attention is made to focus on some shiny objects, respectively arm rings ($33^{a-b}$) and a fine armor ($46^{a}$–$46^{b}$). Within the context of written rhetoric the device is at best inconsequential, since it tells us merely that Hildebrand wears arm rings like most Germanic warriors and that his son, Hadubrand, serves a lord who provides him with the best equipment available. Within the high context of traditional oral-formulaic rhetoric, however, the sight of one or more shiny objects may—and in this case actually does—prove a clue to the presence of a much-attested theme in which the hero (here Hildebrand) at the outset or conclusion of a journey (here his returning after thirty years away from home [$50^{a-b}$]) stands in danger (here indicated at the outset by preparations for combat [$4^{a}$–$6^{b}$]) by the demarcation between two areas (here between two hostile armies [$3^{b}$]), while he or the audience sees some kind of shiny thing (here the rings and the armor which have cued us in). The theme, called "the hero on the beach" even when no water is in sight, is one to which we are attuned because scholars have identified a great many instances of it in Germanic literature; and it has an affective impact because of its strong tendency to occur before a scene of slaughter. Here its effect is to foreshadow the concluding duel to the death between father and son and thus to create a tension which must have been deliciously excruciating for audiences drawn from a world in which the relationship between generations was still of extreme importance. In this case the oral-formulaic approach has provided us with a timeless context to enable us to interpret and appreciate an important aspect of a great poem for which we have no historical context.

In the foregoing illustration I have taken my own cue from a magisterial essay published in 1955, in which Stanley Greenfield argued that "the association with other contexts using a similar formula will inevitably color a particular instance of a formula so that a whole host of overtones springs into action."[7] This basic principle has made it possible for modern readers to understand previously puzzling aspects of ancient texts, and it requires only one alteration to help us understand something of the mechanics which must have governed the original audience's reactions to these particular aspects of these texts. The nature of the alteration stands suggested in an equally important essay, published in 1976, where John Miles Foley argues that oral-formulaic rhetoric will affect the impact of certain elements in the narrative "by locating them in relation to archetypal paradigms."[8] The key word here is the adjective *archetypal,* for we may not reasonably suppose that the members of a society which is constantly exposed to various oral versions of stories known by their contents rather than by a particular treatment thereof would normally associate a given oral-formulaic element with a specific performance. Exceptions are always possible, but in general we must assume that, by the time oral poetry came to be recorded, the age-old formulaic elements therein had acquired an impact of their own regardless of such earlier performances as the audience might happen to recall specifically. For pragmatic and immediate purposes, we may therefore say that the specific formulaic element brought its impact to the performance that used it but that the individual performance contributed little or nothing to the impact of the formulaic element.

Of course the principle does not apply very well today, because we have no opportunity to hear medieval poetry composed orally before us and the extant texts are too few to make it possible for anyone to become as steeped in oral-formulaic rhetoric as the original audiences must have been. As a result, our reaction to oral-formulaic elements is usually conscious, and we decide that this or that theme must have such and such implications because of the circumstances under which it occurs in specific poems which we have studied and call to mind when needed. Yet the chances are that, after encountering the theme

7. Stanley B. Greenfield, "The Formulaic Expression of the Theme of Exile in Anglo-Saxon Poetry," *Speculum* 39 (1955), 205.

8. John Miles Foley, "Formula and Theme in Old English Poetry," in *Oral Literature and the Formula*, ed. Benjamin A. Stolz and Richard S. Shannon (Ann Arbor: Center for the Coordination of Ancient and Modern Studies, 1976).

of the hero on the beach in the *Hildebrandslied, Beowulf, The Dream of the Rood, The Phoenix,* Cynewulf's *Elene,* and other insular and continental Germanic works, a scholar familiar with the mechanics of the theme would not have to evoke all these titles to appreciate its function when he or she encountered it in the Old English *Guthlac,* for example. In short, the oral-formulaic approach may occasionally help us recapture something of the effect which certain medieval poems may have had on their original audiences and thus experience them as live works instead of embalmed corpses.

I have already argued that, from the point of view of the oral-formulaic approach to literary problems, it matters little whether the medieval text under examination was actually composed orally or in writing as long as the rhetoric is oral-formulaic. What does matter is that the oral-formulaic rhetoric be used consistently and skillfully enough to suggest that the text must have been the work of a poet thoroughly steeped in the relevant tradition and—as even the most literate writers tend to work with an eye on their prospective readers—composed for an intended audience presumed capable of reacting accordingly. To return briefly to the theme of the hero on the beach while glancing at works more recent than those we have examined thus far, we find the theme in both the early thirteenth-century *Nibelungenlied* and the late fourteenth-century *Sir Gawain and the Green Knight.* Yet, whereas the telltale mentions of shining objects in the *Hildebrandslied* occur only a few lines ($33^{a-b}$ and $46^{a}$–$46^{b}$) before the beginning of the mortal combat ($63^{a-b}$) which the presence of the theme had led us to anticipate, the *Nibelungenlied* lets 359 lines intervene between the shining object which initially cues us in (1837.2, "einem helm schinen sach") and the beginning of the expected slaughter (1927.1); and the setting has changed enough during this part of the narration to warrant the presence of a separate "aventure" between the two. As for *Sir Gawain and the Green Knight,* it allows no fewer than 1513 lines between the point where we are cued in by the image of a splendid castle which strangely "schemered & schon þurȝ þe schyre okeȝ" (772) and the expected slaughter, which turns out to be nothing more than a nick "þat seuered þe hyde" (2312) on Gawain's neck.

In view of both the space and the interruptions between the initial cue and the expected slaughter, one should not assume that the intended audiences of the *Nibelungenlied* and *Sir Gawain and the Green Knight* could have been expected to sense the relationship between the theme and the action, unless they had come equipped with a prodigious attention span and a fierce determination to study the mechanics of oral-formulaic composition. Even though both poems—perhaps partly under the influence of earlier versions—are heavily indebted to the oral-formulaic tradition, it seems much safer to assume that, within the respective times and places of composition of these poems, oral-formulaic rhetoric had at least in part ceased to be an ongoing productive process. Interpreters wishing to come to terms with the superb narrative skills represented in these masterpieces would probably do well to approach the texts primarily from the point of view of written rhetoric, even though they should also examine the function of the oral-formulaic materials therein.

Unlike the function of Burns's rose, the function of telltale images in the poems examined above remains unspecified, presumably because the oral-formulaic tradition provides enough of a literary high context to make specification unnecessary. Lest this contrast should appear no more than yet another instance of the difference between the Middle Ages and modernity, I should like to look briefly at another traditional theme. It is frequently encountered in Old English and is called "the beasts of battle" because it involves a wolf, a raven, and an eagle or hawk—or at least one of these—which come to the field of battle to feast on the carrion, as we see them do in *The Battle of Brunanburg* after the victorious English have left the field:

> Letan him behindan hræw bryttian
> saluwigpadan, þone sweartan hræfn,
> hyrnednebban, and þane hasewanpadan,
> earn æftan hwit, æses brucan,
> grædigne guðhafoc and þæt græge deor,
> wulf on wealde.
>
> They left behind them to divide the corpses the dark-coated black raven with horned beak, as well as the grey-coated eagle with a white tail, the greedy battle-hawk, to enjoy the carrion along with that grey beast, the wolf in the wood. ($60^a$–$65^a$)

In themselves these animals are not particularly impressive. Yet once we think of them as a theme connected with the aftermath of battle and begin visualizing their tearing of dead human flesh and crunching of bones, the very mention of their presence is enough to make us live through the horror of the scene. We must also recall that Anglo-Saxons would have seen more fields of slaughter and more birds of prey at work than we have, so that the thematic image would have been much more vivid for them than for us.

Whenever the theme of the beasts of battle is implemented before the actual battle, the beasts are shown on the side of the troop which will emerge victorious. This convention is used in *Judith* to make us experience to the full the growing tension which builds up inexorably at the approach of the battle between the Bethulians and the Assyrians. As we are made to foresee the massacre through the expectations of the scavengers advancing with the Bethulian army, we know that the battle will be won but not without blood:

> þæs se hlanca gefeah
> wulf in walde, ond se wanna hrefn,
> wælgifre fugel. Wistan begen
> þæt him ða þeodguman þohton tilian
> fylle on fægum; ac him fleah on last
> earn ætes georn, urigfeðera,
> salowigpada sang hildeleoð,
> hyrnednebba.

> The lean wolf in the wood rejoiced at that, and the dark raven, bird eager for slaughter. They both knew that the warriors intended to provide for them a full meal of those who were yet about to die; but behind them flew the eagle eager for food; dew-feathered, dark-coated, horn-beaked, he sang a battle hymn. ($205^{b}$–$212^{a}$)

Here the message of the image of the beasts of battle is never stated, but it is nevertheless perfectly clear as long as we read or listen within the high context of the appropriate oral-formulaic tradition. Indeed, the image goes beyond itself to make us visualize the slaughter which it does not describe.

With these observations in mind, we may look at a particularly revealing example of the effective potential of oral-formulaic themes when they are skillfully manipulated. Near the beginning of his *Elene,* Cynewulf emphasizes the demoralizing contrast between the diminutive Roman troop ($48^{b}$, "werod læsse") and the formidable army ($35^{a}$, "fyrda mæst") of the invading Barbarians. The Barbarians should unquestionably prove victorious, and it is accordingly fitting that we should be treated to a glimpse of the beasts of battle advancing with them ($27^{b}$–$30^{a}$). But then Constantine has his famous revelation, and no sooner has he ordered a Christian cross ($109^a$, "beacen godes") to be carried forward as his battle standard than the beasts of battle reappear, this time on the side of the Romans:

> Hrefn weorces gefeah,
> unrigfeðra, earn sið beheold,
> wælhreowra wig. Wulf sang ahof,
> holtes gehleða.
>
> The raven rejoiced in the work, dewy-feathered; the eagle beheld the occasion, the warlike action of battle-fierce men. The wolf intoned a song, the forest-dweller. ($110^b$–$13^a$)

At this point, profane readers might legitimately wonder why so many animals are swarming over the page, but initiates of the oral-formulaic tradition will have recognized the theme and will know that the expected victory of the Romans must be credited to their leader's conversion rather than to any military strategy. This observation does not mean that interpreters should feel free to approach the poem without considering the written sources and the influence of their rhetoric on certain aspects of its style. What it means is that Cynewulf must have known what he was doing with oral-formulaic rhetoric and that he must have expected his intended audience to interpret his work accordingly.

The extent to which the message in the foregoing poems depends on the context within which we apprehend the image may be ascertained by comparison with a passage in the fifteenth-century *Life of Saint Alban and Saint Amphibal,* where John Lydgate brings a wolf, an eagle, and sundry "fowlis" (3725) of the kind that "wer disposed to ravyne" (2713) to a field where the carcasses of nine hundred and ninety-nine Christians have been abandoned by the Pagans who have massacred them. If we subscribe to the view that few traditional oral English poets were likely to have found employment with the new Norman masters after the Battle of Hastings, and if we grant any validity to my earlier remarks concerning the rhetoric of *Sir Gawain and the Green Knight,* then the date of *Saint Alban and Saint Amphibal* makes it reasonable to suppose that Lydgate and his intended audience were operating not merely within a low context but indeed within a total noncontext in respect to the Old English formulaic tradition. In this light the mention of the beasts of battle would presumably have evoked no special image or expectation for the audience, and Lydgate acts accordingly. Although he draws a rather striking portrait of the wolf that "cam don with sturdy violence, / Terryble of look, and furious of cheer" (2719–20), he feels the need to enlighten us with a little dissertation on the relevant aspects of lupine behavior: "It is appropid to wolvis of natur, / As clerkis seyn, mannys flessh to attame, / Mong al careyns, whan thei may it recur, / Thei most reioissh & ha therof most game" (3733–36). Not only has the high context of the oral-formulaic tradition been lost, but we are tempted to suspect that Lydgate assumed his prospective readers knew next to nothing about wild fauna.

One might object that Lydgate wrote at a time when the Middle Ages were evolving into the Renaissance, so that his practices are not relevant to the former period. To meet this objection I give the two additional examples below. Because these examples are taken from written works which have no known connection with oral-formulaic rhetoric, they serve to illustrate the absolute opposite of the high-context features which we have examined.

The first example comes from the fourteenth-century *Vox Clamantis*, where John Gower paints the rebellious peasants as asses whose bellies are filled with the furor of lions (I, 183–85; "asinos . . . / . . . Viscera . . . sua repleta furore leonum") and continues in the same vein for more than five hundred lines (I, 186–746). Contrary to what we have noted above in respect to the thematic imagery of oral-formulaic poetry, the relationship between image and message here is anything but hermetic. Yet Gower seems to assume such a low context of communication that he takes the precaution of informing us beforehand that his metaphors stand for the hordes of the rabble transmuted into different kinds of domestic animals (I, Intro., "diuersas vulgi turmas in diuersas species bestiarum domesticarum transmutatas"). The second example is from the twelfth-century *Lanval*, which represents just about the ideal linguistic and cultural mixture for the production of low-context literature, since it is written by Marie de France, who lives in England and turns Celtic tales into French. In this light, it is of interest that her verse is almost devoid of imagery and that the occasional images which we do encounter therein are usually introduced as such, so that the audience has no opportunity to misunderstand the relationship between image and message. When we are allowed a peek at the concupiscible body of a fair damsel, for instance, the entire account is summed up for us with the statement that she was whiter than is the whitethorn flower (196: "Plus ert blanch que flurs d'espine"), so that the function of the image is unequivocally stated for us.

Although medieval works composed squarely within the written tradition may occasionally reflect the influence of oral-formulaic rhetoric, the materials examined in this essay should suggest that approaching the rhetoric of Lydgate, Gower, or Marie de France from a primarily oral-formulaic point of view would be as irresponsible and counterproductive as approaching the rhetoric of the *Hildebrandslied, Judith,* or the *Chanson de Roland* primarily from the point of view of written composition. At the close of the twentieth century the oral-formulaic approach to the study of medieval literature is immensely attractive because it allows us to draw on more than two millennia of Indo-European culture and to link past and present as well as the familiar and the exotic to provide a high context for a great deal of superb poetry for which we would otherwise have no context at all; because it can at times succeed where other approaches have failed to help us with interpretation, aesthetic appreciation, or empirical matters; and because it can act as an effective adjunct to other approaches. It is especially exciting because it is part of a rapidly expanding discipline in which the literary scholar specializing in the western Middle Ages can enjoy rapidly multiplying opportunities to team up with linguists and anthropologists, or at least to make use of their most recent work as well as of the work of literary scholars concerned with practically all languages and periods known to us.

Like all approaches, however, the oral-formulaic approach should be used with discretion. Its proponents—and I include myself among them—should not attempt to impose it upon works better served by other approaches, and they should be willing to use it in conjunction with those other approaches whenever the work under scrutiny warrants such action. As professional scholars of literature, we should hold our first allegiance to the literary tradition. The approaches which we adopt should be those that will do most justice to the works we study rather than those that will do most to raise our reputation and swell our bibliography in the dean's office.[9]

9. Readers specializing in oral-formulaic matters will recognize my indebtedness to innumerable studies which limitations of space prevented me from acknowledging. A less obvious debt is to Sarah L. Higley's dissertation, "The Natural Analogy: Image and Connection in Medieval English and Welsh Poetry of Lament" (University of

California, Berkeley, 1984), in which she applies to medieval poetry the principles of high and low context elaborated in J. Barre Toelken's *The Dynamics of Folklore* (Boston: Houghton Mifflin, 1979). Special thanks are also due to Alexandra Hennessey Olsen, who generously allowed me to draw ideas on Cynewulf from what was then the unpublished manuscript of her *Speech, Song, and Poetic Craft: The Artistry of the Cynewulf Canon* (New York: Peter Lang, 1984). Nonspecialists wishing to check on the origin of the major views which I have expressed are directed to the relevant essays in *Oral Traditional Literature,* ed. John Miles Foley (Columbus, Ohio: Slavica, 1981) and especially to Foley's own masterful introduction, "The Oral Theory in Context," which offers the clearest and most authoritative account available of the history and state of oral-formulaic studies. Attention is further directed to Foley's *Oral-Formulaic Theory and Research: An Introduction and Annotated Bibliography* (New York: Garland, 1985), which sums up and analyzes all the principal studies of oral-formulaic matters.

# Contributors

MARINA SCORDILIS BROWNLEE is chair of Comparative Literature at Dartmouth College in Hanover, New Hampshire, and author of *The Poetics of Literary Theory in Lopé de Vega and Cervantes* (1981) and *The Status of the Reading Subject in the "Libro de Buen Amor"* (1985). She is currently completing a book entitled *Severed Words: Discursive Structure in the "Novela Sentimental."*

SHEILA DELANY is professor of English at Simon Fraser University in Burnaby, British Columbia. While teaching at Queens College, CUNY, she edited *Counter-Tradition: The Literature of Dissent and Alternatives* (1970). She is the author of *Chaucer's House of Fame: The Poetics of Skeptical Fideism* (1972) and of *Writing Woman: Women Writers and Women in Literature, Medieval to Modern* (1983). Professor Delany has published widely on Chaucer and other medieval and modern writers. Her current projects include a collection of her essays on social issues in medieval literature and a study of Chaucer's *Legend of Good Women*.

LAURIE A. FINKE is associate professor of English at Lewis & Clark College in Portland, Oregon. Her articles on literature and feminist theory have appeared in *Theatre Journal, Leeds Studies in English,*

*Tulsa Studies in Women's Literature,* other journals, and several collections of essays. She has also coedited *From Renaissance to Restoration: Metamorphoses of the Drama* (1984). She has recently completed a historical study of feminist criticism between 1975 and 1985 and is currently working on the problem of subjectivity in the literature of the twelfth century.

ROBERT W. HANNING is professor of English and Comparative Literature at Columbia University in New York City. He holds B.A. degrees from Columbia and Oxford and the Ph.D. from Columbia. Author of *The Vision of History in Early Britain* and *The Individual in Twelfth-Century Romance,* he has also translated, with Joan M. Ferrante, *The Lais of Marie de France,* and is coeditor, with David Rosand, of *Castiglione: The Ideal and the Real in Renaissance Culture.* He has published essays on subjects in Old and Middle English, Chaucer, medieval romance and historiography, and Italian Renaissance literature. He is currently completing a study of Chaucer's *Canterbury Tales.*

RACHEL JACOFF is professor and chair of the Department of Italian at Wellesley College in Wellesley, Massachusetts. She has written numerous articles on Dante and, with William Stephany, a monograph on *Inferno* II for the Dante Society of America's series *Lectura Dantis Americana.* She has edited a collection of John Freccero's essays entitled *Dante: The Poetics of Conversion* and is currently editing, with Jeffrey Schnapp, *The Poetry of Allusion: Virgil and Ovid in Dante's Comedy.* She has been codirector of the NEH Dartmouth Dante Institute and is an assistant editor of *Speculum.* She is currently a fellow at the Stanford Humanities Center where she is completing a book entitled *Dante and the Poetics of Literary Influence.*

PEGGY A. KNAPP teaches English at Carnegie Mellon University in Pittsburgh, Pennsylvania, and edits *Assays: Critical Approaches to Medieval and Renaissance Texts.* Her work has appeared in such journals as *PMLA, ELH, Philological Quarterly, Criticism, College English,* and *Modern Language Notes.*

H. MARSHALL LEICESTER is associate professor of English at the University of California, Santa Cruz. His articles on medieval literature have appeared in *PMLA, Chaucer Review, Women's Studies,* and numerous other journals.

ALEXANDRE LEUPIN is professor of French at Louisiana State University in Baton Rouge and the author of *Le Graal et la litterature, étude sur la vulgate arthurienne en prose: L'age d'Homme.* He has published articles on medieval literature and critical theory in a number of journals.

LOUIS MACKEY received his Ph.D. from Yale University in 1954. He now teaches philosophy and comparative literature at The University of Texas at Austin. He is the author of two books on Kierkegaard—*Kierkegaard: A Kind of Poet* (1971) and *Points of View: Readings of Kierkegaard* (1986)—as well as articles on medieval philosophy, literary theory, and contemporary fiction. His chief interest lies in exploring the relationship between philosophy and literature.

ALAIN RENOIR is professor of English at the University of California, Berkeley. He is the author of *The Poetry of John Lydgate,* coauthor of the Lydgate section of *The Manual of Writings in Middle English,* and editor of *Approaches to Beowulfian Scansion.* He has also published some eighty essays, notes, and reviews on Old English, Middle English, medieval German, medieval French, and educational theory.

MARTIN B. SHICHTMAN is an assistant professor of English at Eastern Michigan University in Ypsilanti. He has published articles on Malory, the Grail legend, and *Sir Gawain and the Green Knight.*

PETER W. TRAVIS is professor of English at Dartmouth College in Hanover, New Hampshire, and the author of *Dramatic Design in the Chester Cycle.* He has published extensively on medieval drama and literature.

# Index

*Library of Congress Cataloging-in-Publication Data*

Medieval texts and contemporary readers.

Includes index.
1. Literature, Medieval—History and criticism.
2. Reading. I. Finke, Laurie. II. Shichtman, Martin B.
PN681.M425 1987 809'.02 87-47545
ISBN 0-8014-2003-2 (alk. paper)
ISBN 0-8014-9463-X (pbk. : alk. paper)

EP13X